EUGENE O'NEILL'S ONE-ACT PLAYS

Previous Publications

Michael Y. Bennett
Reassessing the Theatre of the Absurd: Camus, Beckett, Ionesco, Genet, and Pinter

Words, Space, and the Audience: The Theatrical Tension between Empiricism and Rationalism

Refiguring Oscar Wilde's Salome (editor)

Benjamin D. Carson
Sovereignty, Separatism, and Survivance: Ideological Encounters in the Literature of Native North America (editor)

Eugene O'Neill's One-Act Plays

New Critical Perspectives

Edited by Michael Y. Bennett and Benjamin D. Carson

First published in hardcover in 2012 by PALGRAVE MACMILLAN®
in the United States—a division of St. Martin's Press LLC, 175 Fifth
Avenue, New York, NY 10010.

Where this book is distributed in the UK, Europe and the rest of
the world, this is by Palgrave Macmillan, a division of Macmillan
Publishers Limited, registered in England, company number 785998,
of Houndmills, Basingstoke, Hampshire RG21 6XS.

Palgrave Macmillan is the global academic imprint of the above
companies and has companies and representatives throughout the
world.

Palgrave® and Macmillan® are registered trademarks in the United
States, the United Kingdom, Europe and other countries.

ISBN: 978-1-137-47177-2

Library of Congress Cataloging-in-Publication Data

Eugene O'Neill's one-act plays : new critical perspectives / edited by
  Michael Y. Bennett, Benjamin D. Carson.
    p. cm.
  ISBN 978-0-230-33981-1 (hardback)
  1. O'Neill, Eugene, 1888-1953—Criticism and interpretation. 2.
American drama—20th century—Social aspects. I. Bennett, Michael
Y., 1980– II. Carson, Benjamin D.

  PS3529.N5Z639 2012
  812'.52—dc23   2012002675

A catalogue record of the book is available from the British Library.

Design by Scribe Inc.

First PALGRAVE MACMILLAN paperback edition: December 2014

10 9 8 7 6 5 4 3 2 1

To Ben's mentor, Frank R. Cunningham, and Michael's
mentor, Robert Combs, who showed us O'Neill's
"native eloquence" and taught us so much more

Contents

Essay Abstracts

"The Playwright's Theatre: O'Neill's Use of the Provincetown Players as a One-Act Laboratory" by Jeff Kennedy

When the Provincetown Players formally organized in September of 1916, playwright Eugene O'Neill insisted on one thing: that they name the playhouse "The Playwright's Theatre." O'Neill set about writing plays that in performance would help answer questions he had as a playwright, something like a self-imposed curriculum to inform his work. He believed that this amateur company committed to experimenting, and toward the creation of an American identity in theatre, would allow him to test his ideas. Early on, O'Neill exited the daily workings of the Players to concentrate on his writing and maintained a relationship with the Players unlike anyone who called themselves a member of the company. This essay examines the experimentation in his one-act plays performed by the Provincetown Players and how his relationship with the group evolved in the process.

"Rethinking O'Neill's Beginnings: Slumming, Sociology, and Sensationalism in *The Web*" by J. Chris Westgate

Offering a rebuttal to the ahistoricism that governs so much of the criticism on Eugene O'Neill, this essay situates O'Neill's origins firmly in the Progressive Era. This essay demonstrates that *The Web*, O'Neill's first play, reflects a central concern of theater from this period: ethically conflicted depictions of New York lowlife. On the one hand, *The Web* attempts a sociological reading of the conditions of prostitutes, concentrating on how poverty becomes a "category of social being" that defines material circumstances and psychological well-being. On the other hand, *The Web*'s melodramatic design potentially turns Rose's plight into slumming, a popular pastime wherein the wealthy observed the underworld for excitement and titillation.

"Eugene O'Neill's *Abortion* and Standard Family Roles: The Economics of Terminating a Romance and a Pregnancy" by Lesley Broder

While Eugene O'Neill's *Abortion* may seem melodramatic in the twenty-first century, it would have been quite radical had it been performed when it was written in 1914. In the play, Nellie's status as a commodity to be traded and exchanged winds through the discussion between Jack and his father, John, about her abortion. The sanctity of their social position and Nellie's lower-class status preoccupy them. Despite the bold title, abortion is only referred to in hushed euphemisms and is cast as a shameful reality that cannot be addressed openly; instead, abortion runs through the play as representative of the larger issue of women's economic dependence on men.

"*The Movie Man*: The Failure of Aesthetics?" by Thierry Dubost

Like many early works, *The Movie Man* deserves some critical attention not because the passing of time has eventually turned an early dramatic attempt into a masterpiece, but because it exposes a series of threads that O'Neill later wove in different shapes, both thematically and aesthetically. This essay highlights some of the causes—past and present—that explain the lack of success of this clumsy dramatic attempt, contrasting some thematic or aesthetic aspects with O'Neill's future writing modes. Consequently, focusing on how the young playwright failed will help show why *The Movie Man* remains interesting for critics, as a crossroads of genres, a possible starting point to define a new aesthetic frame within which the playwright never included his future plays.

"'God Stiffen Us': Queering O'Neill's Sea Plays" by Phillip Barnhart

Though O'Neill's characters are often men gathered together in confined spaces, few scholars have undertaken a queer reading of his plays. Eve Kosofsky Sedgwick suggests that since the eighteenth century the "path to male entitlement" requires intense male bonding that cannot readily be distinguished from "the most reprobate" bonding. She further suggests that the proximity of intense male friendship to homosexual desire or action fulminates in homosexual panic. This essay examines the homosocial bonds, the homoerotic undertones, the romantic friendships, and the implication of homosexual panic, and its resultant violence in O'Neill's sea plays.

"'The Curtain is Lowered': Self-Revelation and the Problem of Form in *Exorcism*" by Kurt Eisen

With the recent discovery of *Exorcism*, O'Neill's 1920 autobiographical one-act play thought to be lost, scholars can explore not only what it reveals about the playwright's state of mind when he attempted suicide in 1912—the episode from life on which the play is based—but more important, what it reveals about his development as an artist when he wrote, staged, and immediately suppressed the play by gathering all known copies and destroying them. The newly discovered text shows O'Neill on the verge of his mature experimentation with the full-length form but also offers glimpses of the major autobiographical plays of his final period, revealing why the one-act form of *Exorcism* was inadequate to his aims.

"'Ain't Nothin' Dere but de Trees!': Ghosts and the Forest in *The Emperor Jones*" by Paul D. Streufert

Though many critics of Eugene O'Neill's 1920 play *The Emperor Jones* approach the play in terms of race or psychology, this essay examines how O'Neill uses fear and terror in the play, focusing on its ghost characters and the medium of the forest, that supernatural place that links Brutus Jones's external and interior realities. O'Neill's use of ghosts and the haunted forest reveals both his debt to the European theatrical tradition of ghost plays as well as the religious rhetoric and literary tradition of the Puritans, such as Mary Rowlandson's captivity narrative. Reading the ghosts in *The Emperor Jones* suggests a new way to read the literal and symbolic ghosts in the playwright's later works.

"Neither Fallen Angel nor Risen Ape: Desentimentalizing Robert Smith" by Thomas F. Connolly

The Hairy Ape is not primarily social commentary; Yank is not merely an exploited worker. Conventional analysis insists that even as the play's staging is somewhat expressionistic, its philosophy is deterministic: Yank stands for all humanity. Even if he does not understand the universe, or his part in it, Yank wants to dominate his surroundings. Therefore it is interesting that Mildred is able to shatter Yank's confidence effortlessly. Thus broken, he becomes genuinely alien. O'Neill uses the theatrical convention of the ape-man, but rejects sentimentality and overcomes melodrama (and Darwin or Freud). The play is an inverse *Pygmalion*: Mildred is Pygmalion, and Yank is Galatea. The play's subtitle lacks attention; thus the finale ought not be taken as pathetic, but as the inevitable conclusion to the life of someone who has displaced himself.

"Waiting for O'Neill: The Makings of an Existentialist" by Steven F. Bloom

This essay considers how elements similar to those of Beckett's *Waiting for Godot* characterize some of the early one-act sea plays of Eugene O'Neill, including *Bound East for Cardiff*, *Ile*, and *A Long Voyage Home*, which were written over forty years before Martin Esslin included *Godot* among the plays he labeled "the Theatre of the Absurd." The characters in the sea plays repetitively pass the time with others waiting for something to happen, with the inevitability of death hovering over them. Although the ironic endings of O'Neill's early plays ultimately distinguish them from the so-called absurdist dramas, these one-act plays can be seen as early precursors of existential drama and demonstrate that the young O'Neill had the makings of an existentialist.

"Epistemological Crises in O'Neill's SS *Glencairn* Plays" by Michael Y. Bennett

This essay argues that O'Neill's SS *Glencairn* plays display a generic tension between realism and naturalism. The sailors—neither good nor bad—act as solitary and free individuals, and yet O'Neill seems to also suggest that they are bound by the harsh realities of the world. Through this tension between naturalism and realism in these sea plays, O'Neill anticipates Bertolt Brecht's notion of the alienation effect. This alienation effect is achieved by subtly forcing the audience to oscillate between accepting the worldviews of naturalism and realism, thereby destroying the stability of either worldview.

"O'Neill's *Hughie*: The Sea Plays Revisited" by Robert Combs

O'Neill is famous for his expansive dramatic techniques, but a contrary impulse—that of the one-act play and its cousin the short story—is also essential to his success as a dramatist. In *Hughie*, a one-act play that belongs in the company of *The Iceman Cometh* and *Long Day's Journey Into Night*, O'Neill revisits his early sea plays where he first explored the individual's inevitable confrontation with self, other, and nothingness. The one-act play, like the short story, focuses on a single dramatic moment that illuminates a lifetime of struggle for individuals living in a world that makes loneliness a form of ironically heroic endurance. Typically, an O'Neill play focuses on some necessary illusion that renders life bearable and makes human contact for his characters possible; O'Neill's dramatic crises render that illusion transparent and thus expose his characters to the destruction of the very ground of their being. In his sea plays, the sailors face themselves, their pasts, and each other against the background of the sea. In *Hughie*, two men in a run-down hotel lobby in midtown Manhattan in 1928 endure the dark night of their souls by means of their contrary impulses to communicate and to lose themselves in private fantasies and fears. This essay uses two other works—Joseph Conrad's *Lord Jim* and the short story it may have inspired, James Thurber's "The Secret Life of Walter Mitty"—to reflect upon O'Neill's ironic presentation of his characters' struggles to survive as their life-sustaining illusions are destroyed.

"Condensed Comedy: The Neo-Futurists perform O'Neill's Stage Directions" by Zander Brietzke

The New York Neo-Futurists produced an original work, *The Complete and Condensed Stage Directions of Eugene O'Neill, Vol. 1, Early Plays/Lost Plays*, at the tiny Kraine Theater in Greenwich Village in the fall of 2011. In keeping with the company's nonrepresentational aesthetic, the troupe of six actors deleted the dialogue in several of the famous playwright's early one-acts and two of his first full-length plays and performed only the stage directions as read verbatim by a stage manager. The overall effect was, first of all, hilarious, parodying the playwright's zeal for packing novelistic details into a dramatic medium. More important, the production demonstrated the need and challenge to interpret imaginatively and creatively O'Neill's texts and dismissed the notion entirely that his work could be taken seriously by simply doing what the playwright said in his lengthy stage directions.

INTRODUCTION

Benjamin D. Carson

Eugene O'Neill's plays were forged in the crucible of suffering—an admixture of abandonment, spiritual loss, homelessness, and guilt—and the sense that life is deeply tragic. O'Neill had, in Edward Shaughnessy's words, "a tragedian's mind-set"[1] rooted in a Catholic sensibility and fostered by knowledge of the classical (Greek) tradition.[2] While O'Neill lacked faith, his work "expresses in symbols" his "search for a faith" that forever eluded him.[3] But the gap between what is longed for and what can be had is the very stuff of tragedy and is at the heart of O'Neill's greatest works. "Man's modern tragedy," Shaughnessy writes, "is to seek a higher life but to know that it cannot be attained,"[4] and for O'Neill, "the one eternal tragedy of Man . . . is the only subject worth writing about."[5]

O'Neill was born in a hotel in New York City on October 16, 1888, but he was reborn a playwright at the Gaylord Farm Sanatorium, in Wallingford, CT, in late 1912 and early 1913. His "second birth," he wrote to Gaylord's Dr. Lyman, "was the only one which had [his] full approval."[6] At Gaylord, O'Neill, like his double, Stephen Murray in *The Straw*, had nothing but time; time to think about his future and reflect on his past. It was at Gaylord that his "mind got the chance to establish itself,"[7] and before long he determined to become "an artist or nothing."[8] O'Neill, always a voracious reader, began to study seriously the works of Synge, Yeats, Lady Gregory, Brieux, Hauptmann, Ibsen, and Strindberg,[9] and soon after leaving Gaylord, his tuberculosis having been arrested, he started to write.

While, incredibly, O'Neill would win his first Pulitzer Prize (for *Beyond the Horizon*) seven years after he began writing, the prize was certainly hard won. His early efforts were "inexpertly"[10] composed and melodramatic; many are unstageworthy and remain unproduced. But with time and an effort that bordered on obsession, amid the din of Greenwich Village and later the semisolitude of Provincetown, O'Neill found his voice. The early plays, for all of their inadequacies, not only "set forth the initial terms of the playwright's artistry and thought," but they are the first utterances of a true American theater.[11] If, as Edmund claims, in *Long Day's Journey into Night*, "stammering is the native eloquence of us fog people," then O'Neill's one-acts are his first stammerings, his first attempt as an artist to cut through the fog, to give form to a vision that cried out for expression but, in its opacity, its intangibility, was so difficult to articulate. O'Neill would eventually give shape to his vision, but as even he acknowledged, the "germ of the spirit, life-attitude, etc.," of all his greatest artistic achievements, was cultivated "practically within my first half-year as a playwright."[12]

Arthur and Barbara Gelb have written that, "looking back, it seems to us that from the very beginning O'Neill was writing drafts for the final masterworks that have stamped him as America's foremost dramatist,"[13] so it is surprising that O'Neill's one-acts have received so little attention from scholars. This is undoubtedly because, as Travis Bogard argues, with the exception of *Bound East for Cardiff*, "no one of his plays of the period [1913–14] is worth consideration in its own right."[14] What Russell Carl Brignano says of Richard Wright's uneven body of work could just as easily apply to O'Neill's: "His successes are colossal, his failures dreadful."[15] Even though O'Neill subscribed to the "Arts of [sic] Art's sake credo,"[16] his earliest plays are best read in light of his political commitments, the sociopolitical, cultural, and historical milieu in which they were written, the history of dramaturgy, and recent critical theories.

It is fair to say that O'Neill's early plays are portraits of an artist as a young man, but they are portraits deeply rooted in time. O'Neill's nascent artistic sensibility began to bloom at a world-historical moment, a period of intense transformation that would redraw the political, economic, and cultural landscape of the Western world. The completion of *The Movie Man*, in the summer of 1914, for example, marks "the final effort of O'Neill's first year as [a] fledgling dramatist."[17] Coincidentally, O'Neill completed the play just weeks before the assassination, on June 28, 1914, of Archduke Ferdinand and his wife, Sophie, in Sarajevo, which sparked World War I. When the Treaty of Versailles was signed five years to the day later, on June 28, 1919, a new Europe had emerged from the ashes of the old. On the economic front, 1913 sees the implementation by Henry Ford of assembly line production in Dearborn, Michigan; though for David Harvey, "the symbolic initiation date of Fordism must, surely, be 1914, when Henry Ford introduced his five-dollar, eight-hour day as recompense for workers manning the automated car-assembly line he had established the year before at Dearborn, Michigan."[18] The effects of Fordism, however, go far beyond economics. For Antonio Gramsci, the "American phenomenon" of Fordism represented "the biggest collective effort to date to create, with unprecedented speed, and with a consciousness of purpose unmatched in history, a new type of worker and of man."[19] The "new methods of work," which here are synonymous with new methods of capitalist accumulation, are, Gramsci argues, "inseparable from a specific mode of living and of thinking and feeling life."[20] This new mode of production, then, had its correlate in the cultural sphere, a new "structure of feeling," what we might call the cultural logic of modernism.

There is little question that the second decade of the twentieth century saw a revolutionary transformation in representational modes in art, music, and literature. If 1914 marked the symbolic initiation date of Fordism (and thus a new mode of production), it could be argued that the 1913 International Exhibition of Modern Art (featuring the work of Matisse, Picasso, Duchamp, Klee, Kandinsky, etc.) at the Regiment Armory in New York marks the symbolic initiation of modernism—a date that falls squarely between Virginia Woolf's preferred date for this initiation (1910) and D. H. Lawrence's preference (1915). This is not to suggest, however, that experimentation in art and literature was not going on before 1913. Quite the contrary, in the late nineteenth century Baudelaire, Flaubert, Wilde, Yeats, Ibsen, and Strindberg, in literature, and Manet, Renoir, and Cezanne, in art, were already breaking away from the Victorian aesthetic sensibility and setting the stage for what was to come. But in terms of instantiating new modes of seeing, of representing the rapidity and unpredictability of modern life, 1913 is pivotal. The year O'Neill would first try his hand at drama, 1913, the literary world saw the publication of Marcel Proust's *Swann's Way* and D. H. Lawrence's *Sons and Lovers*. By the end of 1914, the year O'Neill declared (to George Pierce Baker) his intention to be "an artist or nothing," James Joyce's *Dubliners*, Thomas Mann's *Death in Venice*, and Ezra Pound's Vorticist manifesto had been published.[21]

O'Neill's transformation from a down-and-out sailor and would-be suicide to an artist was contemporaneous, then, with the "qualitative transformation in what modernism was about," which "most commentators agree" took place "somewhere between 1910 and 1915."[22] While O'Neill was new to his craft, and though it would take some time for O'Neill to find his footing, his instinct for experimentation (evident as early as *Bound East for Cardiff* [1914]) certainly mirrored that of his modernist contemporaries. Not all of his early plays, however, were experimental. His earliest efforts contained the hallmarks of the kind of melodrama characteristic of mainstream American theater at the turn of the century. They also reflect O'Neill's sociological awareness, at least in part a consequence of his association with penniless sailors, bar flies, and characters the likes of Hippolyte Havel, Terry Carlin, Dorothy Day, and John Reed. O'Neill, sociologically speaking, had his finger on the pulse of the moment, but more important, his work does more than just record "the body politic" of his time.[23] In a comparative reading of certain of O'Neill's and Reed's works, John S. Bak argues, "Although just as effective in capturing the social concerns of the times—including the workers' struggle, women's work opportunities and suffrage, and the atrocities of the First World War—O'Neill never seemed as devoted to changing them as Reed was. Instead, O'Neill was content simply to record what he saw happening around him, exploring instead the effects these social ramifications had on the struggles that confronted the individual daily. In short, Reed's works never transcended their social message as O'Neill's did, and that is why he is remembered more as an historian than, like O'Neill, as a literary artist."[24]

This focus on the individual, rather than the broader "social concerns of the times," is evident in all of O'Neill's plays, even those that most overtly address social themes. While certainly a play about the injustices endured by Africans and African Americans throughout history, *The Emperor Jones* (1920), for example, as an expressionist drama, emphasizes the plight of one Brutus Jones. Expressionism was "at its height between 1910 and 1925,"[25] and thus coincided with the first third of O'Neill's career (1913–20). And as an artistic form, expressionism was a good fit for O'Neill, who from the beginning sought objective correlatives to inner emotions. As M. H. Abrams notes, "The expressionist artist or writer, undertakes to express a personal vision—usually a troubled or tensely emotional vision—of human life and human society. This is done by exaggerating and distorting what, according to the norms of artistic realism, are objective features of the world, and by embodying violent extremes of mood and feeling. Often the work implies that what is depicted or described represents the experience of an individual standing alone and afraid in an industrial, technological, and urban society which is disintegrating into chaos."[26] *The Hairy Ape* (1921), which, according to Travis Bogard, "lies at a half-way point [between realism and the new expressionism] in O'Neill's career," is about "man's attempt to come into harmony with his world, to find to whom, to what he can belong."[27] In this sense, then, O'Neill's concerns in *The Emperor Jones* and

The Hairy Ape are "emotional, even spiritual, and less political."[28] Though these two plays engage social problems, their emphasis is on the subject of nearly all of O'Neill's plays, the "fate of that alienated individual."[29]

***

This collection gives long overdue attention to O'Neill's one-acts— from the melodramatic *A Wife for a Life* (1913) to his minor master-piece, *Hughie* (1942). Given their central place in O'Neill's oeuvre, it also includes essays on *The Emperor Jones* and *The Hairy Ape*. While not technically one-acts, these two short plays (of eight scenes each) were meant to be performed in one sitting and are two of the finest plays of O'Neill's early career. Their inclusion here is meant to underscore the larger theme of the collection, the continuity between O'Neill's early works and those of his mature years. O'Neill's early plays are the birth pangs of the American theater and, in embryonic form, embody all of O'Neill. The child gives birth to the man, and without these first plays, it is safe to say there would be no Theodore Hickman, no *Long Day's Journey into Night*.

In "The Playwright's Theatre: O'Neill's Use of the Provincetown Players as a One-Act Laboratory," Jeff Kennedy shows how O'Neill's early experiments as a playwright were tested within the confines of "the Playwright's Theatre." The new American theater that the Provincetown Players set out to create demanded new techniques, and the Playwright's Theatre functioned, Kennedy argues, as a laboratory for O'Neill to test the effectiveness of the monologue, to see if mood can take priority over action, and to challenge an audience's willingness to suspend disbelief. Along with the use of expressionistic techniques, O'Neill wrote plays for and then boldly cast African Americans in primary roles at a time when doing so not only was controversial, to which the production history of *All God's Chillun Got Wings* attests, but was also, Kennedy notes, "not part of the professional American theatre." Kennedy's "The Playwright's Theatre" examines O'Neill's unique relationship with the Provincetown Players and the way in which O'Neill used this amateur theater company to test what Kennedy calls O'Neill's "curriculum of experimentation."

J. Chris Westgate, in "Rethinking O'Neill's Beginnings: Slumming, Sociology, and Sensationalism in *The Web*," examines *The Web* from within the context of the Progressive Era, a time when the new science of sociology was on the rise. To be sure, O'Neill's sympathies were always with the poor and downtrodden, but *The Web*, Westgate argues, reflects Progressive Era ambivalence toward what Jacob

Riis called "the other half." On the one hand, *The Web* exposed the vicissitudes of poverty, and in so doing, O'Neill hoped could work to effect change; on the other hand, it risks turning the poor into spectacles for the amusement of the wealthy. By situating *The Web* in its historical moment, Westgate provides an overdue corrective to the scholarship that tends to "dehistoricize" the play and consequently overlook its central tension: how to stage the slums in a way that does not exploit the poor. Westgate's examination of the dialectic between staging for social justice and staging as sensationalism opens up new ways to interpret O'Neill's later social dramas such as *Anna Christie*, *The Hairy Ape*, and *All God's Chillun Got Wings*.

Lesley Broder's "Eugene O'Neill's *Abortion* and Standard Family Roles: The Economics of Terminating a Romance and a Pregnancy" examines the way in which O'Neill uses the issue of abortion to illuminate women's economic dependence on men. It is worth noting that O'Neill wrote *Abortion* at a time when defending the use of birth control and the right to an abortion was a criminal offense. The National Birth Control League (NBCL) was formed in March 1915 and was dedicated to "reforming the federal and state Comstock statutes" that made illegal the distribution of information regarding, among other things, birth control and abortion.[30] O'Neill would most certainly have been aware of the controversy surrounding the NBCL. Margaret Sanger, one of the most (in)famous women associated with the League, contributed articles on birth control to *The Call*, a publication O'Neill read regularly, and she and O'Neill shared friends (like John Reed) and travelled in the same circles.[31] But if O'Neill tended to romanticize the underprivileged, Sanger, who had read Hutchins Hapgood's *Spirit of the Ghetto*, "saw only the degradation and despair wrought of ignorance, poverty, pregnancy, abortion, child abandonment, and child labor."[32] In *Abortion*, O'Neill, in a way that would have resonated with Sanger, dramatizes the "despair wrought" by pregnancy and abortion. Poverty limits Nellie's ability to make choices for herself. In fact, Broder argues that Nellie lacks entirely the power to choose. Jack and his father, John Townsend, choose to end her pregnancy, and it is Mr. Townsend who finds the quack doctor to perform the procedure that results in Nellie's death. Ironically, Broder suggests that Nellie's death prevents Jack from forming a lasting relationship with his fiancée, Evelyn Sands. Despite the blithe unconcern he initially expresses for the welfare of his former lover, an insouciance the all-too well-to-do often show toward the dispossessed, Jack pays for Nellie's death, finally, with his life.

In "*The Movie Man*: The Failure of Aesthetics?" Thierry Dubost is interested in the formal aspects of O'Neill's *The Movie Man* and addresses the significance of this little-studied play within the context of O'Neill's oeuvre. Dubost's evaluation of the aesthetic (or lack of aesthetic) qualities of this play invites critics to better understand the aesthetic framework O'Neill employed when writing this play. Although *The Movie Man* in form and content anticipates O'Neill's later work, Dubost argues that the melodramatic techniques O'Neill relied on when writing *The Movie Man* were inadequate to the unfolding of the plot and, for this reason, abandoned them. Moreover, Dubost argues that O'Neill's inability to resolve the thematic tensions in the play—between love and war—is as responsible for this play's failure as are its aesthetic limitations. O'Neill, not surprisingly, was well aware of this play's gross inadequacies. As Croswell Bowen writes, O'Neill "knew the play was not successful" and did not want it printed.[33] If *The Move Man* was a failed experiment, though, it was one from which O'Neill would learn a great deal; such failures were crucial to the formation of his aesthetic sensibility and his development as an artist.

It is with *Bound East for Cardiff* that O'Neill came into his own as a playwright. Written in 1914, the crucial first year of O'Neill's apprenticeship, and finally staged in 1916, it was the play that gave the Provincetown Players direction. Like *The Moon of the Caribbees*, *The Long Voyage Home*, and *In the Zone*, which, along with *Bound East for Cardiff*, make up the SS *Glencairn* cycle, *Bound East for Cardiff*, despite its brevity and lack of plot, displays a richness and depth that leaves contemporary critics (and lay readers) much to work with. In "'God Stiffen Us': Queering O'Neill's Sea Plays," Phillip Barnhart looks closely at O'Neill's use of homoerotic imagery in three *Glencairn* plays—*The Moon of the Caribbees*, *Bound East for Cardiff*, *In the Zone*—and *A Wife for a Life*. O'Neill's stage directions invite such a reading, as his characters strut about the stage, Barnhart writes, "in various states of undress." Whether on sea or land, the homosocial space in these plays is the scene of intimate companionship, a male bonding that can be coded as, or code for, homoeroticism. The men in the sea plays live in the cramped confines of the forecastle, whereas the men in *A Wife for a Life*, despite the desert expanse surrounding it, occupy a small miner's camp, an isolated space in which sexual intimacy could remain hidden. The source of the anxiety felt by these men, for whom making real connections with others remains elusive, may rest, Barnhart argues, in the inability to give in to a desire that dares not speak its name in the pre-Stonewall era. Importantly,

Barnhart's queer reading of these plays, the first of its kind, opens up new ways of reading O'Neill's later works, including *Strange Interlude*, *The Hairy Ape*, and *Mourning Becomes Electra*.

In "Epistemological Crises in O'Neill's SS *Glencairn* Plays," Michael Y. Bennett draws on Alasdair MacIntyre to argue that the protagonists in the *Glencairn* plays undergo an epistemological crisis, or a moment when assumptions about the way the world *seems* come into conflict with the way the world *is*. As MacIntyre writes, for those undergoing an epistemological crisis, "the relationship of *seems* to *is* becomes crucial."[34] This "relationship" is particularly crucial, Bennett argues, for the protagonists in the *Glencairn* plays, for whom the veil is lifted as their beliefs—their pipe dreams—are proven false or, in MacIntyre's words, shown to be "susceptible of rival interpretations."[35] Bennett links this crisis to the slippage between realism and naturalism in the sea plays: Putatively free individuals (in the mode of realism) are ineluctably bound (à la naturalism). Bennett goes on to argue that the audience also experiences this "two-fold epistemological crisis" (the tension between realism and naturalism), as it, like the protagonists in the sea plays, tries to reconcile two conflicting worldviews, one that allows for freedom and one that does not. For Bennett, this tension—between *seems* and *is*—is the "central tug" of the *Glencairn* plays.

For scholars and fans of O'Neill, the October 17, 2011, issue of *The New Yorker* included a wonderful surprise, O'Neill's *Exorcism*, a one-act play long believed to be lost to history. Written in 1919 and performed by the Provincetown Players in 1920, *Exorcism: A Play of Anti-Climax* is based on O'Neill's suicide attempt by an overdose of Veronal (barbiturate) tablets in January 1912. While there has been much speculation over the years about the veracity of the various accounts (by Agnes Boulton and George Jean Nathan, for example) of O'Neill's attempt to end his life, it was assumed that *Exorcism* would have supplied the most accurate rendering of that dreadful night at Jimmy the priest's. But as with so many of O'Neill's one-acts, this play is as interesting for what it reveals about O'Neill's development as a playwright as it is for what it reveals about his life. In "'The Curtain is Lowered': Self-Revelation and the Problem of Form in *Exorcism*," Kurt Eisen sets *Exorcism* within the context of *The Iceman Cometh* and *Long Day's Journey into Night* to show how O'Neill struggled with dramatic techniques that he was not quite yet able to fully manage. Ambition outpaced ability, in *Exorcism*, as O'Neill sought to transmute the impulse toward confession into art. *Exorcism* shows O'Neill, in Eisen's words, searching "for a sufficient form," a way to give voice to the private self in the language of art.

Between 1919, the year O'Neill completed *Exorcism*, and 1921 O'Neill would craft a series of plays that would not only change his life but push the American theater in a wholly new direction. O'Neill's skill as a playwright—his ability to find sufficient form for his vision—was in full force by 1920, the year he won the Pulitzer Prize for *Beyond the Horizon*. But even as *Beyond the Horizon* was in production (in 1919), O'Neill was hard at work on *Anna Christie* and *The Emperor Jones*, and before *Anna Christie* opened on Broadway in 1921, the first drafts of *The Hairy Ape* were well under way.[36] While *Anna Christie* won O'Neill his second Pulitzer Prize, in O'Neill's catalog *The Emperor Jones* and *The Hairy Ape* have stood the test of time in a way that *Anna Christie* hasn't; and purely in terms of theatricality, it is impossible to overstate the importance of *The Emperor Jones* and *The Hairy Ape* in O'Neill's oeuvre. They are some of his most exciting plays, and they continue to be produced in new, experimental, if sometimes controversial, ways.[37] And the attention they still garner from scholars attests to their staying power as innovative theater.

In "'Aint' Nothin' Dere but de Tress!': Ghosts and the Forest in *The Emperor Jones*," Paul D. Streufert sets *The Emperor Jones* within the context of dramatic traditions that stretch back to Aeschylus and forward, through the Puritans, to Ann Radcliffe. It is through ghost-inspired fear and terror that Brutus Jones, in Streufert's words, is driven back "through his personal and collective past." By employing ghosts as he does, O'Neill's play finds itself in the company of ghost dramas from Aeschylus's *Persians* (472 BCE) to Strindberg's *The Ghost Sonata* (1907) and Angela Gimke's *Rachel* (1916); O'Neill's forest, for which, in Streufert's reading, Mary Rowlandson's captivity narrative serves as a model, is the wilderness of the Puritan imagination—an uncanny place of darkness, chaos, and sin—and "functions as the primary agent of terror in the play." A deeper understanding of O'Neill's use of ghosts and the forest in *The Emperor Jones* invites a reexamination of later plays, like *Long Day's Journey into Night*, in which the ghosts of the past are almost always present.

In "Neither Fallen Angel nor Risen Ape: Desentimentalizing Robert Smith," Thomas Connolly argues that *The Hairy Ape* deserves to be read in terms of its "absolute theatricality" and not simply as social commentary or as a "fitfully expressionistic American play." Against biographical readings that emphasize the "person" of Robert Smith, Connolly insists on reading Yank as a theatrical character who functions less as a representative of the proletariat than as a character "within the convention of the theatrical ape" that runs from *Jocko, où le singe du Brésil* to the recent *The Planet of the Apes*. Such a reading refuses to sentimentalize (or insist on sympathy for) Yank and instead reads his character as a rhetorical construction performing as an "ape-man." Connolly's formalist reading, then, emphasizes theatricality over the traditional sociological or biographical readings of *The Hairy Ape*, one of O'Neill's most frequently staged and most beloved plays.

If O'Neill's one-acts thematically and stylistically telescope his later works, they also adumbrate theatrical developments that would not take root in the American or European theater for decades. In "Waiting for O'Neill," Steven Bloom considers elements in Beckett's work—codependent relationships, enslavement to repetition, the presence of death—that hark back to O'Neill's early plays, and argues that O'Neill's vision of an isolated man "bemoaning his fate" prefigures existential drama and the Theater of the Absurd. Bloom shows how O'Neill's sea plays are Janus-faced, looking back to the conventions of his father's theater, while, at the same time, capturing a Hemingwayesque "winner take nothing" sensibility that would become a hallmark of twentieth-century drama. In a similar vein, Robert Combs, in "O'Neill's *Hughie*: The Sea Plays Revisited," traces a number of thematic concerns that appear over the arc of O'Neill's career as a playwright. The isolated man in the sea plays—surrounded by an uncaring, unforgiving sea—becomes, in *Hughie*, a lonely man surrounded by a vast, indifferent city. O'Neill's use of the monologue in the Sea Plays and *Hughie*, Combs argues, expresses human isolation and the difficulty of making human connections in the modern world, a world in which the individual seeks, often in vain, to know where he fits in; and out of despair, out of a deep need to bury the reality of his insignificance, he creates a pipe dream as a buffer against the abyss. The style and substance of these plays, as Combs makes clear, capture the quintessence of O'Neill's art.

That so many of O'Neill's one-acts have never been staged has everything to do with their acknowledged lack of theatrical merit; it's fair to say that the "lost plays" were lost for a reason. O'Neill's penchant for melodrama early on in his career often conspired with an exaggerated literary sensibility to make plays that were not just bad but unstageable. Whereas stage directions are meant to give actors cues—what to do and when—O'Neill's stage directions often consisted of thematic content or commentary with little pragmatic value for producers, directors, or actors. What might make for inter-esting reading can just as easily make for strange theater, and this is precisely what the Neo-Futurists' original production, in the fall of 2011, of a number of O'Neill's one-act plays exposed to comic effect. In "Condensed Comedy: The Neo-Futurists Perform O'Neill's

Stage Directions," Zander Brietzke gives a firsthand account of the limitations of O'Neill's dramatic craft, or, to put it another way, the incommensurability between a play as O'Neill imagines it and how it is or can be performed. As the title of Brietzke's essay suggests, The Neo-Futurists performed only the stage directions of O'Neill's plays, leaving out the dialogue completely. O'Neill's intentions, as indicated in detailed stage directions, are often difficult, if not impossible, to translate onto the stage, and as Brietzke observed, moments in the one-acts that are meant to evoke pathos are, without dialogue, rendered comic or absurd. It is well known that O'Neill disliked producers, directors, and actors, and found nearly everyone involved in the staging of his work inadequate to the task of making his vision come alive. O'Neill thought his plays better when read, and as his elaborate stage directions evidence, he felt little compelled to put the needs of actors before his dramatic vision. Ironically, the Neo-Futurist production, by putting the emphasis on what was to be unsaid, put the actors—at the expense of plot and character—on center stage.

★★★

Although not all of O'Neill's early plays were successful, it is a great credit to his inborn talent, his native eloquence, that a close study of his earliest efforts unearths an embarrassment of riches. We, as children, babble our way to articulateness; we all clear our throats before we sing. So it is no surprise that O'Neill's first stammerings as a playwright were as mellifluous as they were off-key. Art, though, isn't born of nothing. Its wellspring is deep and mysterious, and as O'Neill knew well, giving shape to an intangible life force is a daunting proposition. O'Neill sacrificed all to his muse. He turned the ghosts of his past into art, and the spectral fingerprints of O'Neill's singular touch can be detected in twentieth- and twenty-first-century American drama from Albee to Lindsay-Abaire. But when we read O'Neill deeply, we find more than just influence. We find ourselves at our best and at our worst reflected back at us. For this reason alone it is worth returning again and again to O'Neill, a playwright whose vision tells the tale of man's suffering, his triumph over suffering, and his triumph through suffering. It was, for O'Neill, the only tale worth telling.

NOTES

1. Edward L. Shaughnessy, *Down the Nights and Down the Days: Eugene O'Neill's Catholic Sensibility* (Notre Dame, IN: University of Notre Dame, 2000), 5. O'Neill's view of tragedy is, as has been

well documented, deeply indebted to the Greeks. In her introduction to the Lombardo translation of Homer's *Iliad*, Sheila Murnaghan writes, "In his dealings with Zeus, Achilles confronts the painful lessons—the gap between what humans can imagine and long for and what they can actually have, the difficulty of learning except too late and by suffering—that were later to be explored in classical tragedy, and he has experiences that we have come to label 'tragic.' Like many later tragic characters"—say, Robert Mayo, in *Beyond the Horizon*—"and like many of the heroes of the *Iliad* . . . Achilles performs his most memorable and most valued actions when he feels the gods have abandoned him" (Sheila Murnaghan, introduction to *Iliad*, by Homer, trans. Stanley Lombardo [Indianapolis: Hackett, 1997], xvii–lviii). The Greek hero is, in O'Neill, a Nietzschean Übermensch who succeeds by failing. Robert Mayo becomes, in the absence of God, a hero by struggling to attain the unattainable. He, O'Neill writes, "wills his own defeat when he pursues the unattainable. But his struggle is his success" (Ulrich Halfmann, ed., *Eugene O'Neill: Comments on the Drama and the Theater: A Source Book* [Tubingen: Gunter Narr, 1987], 26).

2. Eugene O'Neill, *Selected Letters of Eugene O'Neill*, ed. Travis Bogard and Jackson R. Bryer (New Haven, CT: Yale University Press, 1988), 332.
3. Shaughnessy, *Down the Nights*, 41.
4. Shaughnessy, *Down the Nights*, 41.
5. O'Neill, *Selected Letters*, 195. For O'Neill, and others of his "mindset," the tragic was built into the structure of the human experience. It was "part of the nature of things" (Shaughnessy, *Down the Nights*, 38). As Edward Farley writes, in *Divine Empathy: A Theology of God*, "suffering, frustration, and nonfulfillments are not occasional or accidental but are built into the organic, historical, and psychological existence" ([Minneapolis: Fortress, 1996], 64). There is, O'Neill recognized, no escaping "nonfulfillments." There is only coming to terms with them.
6. O'Neill, *Selected Letters*, 25.
7. Louis Sheaffer, *O'Neill: Son and Playwright* (New York: Cooper Square, 2002), 252.
8. O'Neill, *Selected Letters*, 26.
9. Sheaffer, *O'Neill: Son and Playwright*, 252.
10. O'Neill, *Selected Letters*, 9.
11. Travis Bogard, *Contour in Time: The Plays of Eugene O'Neill* (New Haven, CT: Yale University Press, 1988), 16.
12. O'Neill, *Selected Letters*, 438.
13. Arthur Gelb and Barbara Gelb, afterword to *Four Plays by Eugene O'Neill*, by Eugene O'Neill (New York: Signet, 2007), 309
14. Bogard, *Contour in Time*, 16.

15. Russell Carl Brignano, *Richard Wright: An Introduction to the Man and His Works* (Pittsburgh: University of Pittsburgh Press, 1982), x.

16. O'Neill, *Selected Letters*, 25.

17. Virginia Floyd, *The Plays of Eugene O'Neill: A New Assessment* (New York: Ungar, 1985), 76.

18. David Harvey, *The Condition of Postmodernity: An Enquiry into the Origins of Cultural Change* (Malden, MA: Blackwell, 1990), 123.

19. Antonio Gramsci, *Selections from the Prison Notebooks*, trans. Quintin Hoare and Geoffrey Nowell Smith (New York: International Publishers, 1972), 302.

20. Ibid.

21. This paragraph draws heavily on David Harvey, *The Condition of Postmodernity*, 28.

22. Ibid.

23. John S. Bak, "Eugene O'Neill and John Reed: Recording the Body Politic, 1913–1922," *Eugene O'Neill Review* 20.1–2 (1996), 32.

24. Ibid.

25. M. H. Abrams, *A Glossary of Literary Terms*, 7th ed. (Boston: Heinle & Heinle, 1999), 85.

26. Ibid.

27. Bogard, *Contour in Time*, 245, 242.

28. Deanna M. Toten Beard, "American Experimentalism, American Expressionism, and Early O'Neill," in *A Companion to Twentieth-Century American Drama*, ed. David Krasner (Malden, MA: Blackwell, 2005), 63.

29. Ibid.

30. Ellen Chesler, *Woman of Valor: Margaret Sanger and the Birth Control Movement in America* (New York: Simon and Schuster, 2007), 130. The NBCL was established in March 1915 by Mary Ware Dennett, Clara Gruening Stillman and Jessie Ashley. For this reference, I am grateful to Dr. Cathy Moran Hajo, professor of history at New York University and associate editor and assistant director of The Margaret Sanger Papers Project. See Constance M. Chen, *"The Sex Side of Life": Mary Ware Dennett's Pioneering Battle for Birth Control and Sex Education* (New York: New Press, 1996), 181.

31. Sanger and O'Neill, for example, were both involved with the Ferrer Center in New York City. The Center was a "forum for labor and cultural radicalism" (Chesler, *"The Sex Side of Life,"* 101). At the Center, Chesler writes, "Eugene O'Neill and Theodore Dreiser taught writing, and Margaret lectured on sexuality and family limitation" (Chesler, *"The Sex Side of Life,"* 101).

32. Chesler, *"The Sex Side of Life,"* 62.

33. Croswell Bowen, *The Curse of the Misbegotten: A Tale of the House of O'Neill* (London: Rupert Hart-Davis, 1960), 81.

34. Alasdair MacIntyre, *The Task of Philosophy: Selected Essays*, vol. 1 (Cambridge: Cambridge University Press, 2006), 3.
35. Ibid.
36. Gelb and Gelb, afterword, 314–16.
37. For a very fine treatment of the Wooster Group's production of *The Emperor Jones*, see Aoife Monks, "'Genuine Negroes and Real Bloodhounds': Cross-Dressing, Eugene O'Neill, the Wooster Group, and *The Emperor Jones*," *Modern Drama* 48 (2005): 540–64.

WORKS CITED

Abrams, M. H. *A Glossary of Literary Terms*. 7th ed. Boston: Heinle, 1999.
Bak, John S. "Eugene O'Neill and John Reed: Recording the Body Politic, 1913–1922." *Eugene O'Neill Review* 20.1–2 (1996): 17–35. Print.
Beard, Deanna M. Toten. "American Experimentalism, American Expressionism, and Early O'Neill." *A Companion to Twentieth-Century American Drama*. Ed. David Krasner. Malden: Blackwell, 2005. 53–68. Print.
Bogard, Travis. *Contour in Time: The Plays of Eugene O'Neill*. New York: Oxford UP, 1988. Print.
Bowen, Croswell. *The Curse of the Misbegotten: A Tale of the House of O'Neill*. London: Rupert Hart-Davis, 1960. Print.
Brignano, Russell C. *Richard Wright: An Introduction to the Man and His Works*. Pittsburgh: U of Pittsburgh P, 1982. Print.
Chen, Constance M. *"The Sex Side of Life": Mary Ware Dennett's Pioneering Battle for Birth Control and Sex Education*. New York: New, 1996. Print.
Chesler, Ellen. *Woman of Valor: Margaret Sanger and the Birth Control Movement in America*. New York: Simon, 2007. Print.
Farley, Edward. *Divine Empathy: A Theology of God*. Minneapolis: Fortress, 1996. Print.
Floyd, Virginia. *The Plays of Eugene O'Neill: A New Assessment*. New York: Ungar, 1985. Print.
Gelb, Arthur, and Barbara Gelb. Afterword. *Four Plays by Eugene O'Neill*. By Eugene O'Neill. New York: Signet, 2007. 309–17. Print.
Gramsci, Antonio. *Selections from the Prison Notebooks*. Trans. Quintin Hoare and Geoffrey Nowell Smith. New York: International, 1972. Print.
Halfmann, Ulrich, ed., *Eugene O'Neill: Comments on the Drama and the Theater: A Source Book*. Tubingen: Gunter Narr, 1987. Print.
Harvey, David. *The Condition of Postmodernity: A Enquiry in the Origins of Cultural Change*. Malden: Blackwell, 1990. Print.
MacIntyre, Alasdair. *The Tasks of Philosophy: Selected Essays*. Vol. 1. Cambridge: Cambridge UP, 2006. Print.
Monks, Aoife. "'Genuine Negroes and Read Bloodhounds': Cross-Dressing, Eugene O'Neill, the Wooster Group, and the Emperor Jones." *Modern Drama* 48 (2005): 540–64. Print.

Murnaghan, Sheila. Introduction. *Iliad*. By Homer. Trans. Stanley Lombardo. Indianapolis: Hackett, 1997. xvii–lviii. Print.

O'Neill, Eugene. *Selected Letters of Eugene O'Neill*. Ed. Travis Bogard and Jackson R. Bryer. New Haven: Yale UP, 1988. Print.

Shaughnessy, Edward L. *Down the Nights and Down the Days: Eugene O'Neill's Catholic Sensibility*. Notre Dame: U of Notre Dame P, 2000. Print.

Sheaffer, Louis. *O'Neill: Son and Playwright*. Vol. 1. 1968. New York: Cooper Square, 2002. Print.

CHAPTER 1

THE PLAYWRIGHT'S THEATRE
O'NEILL'S USE OF THE PROVINCETOWN PLAYERS AS A ONE-ACT LABORATORY

Jeff Kennedy

When the Provincetown Players formally organized in September of 1916, just prior to starting a working theatre in New York City, young playwright Eugene O'Neill insisted on one thing: that they name the playhouse they were to create "The Playwright's Theatre." If his intentions for participating in this new theatrical venture were not clear from this, O'Neill soon set a pattern of writing plays to be performed that would help answer questions he had as a playwright, something like a self-imposed curriculum to inform his work. O'Neill wanted to try new approaches, wondering how an audience would respond and what their limits were with certain structures and techniques. He believed that this amateur company committed to experimenting, and geared toward the creation of an American identity in theatre, would allow him to test his ideas. His investigating included finding out how long an audience would allow a monologue, whether he could hypnotize the audience into believing they were mad, the use of mood versus action, the use of African American characters when this was not yet part of the professional American theatre, and the use of expressionistic techniques.

After the first summer of plays presented by the amateurs in Provincetown, Massachusetts, George Cram Cook began to have a vision for how he could establish what he often called his "Beloved Community of Life-Givers." Cook had dreamed they could create a place where they would write their "own plays and put them on ourselves, giving writers, actors, designers, and a chance to work together without the commercial thing imposed from without. A whole community working together, developing unsuspected talents."[1] Cook also saw the need for an American identity to emerge in the writing styles and structures of literature and plays, having fostered and encouraged many writers while an editor at the *Friday Literary Review* with Floyd Dell in Chicago. This was further encouraged by his 1912 viewing of the Irish Players from the Abbey Theatre in Dublin, who presented an Irish identity in the plays written by their countrymen (this company inspired O'Neill as well). It was Cook's belief, one that was tested over his years with the original Provincetown Players, that only a truly amateur group could provide the environment necessary for the experimentation needed to develop an American voice in theatre. So when the original constitution of the Provincetown Players was drawn up at the end of their second summer in Provincetown, Massachusetts, it states immediately that their purpose was "to produce plays written by active members or by others in whose work the active members may be interested." In the second section of resolutions, it is clear that from the beginning that the group wanted the author of the plays they presented to have full authority of its production. Resolution 1 states that the "President shall cooperate with the author to produce a play like its author prefers. All aspects of the theatre (i.e. actors, sets, costumes, etc.) shall be at the disposal of the author . . . The author shall produce the play without hindrance, according to his own ideas." Resolution 2 determines that the "Author must select his own cast, with the assistance of the President, and supervise rehearsals and direct the production."[2] The officially organized group was both the type that Cook desired to helm and one by whom O'Neill wanted his plays produced.

O'Neill's first play to be presented in Provincetown, and likewise when they moved to New York City, was the sea play *Bound East for Cardiff*, the play that, when heard, playwright and original member Susan Glaspell claims the Players "knew what we were for."[3] What was unique about the play, causing the Players to feel as if they'd found something they could rally around, is what O'Neill scholar Travis Bogard attributes as O'Neill's ability to capture the "dramatic reality" of life at sea. What O'Neill was able to do with his story of Yank and Driscoll—one a sailor dying at sea, the other his loyal shipmate of five years—was to create the truth of this situation for the stage in a way that had only previously been created in novels and poems, "leaving fertile opportunity for one of Eugene's experiences."[4] Louis Sheaffer comments that the play is "told in crude, flavorsome sailor talk" and is "more truly poetic than any of O'Neill's poetry; more to the point it reflected the spirit of brooding compassion, of tragic inevitability, that would distinguish his mature writings."[5] Brenda Murphy points out that "the play's action is at once the simplest and the most meaningful one can imagine. A man dies in the midst of the milieu in which he has lived a life that was the opposite of the one he dreamed of. The action consists of his talking about it to his best friend" and she believes that with this play O'Neill "captured a new authenticity in its rejection of the theatrical conventions of what was currently realism."[6] Once *Bound East for Cardiff* opened at the "The Playwright's Theatre" in New York on November 3, 1916, giving O'Neill his first production in the city, he turned his attention toward writing plays that tested the limits of audiences using devices he wanted to explore.

The next new play O'Neill contributed was a piece he'd begun in Provincetown that past summer of 1916: *Before Breakfast*. The play is unique in that it presents only one character onstage and another who does not speak and remains offstage, save for one appearance of his hand. O'Neill read and was inspired by the works of Swedish playwright August Strindberg while he was convalescing after his bout with tuberculosis during the fall of 1913 to early 1914. Bogard writes that

> what Strindberg dramas would have meant to a young American writer in the early years is not difficult to imagine. In the naturalistic plays, the extraordinary sharpness of focus, the strength of the major lines of action, the shocking sexuality and the psychological force of the characterization would have combined to make the work of every other contemporary dramatist pallid by comparison. To one like O'Neill, whose taste was for a subject matter much stronger than the routines of sin and redemption that had passed for an image of life in much American theatre, Strindberg must have seemed like Truth's original . . . he felt an instinctive, personal sympathy for what he found in Strindberg's work.[7]

Most scholars believe that O'Neill used Strindberg's *The Stronger* as a model for writing *Before Breakfast*, imitating the fact that only one person speaks during the play, though in Strindberg's play there is another nonspeaking character onstage, which he later modeled in his play *Hughie*. When accepting the Nobel Prize in 1936, O'Neill said that "it was reading [Strindberg's] plays . . . that first gave me the urge to write for the theatre myself. If there is anything of lasting worth in my work, it is due to that original impulse from him, which has continued as my inspiration down all the years since then."[8] Bogard qualifies that when compared with Strindberg's *The Stronger*, O'Neill's play "is a paltry affair," and that he "aped the technical manner and the superficies of Strindberg's subject matter but caught none of its sophistication," particularly Strindberg's "sharply focused conflict," of which he believes *Before Breakfast* has none.[9]

The Players' executive committee member Edna Kenton reports that O'Neill one evening asked with a grin, "I wonder how long an audience will stand for a monologue?" and *Before Breakfast* was his experiment to find out. She continues that as rehearsals went on, he asked, "How much are they going to stand before they begin to break?" and that by casting himself in the silent offstage role he was going to find out. Though she calls it one of O'Neill's "very minor plays," she also defends it as a "deliberate experiment for a definite result—the endurance of the audience," and the results of the experiment helped him write future plays, including *The Emperor Jones*, in which he uses monologues extensively.[10]

Before Breakfast is set in the early fall in a Village flat on Christopher Street beginning at 8:30 a.m. The play presents Mrs. Rowland, who directs all her comments onstage to her husband, Alfred, who is offstage in the bedroom. The unhappy Mrs. Rowland is described as shrewish by most critics as she spends the entire play berating her sensitive poet husband whose only success seems to be wooing other women. She reveals that pregnancy forced their marriage and she bemoans the extent to which they have fallen from their former selves. She condemns her husband's drinking, his inability to get a job, even the flat in which they live. At one point, the husband's hand reaches out to be seen onstage to accept some shaving water from the wife. As she continues, the wife reveals she's found a letter from his lover and that she will never give him a divorce. We hear a "stifled groan of pain" and then "the noise of a chair being overturned and something [crashing] heavily to the floor" from offstage, to which the wife goes to investigate when she receives no response to her inquiry. She discovers the husband on the floor of the bedroom, having committed suicide by slashing his throat, which sends the wife "shrieking madly," and the play ends as she runs out their front door.[11] Arthur and Barbara Gelb feel that "O'Neill himself obviously was the model of the suicidal husband," from the wife's description of the husband as someone who was Harvard-educated but now loafs around barrooms, to him killing time "with that good-for-nothing lot of artists from the Square," down to the description of the "sensitive hand with slender fingers. It trembles."[12] Arthur Feinsod sees this play, along with Strindberg's, as prefiguring "an extreme simplicity later to be seen in the works of Samuel Beckett." He sees *Before Breakfast*, combined with Alfred Kreymborg's *Lima Beans*, which attempted to treat its three characters like musical instruments in a sonata, as allowing the third bill of the Players' first New York season to offer "a common style around self-imposed limitation."[13]

Ironically, the older style of acting that O'Neill was trying to steer away from in his plays came into conflict while rehearsing the play when his famous actor father, James, attended a rehearsal and proceeded to instruct the young actress Mary Pyne in the role of Mrs. Rowland. Many who were there remember the seasoned actor's "grandiose presence," describing him as "a striking figure with fur-collared coat, gold-headed cane and a diamond ring on his finger."[14] Hutchins Hapgood describes that the elder O'Neill "did not approve the diction or 'business' of the actress; he began to show her how acting was done, how points were made, with the voice and gesture of Monte Cristo."[15] Pyne wisely did everything he instructed, "grandiloquent gestures, melodramatic inflections and all," and James told her, "You are a most intelligent young actress. I don't need to give you any further instruction."[16] Helen Deutsch and Stella Hanau describe that while the elder O'Neill was instructing, the younger "stalked up and down, muttering his displeasure," disagreeing with his every point "in a perfect Freudian patter."[17] William Zorach recalls that while James was critiquing, "Gene slumped down in his seat. 'That old fogy!' he said when he left."[18] It's reported that "as soon as he had done," Eugene "redirected her from the beginning to end."[19] O'Neill cast himself in the offstage role of the husband and his participation, sliding out his arm during the play, was his last as an actor on any stage. However, from his vantage point backstage, O'Neill could gauge the audience's response to this extended monologue and this informed his future use of the device.

In the fall of 1918, the Provincetown Players were forced to move from their location at 139 Macdougal Street in Greenwich Village, New York City and they secured a building just a few doors down at 133. O'Neill very much wanted to be represented in the first bill of the Players' new season in a new theatre and ultimately wrote the play *Where the Cross Is Made*. By this point in his life, O'Neill had married Agnes Boulton and was almost completely separated from the daily processes of the Players, which were primarily in the care of George Cram Cook and the company's executive committee. Instead, O'Neill spent his time with Boulton either in Provincetown or at her home on the Jersey shore and concentrated almost exclusively on his writing. While in Provincetown in early November 1918, O'Neill received a letter from Cook that insisted he come to New York to supervise the casting and rehearsals of *Where the Cross Is Made*. Cook reported there were "strong disagreements" between many members as to how O'Neill's play should be staged, and Cook wanted O'Neill there to "back him up."[20] The O'Neills journeyed to New York City and were greeted with the flurry caused by the company converting the inside of 133 Macdougal into a theatre, as well as the announcement of the end of World War I, which had launched the city into a mode of joyous frenzy. Boulton describes Cook taking about an hour to describe to O'Neill what the finished theatre would look like and to discuss the technical aspects of *Where the Cross Is Made* on the new stage. As O'Neill rejoined Boulton in the back of the theatre, Ida Rauh, who was directing and performing in *Cross*, entered and began verbally attacking O'Neill: "You'll have to do something about the ghosts, Gene. The boys never *can* look like ghosts, and you know it. The audience will simply laugh at them."[21] O'Neill responded, "Everyone in the play is mad except the girl. Everyone sees the ghosts except the girl. What I want to do is hypnotize the audience so when they see the ghosts they will think they are mad too! And by that I mean the whole audience! Remember—[quoting from the Players' by-laws] 'The author shall produce his plays without hindrance, according to his own ideas.'"[22]

Where the Cross Is Made portrays a sea captain who obsessively stands looking out to sea every night on the roof deck of his house. Having gone mad, he claims he's waiting for his ship to return with a treasure he and his crew had buried on a South Pacific island. His son, Nat, aware of his father's madness, goes so far as to burn the map with the cross that shows where the treasure is buried. Eventually, however, his father's relentlessness has caused Nat to become equally possessed. Only his sister seems able to stand apart from the delusion and tries to help them. At the climax of the play, O'Neill calls for all the lights to turn green and the ghosts of three sailors who were killed in the shipwreck to appear, carrying a treasure chest. O'Neill's stage directions read, "The forms [of the ghosts] rise noiselessly into the room from the stairs . . . Water drips from their soaked and rotten clothes. Their hair is matted, intertwined with slimy strands of seaweed. Their eyes, as they glide silently into the room, stare frightfully wide at nothing. Their flesh in the green light has the suggestion of decomposition. Their bodies sway limply, nervelessly, rhythmically as if to the pulse of long swells of the deep sea."[23] As the ghosts enter, both the father and son believe their ship has come home. The father dies of a heart attack and his son sadly replaces him, now mad with his own nightly watch of the sea.

Kenton called rehearsals for *Cross* "one prolonged argument."[24] As the play was rehearsed, it became evident that the last thing the ghosts could do on a wood-slat stage was carry a chest up the stairs "noiselessly" and "glide silently." Most of the company pleaded with O'Neill at the dress rehearsal to get rid of the ghosts "as if it were a favor to the dying." O'Neill refused and said that "perhaps the first rows will snicker—perhaps they won't. We'll see."[25] O'Neill did not wait to find out if they did or not: as was typical for him, he and Boulton left town after that final dress rehearsal on November 21, 1918. Critical response to the play was mixed. Heywood Broun praised the play as "among the best things which the Players have done" and singles out the final scene saying, "We sat so close that there was little visual illusion, but the sweep of the story and the exceptional skill with which the scene of the delusion is written made us distinctly fearful of the silent dead men who walked across the stage."[26] Other reviews were not as generous. *The Morning Telegraph* headline read, "Only the Captain's Daughter Stays Sane," and the review states, "If you would like to enjoy the sensation of going mad you'll find the want supplied in the bill with which the Provincetown Players began their fifth season."[27] The *Dramatic Mirror* called *Cross* the "latest of Eugene O'Neill's remarkably vital sea plays," and that it was the "most notable" of the evening. The review goes on to say that "the room, fitted up to resemble a ship's cabin, provides a realistic setting," and that the play "is written with the skill and directness O'Neill usually employs and may be ranked among his best works."[28]

During the period of 1916–17, O'Neill wrote three new sea plays in addition to *Bound East for Cardiff*, two utilizing the same ship, SS *Glencairn*, and the same company of characters with minor additions and subtractions, many of whom had appeared in *Bound East*. These plays were *The Long Voyage Home*, *In the Zone*, and *The Moon of the Caribbees*. In spite of their obvious connections, O'Neill never intended to have them performed together, nor is there any connecting narrative between them. He explained his choice of continuing characters and vessel in a letter to a magazine publisher in 1917: "I have used members of the same crew throughout [the cycle], because judging from my own experience as a sailor, I thought I had . . . picked out the typical mixed crew of the average British tramp steamer."[29] O'Neill's "own experience" began in June 1910 when, as a 21-year-old, he became determined to taste the romance of life on the sea, his desire having been fueled by his reading Joseph Conrad's 1897 novel *The Nigger of Narcissus*. While working as the assistant company manager for his father's touring production of *The White Sister*, the young

O'Neill's first job in the theatre, he visited the docks in Boston. There he met the captain of the *Charles Racine*, a 220-foot long Norwegian square-rigger[30] with a crew of mates and 19 others, and he was offered passage on the ship for a small fee and the promise of doing light work. After completing the show's tour and revisiting Boston to pursue the possibility, O'Neill's father gave him the $75 needed to book passage, hoping it would improve the young O'Neill's health and teach him some much-needed discipline. O'Neill set out on a two-month, 5,900-mile journey to Buenos Aires. Once he arrived in Argentina, O'Neill lived as a vagrant for ten months, taking a series of unusual jobs to earn just enough money to survive. His lowest point came from a reoccurrence of the malarial fever he had contracted while traveling a few years before in Honduras. He returned to the United States as a crewman on the British merchant tramp freighter *Ikala*, which became the model for the SS *Glencairn*. O'Neill arrived back in New York on April 15, 1911, but not before the ship made a stop at the Port of Spain in Trinidad to pick up 250 tons of coal and more than 500 bags of coconuts. It was this stop, with the ship anchored off a half-mile from the jetties, that inspired the setting for *The Moon of the Caribbees*.

The Moon of the Caribbees premiered in the second bill of the 1918–19 season on December 20. In the winter of 1917–18, O'Neill showed Nina Moise, who had become the Player's first professional staging director, a script of *Moon*. It had already been decided, though, that the play could not be produced without a larger stage, which the Players hoped to have by their next season. After the opening of *Where the Cross Is Made*, O'Neill and Boulton stayed in a house she owned in West Point Pleasant on the Jersey shore. While there, and similar to his experience with *Cross*, O'Neill received a letter from Cook, again insisting upon his return to New York, this time because rehearsals of *Moon* were not going well and, again, he returned to assist.

O'Neill clearly thought *The Moon of the Caribbees* was his best work to date, often carrying a copy of the script with him and judging people's aesthetic depth by their response to it. He had boasted to Moise that "no one else in the world could have written that one."[31] Bogard calls the play a "nearly flawless dramatic poem"[32] and believes that, with this play, O'Neill "perfected in one-act form what he had earlier called a 'tragedy of fate.'"[33] Unlike *Zone* and *Voyage*, *Moon* has almost no narrative, depending instead on poetic mood for its dramatic effect, a departure from his Harvard playwriting teacher George Pierce Baker's axioms and Aristotelian rules. O'Neill wrote Bennett Clark that the play was his "first real break with theatrical traditions."[34] Bogard believes that it was "the end of the first phase of

O'Neill's career," that from this play on he "would begin to test other directions other than realism."[35] Brooks Atkinson would later describe *Moon* as a "drama of silences."[36]

The Moon of the Caribbees opens as the "full moon, half-way up the sky, throws a clear light on the deck. The sea is calm and the ship motionless." The play is set on the forward section of the main deck of the SS *Glencairn*, anchored off an island in the West Indies. In the distance, a "melancholy Negro chant, faint and far-off, drifts, crooning, over the water." As the curtain opens, almost all the crew of the ship are on deck, smoking pipes or cigarettes, with the "low murmur" of conversations going on, followed by "a sudden silence in which the singing from the land can be plainly heard."[37] The constancy of the chant, performed in the December 1918 performance by Edna St. Vincent Millay, her two sisters and their mother,[38] makes it a formidable character in the play; Bogard calls it the "central agent of the conflict in the play, the protagonist against whom the men react . . . It never goes away. The men are defined by their relationship to the offstage song."[39] O'Neill's final stage direction of the play likens the music to "the mood of the moonlight, made audible."[40] This kind of aural device used here by O'Neill suggests the similar uses of sounds and music in many of his other plays, like the constancy of the drums in *The Emperor Jones* and the fog horns surprising the silences in *Long Day's Journey into Night*.

In a letter to Barrett Clark, O'Neill compares *Moon* with his other sea plays and explains his reason for it being his "favorite": "The spirit of the sea—a big thing—is in this latter play the hero . . . In *The Moon*, posed against a background of that beauty, sad because it is eternal, which is one of the revealing moods of the sea's truth . . . To me *The Moon* works with truth . . . *The Moon* [is] an attempt to achieve a higher plane of bigger, finer values."[41] Margaret Loftus Ranald, agreeing that in the play O'Neill develops mood, also sees *Moon* as his first experiment "with the impact of black culture upon whites, and this, his first truly multicultural play, foreshadows also his interest in 'total theatre.' Character, theme, and mood become interdependent . . . The clash of cultures leads to a bacchanal and consequent violence, reinforced by music and dance."[42] While Ranald's observation may be true, the characters of the Negro women were played in blackface by white actresses, and the use of actual black actors in black character roles by the Players had to wait until the production of O'Neill's *The Dreamy Kid* in the fall of 1919.

The new 1919–20 Provincetown Players season has been referred to as the "Season of Youth" because Cook stepped aside for a year, taking a sabbatical to Provincetown to write, and allowed the younger members of the organization to run the company, primarily led by James Light and, initially, Ida Rauh. The season began on October 31, 1919, and opened with a play by O'Neill, as had been the tradition, but rather than open with a totally new play, they opened with a play that had been written for the year prior yet not produced. *The Dreamy Kid* had been rejected because Cook felt they needed a "stronger" play; O'Neill had complied by writing *Where the Cross Is Made*. However, by this time O'Neill was writing full-length plays and *The Dreamy Kid* was one of the last one-acts he would write until *Hughie* in 1942, so if the company wanted a new O'Neill one-act, this would have to be it. The play began when O'Neill's imagination was caught by the story of a black gangster named Dreamy that drinking buddy Joe Smith told him. O'Neill initially began to write the idea as a short story in the summer of 1918 and, after writing a page, typed a letter to Lee Foster Hartman of *Harper's Magazine*, dated July 6, 1918, regarding the submission of the story for possible publication.[43] Boulton tells that it started as a short story because O'Neill felt "he could better emphasize . . . the psychological split in the young Negro," writing inner dialogue from inside his mind. However, the desire of the Players for a new play, as well as "the dramatist in him" overcoming "the psychological aspect of the story," led him to begin writing it as a play.[44] After it was finished, O'Neill read the play to the Cooks one night and there was "enthusiasm" for it, but later this turned to doubt, Boulton not remembering if it was because they felt the play wasn't as good as his others or "if there was some difficulty in regard to the Negro cast."[45]

The Dreamy Kid tells the story of a Negro gangster named Dreamy who has killed a white man the night before, but whose grandmother is dying and he risks coming to see her rather than live with a feared curse on his life. Though O'Neill had written dark-skinned women of the Caribbean into *The Moon of the Caribbees*, this was his first time writing a play in which all the characters were African American. Bogard calls the dialect O'Neill wrote for the characters a crude experimentation toward the "authentic language" he later uses in *The Emperor Jones*. Sheaffer tells that O'Neill had originally written a white prostitute as Dreamy's girlfriend Irene, but "since this would have added a distracting element to the story," he changed her to a black character.[46] Though the current Harlem Renaissance was creating a surge of literary work by African American writers, including plays, these were relegated to theatres out of the mainstream, mostly in Harlem and with no possibility of Broadway runs. Musical entertainments were another story, however, and that year *Maid of Harlem*, an all-black musical starring Fats Waller, Mamie Smith, Johnny Dunn, and Perry Bradford, was a hit at the Lincoln Theatre. Ironically, just days after the opening of *The Dreamy Kid*, Al Jolson sang for the first time the Gershwin song "Swanee" that would become his signature number, performing it in blackface makeup. In plays, a white actor "blacking up" when playing a Negro character was typical theatre practice. A momentous occasion in the spring of 1917 was the use of an all-black cast on Broadway in an evening of three one-act plays that dealt with black themes by white playwright Ridgely Torrence. Opening on April 5, 1917, in the seldom-used Garden Theatre and directed by Robert Edmond Jones, the plays incurred the ire of many critics because the actors were not up to their standards for Broadway and the production closed after three weeks. *The Dreamy Kid* was the next occurrence of using all black actors in a play produced by a white theatre company.

Ida Rauh, now one of the two directors of the new season, decided that she would direct *The Dreamy Kid* once it was placed on the bill. O'Neill couldn't possibly have wanted or asked Rauh to direct given all the badgering and argument he'd encountered with her the year before during *Where the Cross Is Made*. Regardless, once at the helm, Rauh insisted on having African American actors play all the roles; whether it was her own sense of racial equality or simply a way to make unique a lesser O'Neill play, is not on record. Regardless, Rauh went to Harlem and searched "the YMCA, the library, the churches, and everywhere else" to find her four actors for the play. Harold Simmelkjaer—"despite the Dutch name, is a negro" said James Weldon Johnson[47]—played the role of Dreamy ("Abe"), Ruth Anderson played Mammy, Leathe Colvert played Ceely Ann, and Margaret Rhodes played Irene.[48] Critic Rebecca Drucker in the *Tribune* said the casting "illumines in a great many ways the psychological values of the piece."[49] Alexander Woollcott for the *Times* mentions the use of an all-black cast but called them "amateurs mostly," consistent with the production, which was "on the quasi-amateur level and pretends to no more." He does, however, compare their acting favorably to the "preposterous production" of the Torrence plays mentioned earlier.[50] Cheryl Black rightly makes the point that Rauh should be given her due for her casting of *The Dreamy King* as making a "singularly influential contribution to American theatre history."[51]

Drucker calls the play by O'Neill "as fine a thing as he has ever done."[52] Critic Woollcott writes that it's a "good" play by the "oncoming" O'Neill, and that "it is interesting too how . . . the author . . .

induces your complete sympathy and pity for a conventionally abhor-rent character."[53] O'Neill was not there for the opening, as he was in Provincetown; his son Shane was born the night before. He would respond to a friend's congratulations for *The Dreamy Kid* by saying, "Of course, I by no means rate it among my best one-act plays for genuine merit, but I did think it would prove theatrically effective and go over with a bang to the audience."[54]

O'Neill's experiments of monologue, portraying ghosts seen in madness, mood, expressionistic devices, and using African American characters conducted with the Provincetown Players were are all put to use significantly in an integrated and culminating way in the 1920 play *The Emperor Jones.* Though he'd already had *Beyond the Horizon* produced on Broadway earlier in 1920, O'Neill knew that the unusual structure and experimental approach of *Jones* would be a real stretch for Broadway and would need to be done in Provincetown, at least initially, to test it out. The demands of the play caused the company to put forward their very best for its production, though they were in terrible financial straits at the time. Their work included Cook build-ing a plaster dome to serve as a cyclorama that made the stage look exceedingly larger, the unique and detailed set design created at the last moment by Cleon Throckmorton, the demands of a larger cast than the Players' typically required (though only three characters had dialogue), and the hiring of Harlem actor Charles Gilpin to play the lead role.

The Emperor Jones is presented in eight scenes, set on a West Indies island, and tells the story of Brutus Jones, an African American Pull-man porter who has escaped a chain gang in the United States after being sentenced for murder. He has come to this West Indian island and taken power after appearing to them to escape death and by tell-ing the natives that he can only be killed by a silver bullet. Jones has taxed the people to his own advantage and realizes his reign will be limited before the people revolt, planning an escape route and provi-sions to facilitate his safe departure with his riches. Though happening sooner than he thought it would, Jones confidently leaves the palace to begin his escape, bequeathing all that is left to an English trader named Smithers. Jones is visibly shaken, however, when the tom-toms of the natives begin and can be heard in the distance. The tom-toms continue from this moment until the end of the play, progressively increasing in tempo, volume, and intensity. From scene two to seven the play is an extended monologue with action for Jones as he attempts his escape, running through the dark of the forest and progressively losing his sense of direction. With each scene, Jones removes more clothing, either from it being torn off or because it becomes cumbersome, so that by the final scenes he is wearing only a breechcloth. In each scene he is confronted by the ghosts of his and his ancestors' past and shoots one of his remaining six bullets to make them go away. Throughout each of these scenes, Jones progressively becomes more penitent, asking God for forgiveness for his deeds and pleading for his protection. The final scene is the next morning back at the edge of the forest, with Smithers and a large native named Lem whose men are in the forest looking for Jones. When gunshots are heard, the tom-tom ends its beating and Jones is carried out of the forest dead; it turns out he'd been running in a circle through the night and ended up near his entrance to the forest.

Ranald summarizes O'Neill's theatrical approach to the play as going "beyond language into total theatrical experience." She calls the play "essentially an expressionistic psychodrama" that not only presents "a reverse historical account of African American history" but "draws the audience into sensory and emotional participation."[55] Lawrence Langner remembers "the insistent beat of the tom-toms worked the audience and the critics into a state of hysterical excitement," and then when the curtain came down, there was an "avalanche of applause for O'Neill's masterpiece."[56] Kenton, understanding their risk in presenting the play, reports that "it was good to hear the acclamation ring through the Playwright's Theatre when the last curtain fell," and that "the audience would not go home."[57] Critics also embraced the play enthusiastically, Broun writing that it was "the most interesting play which has yet come from the most promising playwright in America."[58] Woollcott wrote that the play was "an extraordinarily striking and dramatic study of panic fear" that "reinforces the impression that for strength and originality . . . [O'Neill] has no rival among the American writers for the stage."[59] Maida Castellun in *New York Call* wrote the play was "a rare and richly imaginative feast for lovers of true drama."[60] African American response to the play generally can be summed up by James Weldon Johnson when he writes that with the opening of *The Emperor Jones* an "important page in the history of the Negro in the theatre was written."[61] The success of *The Emperor Jones* was such that it soon transferred to a Broadway theatre, bringing professional recognition to the Provincetown Players and solidifying O'Neill's standing as the country's most important new playwright.

Though various theatrical ideas likely also influenced O'Neill's experimenting in *The Emperor Jones*, from Gordon Craig's book *The Theatre Advancing* to Ibsen's *Peer Gynt*, primarily the play was a

culmination of the many innovations he had tested with the Provincetown Players. From the use of extended monologue he attempted
in *Before Breakfast*, to the portrayal of ghosts seen in a character's
madness in *Where the Cross Is Made*; to the mood versus action scenes
and expressionistic devices of *The Moon of the Caribbees*, and the successful use of African American characters in *The Dreamy Kid*, as well
as a specific written dialect and the making sympathetic an otherwise
unsympathetic character; all these can be directly seen being used in *The
Emperor Jones*. O'Neill would further use expressionistic devices in his
writing of *The Hairy Ape*, also produced by the Players before moving
uptown to a professional theatre. The Players had celebrated O'Neill's
debut on Broadway earlier in the year, feeling they had witnessed the
birth of a new American drama that they had been intricately a part
of by giving O'Neill a place to try out his ideas. However, the truth
is that *The Emperor Jones*, which premiered just months later at the
Provincetown Playhouse, was even more a culmination and justification of the experimental work they had committed to from their start.
Cook had fought continuously to remain amateur so they could allow
experimentation while many of the younger members of the company
saw the Players as a stepping-stone to their budding careers, want-
ing to seek publicity and professional recognition. Ironically, once
the Players started regularly having their plays produced on Broadway, their focus changed and simultaneously new playwrights of merit
became harder to find; this led to Cook's decision to dismantle the
company at the end of the 1921–22 season, even as O'Neill's *The
Hairy Ape* was enjoying success on the professional stage. Though
in the end Cook felt that their great experiment had failed, with the
caveat that "failure" if in the "inevitable price of many an experiment"
could still be considered a success,[62] he also understood that their
laboratory had given the world O'Neill and, in doing so, ushered
American theatre into the modern era.

NOTES

1. Susan Glaspell, *The Road to the Temple* (New York: Frederick A. Stokes, 1927), 251.
2. Minutes of the Provincetown Players, Billy Rose Theatre Collection, New York Public Library.
3. Glaspell, *Road to the Temple*, 254.
4. Louis Sheaffer, *O'Neill: Son and Playwright*, vol. 1, 1968 (New York: Copper Square, 2002), 271. In 1914, playwright Clayton Hamilton had pointed this out to O'Neill.

5. Sheaffer, *O'Neill: Son and Playwright*, 279.
6. Brenda Murphy, *The Provincetown Players and the Culture of Modernity* (New York: Cambridge University Press, 2005), 1–14.
7. Travis Bogard, *Contour in Time: The Plays of Eugene O'Neill* (New York: Oxford University Press, 1972), 76–77.
8. Arthur Gelb and Barbara Gelb, *O'Neill: Life with Monte Cristo* (New York: Applause Books, 2000), 404.
9. Bogard, *Contour in Time*, 77.
10. Edna Kenton, *The Provincetown Players and the Playwright's Theatre, 1915–1922*, ed. Travis Bogard and Jackson R. Bryer (Jefferson, NC: McFarland, 2004), 44.
11. Eugene O'Neill, *Complete Plays 1913–1920*, ed. Travis Bogard (New York: Library of America, 1988), 398.
12. Gelb, *O'Neill: Life with Monte Cristo*, 566.
13. Arthur Feinsod, *The Simple Stage: Its Origins in the Modern American Theater* (New York: Greenwood, 1992), 118.
14. Gelb, *O'Neill: Life with Monte Cristo*, 588; Hutchins Hapgood, *A Victorian in the Modern World* (New York: Harcourt, Brace, 1939), 399.
15. Hapgood, *A Victorian*, 399. James O'Neill was most famous nationally for his lead role in the melodramatic action play *The Count of Monte Cristo*.
16. Gelb, *O'Neill: Life with Monte Cristo*, 589.
17. Helen Deutsch and Stella Hanau, *The Provincetown: A Story of the Theatre* (New York: Farrar and Rinehart, 1931), 22.
18. William Zorach, *Art is My Life: The Autobiography of William Zorach* (Cleveland: World Publishing, 1967), 47.
19. Arthur Gelb and Barbara Gelb, *O'Neill* (New York: Harper and Row, 1987), 322–23.
20. Agnes Boulton, *Part of a Long Story: Eugene O'Neill as a Young Man in Love* (London: P. Davies, 1958), 219.
21. Ibid., 242.
22. Ibid., 242.
23. O'Neill, *Complete Plays*, 709–10.
24. Kenton, *The Provincetown Players*, 82.
25. Ibid.
26. *New York Tribune*, November 25, 1918, col. 4: 9.
27. *The Morning Telegraph*, November 23, 1918.
28. *Dramatic Mirror*, December 14, 1918, col. 2: 865.
29. Gelb, *O'Neill*, 159–60.
30. A square-rigger is a ship fitted with square sails as the principal sails and was one of the last ships to compete with steamers at the end of the nineteenth century.
31. Sheaffer, *O'Neill: Son and Playwright*, 395.
32. Bogard, *Contour in Time*, 85.
33. Ibid., 90.

34. Barrett H. Clark, *Eugene O'Neill: The Man and His Plays* (New York: Dover, 1947), 60.
35. Bogard, *Contour in Time*, 90.
36. Gelb, *O'Neill*, 327.
37. O'Neill, *Complete Plays*, 527.
38. Malcolm Cowley, in an interview with Anne Cheney, claims the Millay sisters "sometimes broke into a folk song about cocaine" (Anne Cheney, *Millay in Greenwich Village* University of Alabama Press, 1975], 38).
39. Bogard, *Contour in Time*, 87.
40. O'Neill, *Complete Plays*, 544.
41. Clark, *Eugene O'Neill*, 58–59.
42. Michael Mannheim, ed., *The Cambridge Companion to Eugene O'Neill* (Cambridge: Cambridge University Press, 1998), 55.
43. Eugene O'Neill, letter to Lee Foster Hartman, 6 July 1918, Theatre Collection, Museum of the City of New York.
44. Boulton, *Part of a Long Story*, 160.
45. Ibid., 164.
46. Sheaffer, *O'Neill: Son and Playwright*, 430.
47. James Weldon Johnson, *Black Manhattan* (New York: Atheneum, 1972), 183.
48. Harold Simmelkjaer would continue as an actor, playing a role in *The Niche* for the Colored Players' Guild, and then playing in *Taboo* on Broadway in 1922. He may have also become a clerk in the New York Supreme Court; a man by that exact nontypical name was part of a survey conducted about black amalgamation in the twenties.
49. Rebecca Drucker, *New York Tribune*, November 16, 1919, col. 2 7.
50. Alexander Woollcott, "Second Thoughts on First Night," *New York Times*, November 9, 1919, XX2.
51. Cheryl Black, *The Women of Provincetown, 1915–1922* (Tuscaloosa: University of Alabama Press, 2002), 109.
52. Drucker, *New York Tribune*.
53. Woollcott, "Second Thoughts."
54. Gelb, *O'Neill*, 381.
55. Margaret Loftus Ranald, "From Trial to Triumph (1913–1924): The Early Plays," in *Cambridge Companion to Eugene O'Neill*, ed. Michael Manheim (Cambridge: Cambridge University Press, 1998), 61.
56. Lawrence Langner, *The Magic Curtain* (New York: E. P. Dutton, 1951), 109.
57. Kenton, *The Provincetown Players*, 126.
58. Heywood Broun, "*The Emperor Jones* by O'Neill Gives Chance for Cheers," *New York Tribune*, November 4, 1920, col 2: 8.
59. Alexander Wollcott, "Second Thoughts on First Nights," *New York Times*, November 7, 1920, 88.
60. Maida Castellun, *New York Call*, November 19, 1920.

61. Johnson, *Black Manhattan*, 184.
62. Deutsch and Hanau, *The Provincetown*, 92.

WORKS CITED

Black, Cheryl. *The Women of Provincetown, 1915–1922.* Tuscaloosa: U of Alabama P, 2002. Print.

Bogard, Travis. *Contour in Time: The Plays of Eugene O'Neill.* New York: Oxford UP, 1972. Print.

Boulton, Agnes. *Part of a Long Story: Eugene O'Neill as a Young Man in Love.* London: Davies, 1958. Print.

Broun, Heywood. "*The Emperor Jones* by O'Neill Gives Chance for Cheers." *New York Tribune* 4 Nov. 1920: col 2: 8. Print.

Castellun, Maida. *New York Call* 19 Nov. 1920. Print.

Cheney, Anne. *Millay in Greenwich Village.* Tuscaloosa: U of Alabama P, 1975. Print.

Clark, Barrett H. *Eugene O'Neill: The Man and His Plays.* 1926. New York: Dover, 1947. Print.

Deutsch, Helen, and Stella Hanau. *The Provincetown: A Story of the Theatre.* New York: Farrar, 1931. Print.

Dramatic Mirror 14 Dec. 1918: col. 2: 865. Print.

Drucker, Rebecca. *New York Tribune* 16 Nov. 1919: col. 2: 7. Print.

Feinsod, Arthur. *The Simple Stage: Its Origins in the Modern American Theater.* New York: Greenwood, 1992. Print.

Gelb, Arthur, and Barbara Gelb. *O'Neill: Life with Monte Cristo.* New York: Applause, 2000. Print.

———. *O'Neill.* 1962. New York: Harper, 1987. Print.

Glaspell, Susan. *The Road to the Temple.* New York: Stokes, 1927. Print.

Hapgood, Hutchins. *A Victorian in the Modern World.* New York: Harcourt, 1939. Print.

Johnson, James Weldon. *Black Manhattan.* 1930. New York: Atheneum, 1972. Print.

Kenton, Edna. *The Provincetown Players and the Playwright's Theatre, 1915–1922.* Ed. Travis Bogard and Jackson R. Bryer. Jefferson: McFarland, 2004. Print.

Langner, Lawrence. *The Magic Curtain.* New York: Dutton, 1951. Print.

Mannheim, Michael, ed. *The Cambridge Companion to Eugene O'Neill.* Cambridge: Cambridge UP, 1998. Print.

Provincetown Players. "Minutes Book." Billy Rose Theatre Collection. New York Public Lib. Print.

The Morning Telegraph 23 Nov. 1918. Print.

Murphy, Brenda. *The Provincetown Players and the Culture of Modernity.* New York: Cambridge UP, 2005. Print.

New York Tribune 25 Nov. 1918: col. 4: 9. Print.

O'Neill, Eugene. *Complete Plays 1913–1920*. Ed. Travis Bogard. New York: Library of America, 1988. Print.

———. Letter to Lee Foster Hartman. 6 July 1918. Theatre Collection. Museum of the City of New York. Print.

Ranald, Margaret Loftus. "From Trial to Triumph (1913–1924): The Early Plays." *The Cambridge Companion to Eugene O'Neill*. Ed. Michael Manheim. Cambridge: Cambridge UP, 1998. 61. Print.

Sheaffer, Louis. *O'Neill: Son and Playwright*. Vol. 1. 1968. New York: Cooper Square, 2002. Print.

Woollcott, Alexander. "Second Thoughts on First Night." *New York Times* 9 Nov. 1919: XX2. Print.

———. "Second Thoughts on First Nights." *New York Times* 7 Nov. 1920: 88. Print.

Zorach, William. *Art Is My Life: The Autobiography of William Zorach*. Cleveland: World, 1967. Print.

CHAPTER 2

RETHINKING O'NEILL'S BEGINNINGS

SLUMMING, SOCIOLOGY, AND
SENSATIONALISM IN *THE WEB*

J. Chris Westgate

The early plays of Eugene O'Neill make for a compelling study in hermeneutics. By early plays, I mean those composed *before* O'Neill went to Provincetown, now anthologized in the tellingly titled *Ten "Lost" Plays*, which includes *A Wife for a Life, Thirst, Warnings, Fog, Recklessness, Abortion, The Movie Man, Servitude, The Sniper*, and most important here, *The Web* (1913). Defining them as "lost" concedes, rather appropriately, O'Neill's dissatisfaction with these plays. But this definition likewise endorses two troubling conclusions that inform O'Neill criticism: first, that the early plays are so burdened by melodrama that they do not merit consideration, and second, that O'Neill gained nothing and had nothing to gain from American theater of the Progressive Era. Demonstrating the problems that follow from such conclusions are the observations by Arthur and Barbara Gelb in *O'Neill: Life with Monte Cristo*. In *The Web*, they contend, "it is possible to discern Eugene's first shaky steps toward exposing social injustice and hypocrisy" about the misbegotten from New York City slums.[1] Yet O'Neill's ambition is compromised by the equivalent of boasting, his "showing off his familiarity with New York's seamy street life."[2] The Gelbs are correct in stressing this contradiction in *The Web*, which intends an indictment of class-based injustice but frequently indulges in cross-class sensationalism. They are right, too, in arguing that this contradiction comes from O'Neill's experiences, likely from

time spent with Jack Reed and Terry Carlin, social and political radicals
that O'Neill befriended while drinking in Lower Manhattan in 1912.
But the Gelbs are wrong in how they interpret this contradiction—
that while plays like *The Web* may "foreshadow the noble themes"
of later works like *The Iceman Cometh* and *Long Day's Journey into
Night*, they were only "frail beginner's efforts" that reflect O'Neill's
immaturity as a dramatist.[3]

Common enough in O'Neill criticism, this conclusion proves
unsatisfactory for several reasons, but none more so than this: the
contradiction was not his alone. In the years leading up to O'Neill's
beginnings, American theater was wrestling with the contradiction
between revealing social injustice and indulging in sensationalism
regarding the slums. The 1908–9 season saw an approval of the former
with the emergence of sociological plays, such as Owen Kildare's and
Walter Hackett's *The Regeneration* (1908), Cleveland Moffett's *The
Battle* (1908), Edward Sheldon's *Salvation Nell* (1908), and Eugene
Walter's *The Easiest Way* (1909). Bringing together such plays were
decidedly progressive attitudes about poverty, drunkenness, and prostitution that defined the misbegotten as victims of environmental and
material circumstances rather than of pathological or inherent failings,
as they had been defined in the Victorian Era. In "The Slum Invades
the Theatre" (1909), Hartley Davis described this proliferation as
unsurprising: "Everybody knows that of late years the slum has been
made the subject of careful study" and that "whatever is dominant in
the thoughts of people finds its way to the stage."[4] Behind the initial point are the founding of social sciences at Columbia University[5]
and the establishment of the United Charities Building at 105 East
Twenty-Second Street, two powerful forces that advanced progressive arguments about reform and philanthropy. Behind the second is
a point that adds to Brenda Murphy's work in *American Drama and
American Realism, 1880–1940*. She argues that the aforementioned
dramatists "were crucial for the establishment of realistic principles in
American drama,"[6] especially in *Salvation Nell*'s conception of setting,
through which Sheldon helped "create the forceful sense of character-
determining milieu" by developing the conflicts for the eponymous
character through a contrast of environments.[7] Driving this concern
was a progressive understanding of the dialectical relationship of character and environment; and the plays, in turn, endeavored to advance
this dialectical understanding for middle-class audiences.

Highly popular for the most part, these plays were, nevertheless, met
with apprehension from theater critics, including Davis, who regrets
this invasion of the slums "with all its hideous reality."[8] Importantly,

this regret is not with the subject but with the method of the sociological plays. Perfectly comfortable with dramatists representing the slums "for . . . contrasts" to the norm of middle-class life, Davis is made uncomfortable by plays confronting audiences with the "real slum." Historically, Davis places these plays against an older tradition that staged slums as locations for adventure or exoticism, such as Robert Neilson Stephens's *On the Bowery* (1895), Joseph Jarrow's *The Queen of Chinatown* (1899), and Theodore Kremer's *The Bowery after Dark* (1899). Ideologically, Davis suggests that when middle-class audiences look at the slums, it should be as entertainment as with these melodramas, not confrontation as with the sociological plays. This assumption is hardly surprising given that "fashionable slumming"—which involved the well-to-do touring slum districts and therefore "encouraged some observers to trivialize poverty, transform[ing] it into self-serving entertainment"—was extremely popular at this time.[9] For Davis, the contradiction emerges diachronically, with the emergence of sociological plays challenging the class-based amusement of melodramas. But for John Corbin, who wrote "The Drama of the Slums" in 1909, the contradiction was evident in the sociological plays alone. One of the elements underlying these plays was attention to details, which produced stunning verisimilitude in representations. Unlike Davis, Corbin did not see this as threatening to the entertainment of slumming. Writing about *Salvation Nell*, Corbin asks, "What is the purpose of this elaborate exploitation of the slums? Or is there any purpose in it?"[10] In this inquiry is concern that greater verisimilitude may enhance rather than challenge the trivialization of poverty that followed from fashionable slumming.

Against this history, the Gelbs' conclusion about *The Web* proves insufficient. Anything but "trivial" or "self-satisfied," American theater was struggling with philosophical and ideological contradictions about how to stage the slums, through either the progressive discourse of sociology or the exploitative discourse of sensationalism. Not connecting the contradictions from *The Web* to this larger debate about theater, poverty, and class demonstrates a significant flaw in O'Neill criticism, specifically the failure to historicize O'Neill's beginnings. This failure is odd given that the very language used by the Gelbs to describe the contradiction in *The Web* corresponds so closely with the discourses of sociology ("exposing social injustice") and of sensationalism (his "showing off his familiarity with New York's seamy street life"). It is odder still when direct and indirect confirmation of the influence of this debate on O'Neill is accessible. In 1926, O'Neill wrote to Sheldon thanking him for a letter of congratulations on the

debut of *The Great God Brown* and noting a "debt of longstanding":
"Your *Salvation Nell* . . . was what first opened my eyes to the existence of a real theatre as opposed to the unreal . . . theatre of my
father."[11] Murphy has already described this opening of O'Neill's eyes,
if only tenuously, in terms of Sheldon's advancements in realism. To
this, I would add that these advancements took place during the time
when American theater was wrestling with the aforementioned issues.
O'Neill's "debt," then, could be considered in terms of Sheldon's
place among the sociological playwrights. If nothing else, O'Neill's
letter demonstrates that he was well aware of what was occurring in
American theater before he wrote *The Web*. Indirect evidence of influence comes with Murphy's noting that O'Neill enjoyed the "privilege
of free passes" to Broadway theaters because of his father.[12] Admittedly circumstantial, this fact would have made "the whole range of
Broadway plays" available to O'Neill during the years when American
theater was struggling with the twin discourses of slumming: sociology and sensationalism.[13]

This argument, then, does what O'Neill criticism has not: it situates *The Web* within the philosophical and ideological debates taking
place in American theater during the Progressive Era. In particular,
it takes the contradiction between sociology and sensationalism as a
starting point to examine how *The Web* struggles to reconcile competing and finally incompatible modes of ethical engagement. The
first is the progressive mode, which begins from the rise of sociology and advances arguments for intervention and reformation as the
mode of engagement between the middle and upper classes and the
misbegotten. Central to this mode is a redefinition of the dialectical
relationship of character and environment, in particular, establishing
that problems of poverty, vice, and crime emerge from circumstances.
With this comes the possibility of "regeneration," a favorite theme
in the sociological plays, one that advocated for redeeming criminals
and fallen women especially by transforming them into decent members of society, and that endorses philanthropy. Competing with this
mode, though, is the decidedly exploitative engagement of the fashionable slummer, who ideologically defines those living in the slums as
sources of entertainment. Under this mode, the misbegotten become
flattened out, part of a picturesque experience and significant only
for what they represent as contrasts to middle-class life. Because *The
Web* had no production during the Progressive Era, I do not examine the specifics of reception. Instead, I consider engagement through
W. B. Worthen's "rhetoric of theater." Worthen argues that dramatic
texts contain a blueprint for engagement—that is, they help define and

legitimate "a certain range of interpretive behavior and experience as the role the audience performs."[14] Considering stage directions and internal cues, I show how *The Web* endorses contradictory modes of engagement in this "range of interpretive behavior," a contradiction that corresponds with competing audiences—the thrill-seekers and the social redeemers of the Progressive Era. All this has radical implications for how O'Neill and American theater have been defined in theater history.

A BUM GAME ALL AROUND: THE MISERY OF THE MISBEGOTTEN

In the initial stage directions for *The Web*, O'Neill underscores a central crux behind the philosophical and ideological argument in American theater. Describing the boarding house on the Lower East Side where Rose lives, he uses the word "squalid," which has important definitions for the Progressive Era. First, "squalid" defines *those* who are "morally degraded," a definition that speaks to the notion of poverty as a reflection of differences in values between the upper and lower classes. Borrowing from Jacob Riis's famous description of the misbegotten, the "other half," under this definition, defined both material and moral difference. Second, "squalid" defines "wretched" or "miserable" *conditions*, a definition that corresponds with progressive attitudes about poverty being created by circumstances. It is doubtful that O'Neill was concerned with these denotative tensions, since he intended the play to be produced rather than read. But he was certainly concerned with the cultural tensions that correspond with these denotations given that he compounds the contrast between moral breakdown and material deprivation. After all, Rose is not just impoverished but further caught up in the social evil of prostitution— purposely or not, she's a conflation of characters (Nell and Myrtle) from *Salvation Nell*. Moreover, O'Neill stresses Rose's suffering from "an advanced stage of consumption,"[15] which may have been inspired by his dalliance with Catherine Mackay, another patient at Gaylord Sanatorium but also suggests a literary inheritance from Alexander Dumas's *Camille*. Consumption was the symptom of and punishment for fallen women of all kinds in Victorian literature. In Rose, then, O'Neill depicts three interlocking concerns about morality: poverty, prostitution, and disease. In this, he introduces the daunting ambition of *The Web*, which is to redefine the other half from threat of moral degeneracy to the victims of material circumstances.

Because of the brevity of the one-act structure, O'Neill could not relocate characters to different environments in his depiction of the other half, a common method in sociological plays like *The Regeneration*, *The Straight Road*, and *Salvation Nell*. Nevertheless, he was trying to make a similar argument, beginning with the opening stage directions, which initially describe the interior of the boarding house, with emphasis on images of deterioration, such as the "wall-paper is dirty and torn in places" and "above the washstand a cracked mirror hangs" while "in the middle of the room stand a rickety table and chair."[16] Details of the room correspond with the second definition of squalid as a derelict environment. It is not until the second paragraph that Rose enters the play, described as "a dark-haired young woman looking thirty but really only twenty-two."[17] Like the room, Rose's body is marked by deterioration (of age and disease), suggesting a metaphorical link between place and person. Notably, O'Neill defines this link in progressive terms. Rose is "discovered"[18] after the lengthy description of the room, suggesting that O'Neill imagined how the play would be produced: initially with Rose sitting in darkness, with lights up on the rest of the stage so that audience attention begins with the environment and moves—with a change in lighting, probably—to Rose. It is not merely that Rose's bodily deterioration mirrors the environment but that it comes *after* the environment— a suggestion of causation, not just correspondence, and an intriguing way of suggesting Murphy's "character-determining milieu" of realism. Not conclusive unto itself, this authorial gesture nevertheless reinforces sociological ambitions. In case the connection was not apparent, O'Neill underscores the link through Rose's first, dejected words: "Gawd! . . . What a chance I got!"[19]

Building on this opening, *The Web* endeavors to reveal how little "chance" Rose has by weaving together layers of environment and circumstance that illustrate the web in which she is trapped. This begins with the entrance of her pimp, Steve. Abusive and petty, Steve berates Rose when he learns that they have no alcohol: "Yuh're always holdin' out on me and yuh got to quit it."[20] Rose denies this by comparing herself to another prostitute, Bessie, who holds out on her pimp, Jack. Briefly mollified, Steve still threatens to tell Jack, who will give Bessie "a good beatin.'" While defending Bessie, Rose falls into a fit of coughing, which leads to her plea, "Let me stay in tonight."[21] She stresses that she's "sick" by describing chest pains and how she gets "dizzy" and then asks for a "couple of dollars" to see the doctor. To this, Steve responds, "If yuh want any coin git out and make it."[22] With this scene, O'Neill extends *The Web* beyond the room toward the milieu of prostitution, which is defined by the interplay of violence, power, and money. The first two emerge through reference to

Jack and Bessie, a veiled threat to dissuade Rose from ever "holdin' out" on him. Later, Steve makes this explicit by threatening to end his "protection" that prevents "the bulls from runnin' yuh in'" and Rose losing her child.[23] Violence and power rest in the hands of male authority, leaving those like Rose little chance except submission. Underlying this interplay is money, which facilitates the commodi- fication of the female body through the material deprivations that precipitate this. Thus Rose finds herself in a catch-22 worthy of any Heller novel: in order to get enough "coin" to keep Steve from beat- ing her, see a doctor, and buy sufficient clothes for the elements, she must sell and destroy her body.

With the entrance of Tim Moran, an escaped convict hiding in the next room, comes the final layering. He kicks the door in when Steve assaults Rose and, pistol in hand, forces Steve to flee. When he asks why she doesn't leave Steve, Rose initially describes the harsh reality of pros- titution: "I never have enough coin to make a good break . . . he'd find me and kill me."[24] Rose then extends her explanation toward her efforts to find "decent work" and how they were sabotaged by class difference. "I got a job at housework—workin' twelve hours a day for twenty-five dollars a month" for an unnamed woman from the middle or upper classes.[25] "One night they have a guy to dinner who's seen me some place when I was on the town"—a common euphemism for prostitu- tion during this period. When he reported this to the unnamed woman, she fired Rose. The man who recognized her and the woman who fired Rose seem to view the other half in terms of Victorian moralizing: once her past is revealed, she deserves no chance for reform. But *The Web* challenges this premise by locating Rose's past in material circumstances that are linked with class stratification. The man who recognized her is one of the "curious thrill seekers" who descended into red light districts "to contrast themselves with the depravity and dilapidation" and "to emulate the sense of social and sexual freedom" there.[26] The interplay of violence, power, and money, then, extends to upper-class slummers who subsidize this illicit economy even while they condemn it. As Rose laments, "They—all the good people—they got me where I am and they're going to keep me there. Reform? . . . They won't let yuh do it."[27] Class stratification becomes another layering of circumstance that undermines her chance.

In *The Web*, then, O'Neill suggests how the three interlocking forces were deeply imbricated with one another and complicit in delimiting the chances that the other half would have for reform. Because of this, no doubt, Rose declares that "it's a bum game all around"[28] and believes that reform "can't be done."[29] O'Neill's play is more cynical than many of the sociological plays of the time in that it endorses this fatalistic conclusion with Rose being arrested for the murder of Tim while Steve, the killer, is free to roam the city. But the play corresponds with the sociological ambition of redefining ethical engagement across classes. In particular, it redefines what might be considered moral questions as material ones by situating prostitution (and consumption) within the "socioeconomic suffering" of poverty.[30] More subversively, it nests that poverty (to which she is sent once fired from housework) and her prostitution (to which she is condemned for the benefit of the man who recognized her) within the social hierarchy of the Progressive Era. As Rose says, reform may be impossible, but it's impossible because of the circumstances that she faces, because the "good people"[31] will not allow it. In this, O'Neill advocates for an Ibsen-like appraisal of society, specifically, the stratification of classes that condemns the poor to ignominy and misery. In all, *The Web* suggests that Rose has little chance, not because of what is wrong with her, but because of what is wrong with society.

ON THE TOWN: THE SPECTACLE OF THE MISBEGOTTEN

In *The Web*, O'Neill makes a compelling argument for sociological redefinition of ethical engagement across class lines, but this argument must be reconciled with the second half of the Gelbs' observation: O'Neill's interest in "showing off his familiarity with New York's seamy street life." It is unlikely that O'Neill was boasting in *The Web*, but he does represent some of the more lurid elements of New York City slums. With Steve's arrival, Rose goes to the mirror and applies more makeup, becoming a caricature of a streetwalker, and soon thereafter Steve and Rose talk about Bessie and Jack, all of which sensationalize the sex industry. With his entrance, Steve brings more sensational subjects, which are highlighted by Rose: "Yuh're half drunk now. And yuh been hittin' the pipe too; I kin tell by the ways your eyes look. D'yuh think I'm goin' to stand for a guy that's always full of booze and hop?"[32] Drunkenness and drug use, in this instance, are condemned by Rose's indignation, but her calling attention to these vices functions in a more complicated way when considering theater audiences of the Progressive Era. After all, the audiences flocking to the sociological plays were the same people joining slumming parties or reading accounts of intrepid slummers with the hopes of glimpsing prostitution, opium use, and drunkenness. While O'Neill surely included these vices as part of a verisimilar portrait of the Lower

East Side, such portraits can also invite excitement or titillation. As Keith Gandal notes about slumming, if not in O'Neill's play, enjoying "photographs of drunkards and description of heroin use" implies "a different ethical relation to others and oneself": it suggests that "there is nothing wrong with treating the poor as spectacles."[33]

To some degree, O'Neill inherits the same problem confronting sociological dramatists like Moffett, Fitch, and Sheldon: a horizon of expectations that privileged thrills instead of truth. Undoubtedly this reality contributed to Corbin's frustrated question. But O'Neill endorses this privileging of spectacle, thrill, and entertainment with his reliance on melodramatic conventions, beginning with the flattening of characters. This is most evident with Steve who, as Zander Brietzke puts it, "is a cartoonish villain who fulfills necessary plot function."[34] Though O'Neill probably meant for Tim to be more complex (he has a speech that describes his start in crime in ways that parallel Rose's descent into prostitution), he becomes just a noble mirroring of Steve, the criminal with a good heart who tries to stake Rose for a new future. Even Rose, despite moments of self-awareness, falls into the stock behavior of the fallen woman. Certainly this flatness owes something to the brevity of the one-act play, which makes it difficult though certainly not impossible[35] to create complexity. Nevertheless, this method of characterization reduces Steve, Tim, and possibly Rose to archetypes that match preconceived and interchangeable images of the misbegotten. They become not individuals in a larger network of circumstances against which they struggle, but rather adornments of exoticism or menace or adventure in the slumming landscape. While this landscape may be one of misery for those living there, it could paradoxically become "pleasingly affective" to the slummer, as William Dean Howell notes, if represented at sufficient "distance."[36] Partly ideological and partly aesthetic, this distance invites audiences to enjoy the spectacle of poverty instead of confront the inequities that produce poverty.

Compounding this alchemy of turning misery into spectacle is O'Neill's reliance on moments of melodramatic violence as the fulcrum for the plot. There are two such moments, the first of which follows the conversation between Rose and Steve wherein O'Neill introduces the world of prostitution: Steve threatens Rose's child sleeping on the bed, telling her to "git dat brat outa here," and when she attacks him in desperation, he knocks her down.[37] Before Steve can do worse, Tim enters and expels him with the threat of his pistol. Out of the following scene between Tim and Rose comes the play's indictment of class stratification, with the tale of the man who recognized Rose.

This scene ends abruptly with Steve on the fire escape, shooting Tim and throwing the pistol into the room to frame Rose when the police burst in. *The Web* divides into three sections (Rose and Steve, Rose and Tim, Rose and the police) delineated by melodramatic violence (Steve assaulting Rose and Steve killing Tim). Structurally, O'Neill includes two types of scenes: discussion scenes, which constitute the three sections of the play and look like something out of Ibsen's or Shaw's plays; and action scenes, which change the alignment and outlooks of the characters and are the typical fare of melodrama. Importantly, the action scenes not only interrupt the discussion scenes but disrupt them—that is, they redirect energy away from the social analysis of discussion scenes. After the first action scene, O'Neill resumes this social analysis by adding the layer about class. But after the second, O'Neill lets the analysis dissipate, leaving only the cynical aftermath of violence. Structurally, it's crucial to recognize that this plotting contrasts moments of excitement with periods of examination, but toward the end it privileges excitement at the expense of examination. In other words, the melodramatic violence muddies sociology and invites audiences toward the slums for excitement and thrills.

This shift from examination to excitement becomes crucial when considering the ending of *The Web*. In fact, the play contains three possible—and competing—resolutions, but finally adopts the one most contradictory to sociological ambition. One emerges with Tim's offer to support Rose: "Go some place in the mountains and git rid of that cough."[38] Admittedly, this is the least likely resolution given the fatalistic tone of the play, but this sort of conclusion would have been consistent with plays like *Salvation Nell*, which end by endorsing sociological definitions of poverty wherein changes in the environment lead to changes in the character. A better possibility, given the play's tone, comes during the second discussion scene, wherein Rose describes what has frustrated her efforts toward reform: "They won't let yuh do it, and that's the Gawd's truth."[39] "They" here refers, within the play, to the woman who hired her and the man who reported her. But "they" could also potentially refer to the sort of audiences that attended sociological plays, such as those with the economic means and ideological interest in philanthropic activities, like the Social Gospel Movements,[40] to help those like Rose instead of victimizing her. This would be the most compelling end for sociological ambitions. But the play ends not with Rose's indictment of the upper classes but with Tim dead, Rose arrested, and her child taken by the police. No doubt, O'Neill meant to underscore how little chance Rose has, but this distracts from the key criticism of *The Web*—namely, that the misery of the misbegotten is subsidized by class hierarchy, slummers in particular. Allowing Steve's violence to end the play minimizes concerns about class by displacing the hostility of the upper classes described by Rose onto corrupt police. Worse, this conclusion could endorse condescending attitudes about the other half by confirming that they were dangerous and needed containment and surveillance.

In the end, *The Web* may reiterate and reaffirm the experience of being "on the town"[41] that the play endeavors to condemn. It is not just that this emphasis on spectacle, thrill, and entertainment is inconsistent with the sociological aspects discussed in the previous section; it is that they are incompatible with them. Part of the problem may have been what the Gelbs suggested: O'Neill's inexperience as a dramatist made him lean too heavily on the tradition of melodrama. But this conclusion is the beginning, not the end, of the contradiction, considering what was happening in American theater before, during, and after O'Neill's beginnings. The contradictions in *The Web* correspond with the contradictions of theater, slums, and slumming during the Progressive Era. Certainly, this contradiction did involve a contrast of realism and melodrama as dramatic and theatrical modes of engagement with poverty: realism privileged sociological assumptions of character and setting about the slums, while melodrama privileged adventure and excitement. But this explanation may be too easy, since *The Web* hints at the larger problem for depictions of the slums in theater: that the advancements of realism could advocate one form of ethical engagement while paradoxically endorsing another. One way this emerges is through the milieu of prostitution, which involves violence, power, and money, as well as alcohol and drugs. On the one hand, these details serve verisimilitude in that they define this environment and explain what little chance the misbegotten have. On the other hand, details about the slums can facilitate the enthusiasm for spectacle, which can even endorse a way of viewing slums and those living there that is exploitative. Perhaps this is why Howells argued that "there is nothing more infernal than the juggle that transmutes for the tenderest-hearted people the misery of their fellows into something comic or poetic."[42] Like other dramatists of the Progressive Era, O'Neill may have been mired between sociology and sensationalism.

CONCLUSION: RETHINKING O'NEILL'S BEGINNINGS

Almost certainly, *The Web* was informed by the contradictions about theater, slums, and slumming, and this conclusion has key implications

for the way in which O'Neill's beginnings have been defined. It is
not just that O'Neill criticism has, by and large, failed to historicize
his beginnings but that it goes out of its way to deny links between
O'Neill and American theater of the Progressive Era. This dehistori-
cizing is evident, first of all, in the Gelbs' observations on *The Web*:
first, in the way they describe its problems as nothing more than the
result of O'Neill's inexperience, and second in how they define links
between O'Neill and American theater only in terms of transformation, such as the "noble themes" of his later plays, which "awaken[ed]
the trivial, contemporary theater from its self-satisfied torpor."[43] It is
evident, also, in Margaret Ranald's reading of the early plays, when she
argues that O'Neill's decision to "become a dramatist" infused American theater with a "new high seriousness" that it was distinctly lack-
ing,[44] and in John Patrick Diggins's book, where O'Neill's beginnings
are *ex nihilo*: "Coming out of nowhere, Eugene O'Neill appeared upon
the scene in 1916."[45] Behind arguments like this is the abiding myth
of American theater. O'Neill had only two points of contact with this
theater: initially, the melodrama of his father's theater, against which
he struggled, and later the transformation of American theater following his return from Provincetown. Necessary for this myth is the idea
that O'Neill gained nothing from theater of the Progressive Era, which
is viewed as torpid, frivolous, and bland. Only Murphy and Daniel J.
Watermeier consider positive links between O'Neill and American theater, but neither considers the pre-Provincetown plays in any depth.[46]

However compelling, this myth of O'Neill and American theater
proves unsatisfactory for two reasons. The first is that this myth,
simply put, is historically unsound. Although the theater of the late
nineteenth and early twentieth centuries was dominated by melodrama and escapism, this theater was neither "torpid" nor "thin and
bland." Well before O'Neill went to Provincetown, dramatists like
Sheldon, Fitch, and Moffett began wrestling with the philosophical
and ideological concerns that would help shape the nature of realism
in American drama and, crucially, O'Neill's beginnings. *The Web* demonstrates indisputable links with the sociological plays described by
Davis and Corbin: on regeneration, or Rose's efforts to "go straight"
(echoed in *The Straight Road*, *The Regeneration*, and *Salvation Nell*);
on prostitution (*Salvation Nell* and *The Easiest Way*); and on slums
and slumming (*Salvation Nell*, *The Battle*, and *The Regeneration*).
Denying the ways O'Neill's beginnings related to American theater
from the first decade of the century involves deliberate myopia. Just as
important, this myth about O'Neill and American theater is heuristi-
cally sterile. Once this is established, as it has become, it closes more

doors than it opens because it denies historical and cultural roots for O'Neill, except through rebellion against those roots (a critical position that is nearing exhaustion, if not already there). Arguing that O'Neill's plays emerge "out of nowhere" means minimizing work in cultural studies or theater history. More than that, it creates an odd problem for criticism when it comes to the early plays: writing about them at all seems to require rationalization as demonstrated by Charles Fish's "Beginnings: O'Neill's 'The Web.'" Beginning with an apology for his "critical prowling in the obscure regions" of O'Neill's "early attempts to become a writer," he justifies this by arguing for links to the "brilliance of [the] later plays."[47] In other words, the only justification for considering pre-Provincetown plays is to reiterate the genius of O'Neill's mature works.[48]

My ambition here was never to question the importance of O'Neill to American theater. O'Neill stands out among (towers over, in my opinion) the best of his or of any generation of dramatists regardless of how accomplishment is measured, whether it be by the number of successful plays, the quality of individual plays, their engagement with a range and depth of themes and issues, or their accolades and awards. Reaffirming O'Neill's importance, in other words, hardly seems necessary. Instead, my ambition was to rethink O'Neill's beginnings and, consequently, advocate new modes of "critical prowling in the obscure regions" of these plays. This reading of *The Web* suggests O'Neill's engagement with difficult questions about composition, staging, and the social implications of theater from his first play. That he could not resolve these questions requires no apology. Instead, it suggests a new thread of investigation for O'Neill criticism and theater history, particularly the issues involved in staging poverty, vice, and class stratification. In fact, new efforts at resolving problems like these recur in later plays such as *Anna Christie* (prostitution and saloons), *The Hairy Ape* (slumming and class), *All God's Chillun Got Wings* (race and racism), *The Iceman Cometh* (drunkenness and the defeated)—among others. Additionally, this argument intends to redefine O'Neill's beginnings along the lines of Murphy's argument that we should not be denying the influence of Europeans on O'Neill's dramaturgy but complementing it with the influence of Americans. If O'Neill did help transform theater after Provincetown (and surely he did), then he, too, was transformed years earlier by the philosophical and ideological wrestling at work with the daunting questions underlying American theater. Hopefully this argument demonstrates the long-overdue investigation of a more dialectical relationship between O'Neill and American theater during the Progressive Era.

NOTES

1. Arthur Gelb and Barbara Gelb, *O'Neill: Life with Monte Cristo* (New York: Applause Theatre and Cinema, 2000), 398.
2. Ibid.
3. Ibid.
4. Hartley Davis, "The Slum Invades the Theatre," *Everybody's Magazine*, April 1909, n.p.
5. See John Louis Recchiuti, *Civic Engagement: Social Science and Progressive-Era Reform in New York City* (Philadelphia: University of Pennsylvania Press, 2007) for a discussion of the origins of social sciences.
6. Brenda Murphy, *American Realism and American Drama, 1880–1940* (Cambridge: Cambridge University Press, 1987), 86.
7. Ibid., 88.
8. Davis, "The Slum Invades."
9. Robert Dowling, *Slumming in New York: From the Waterfront to Mythic Harlem* (Chicago: University of Illinois Press, 2007), 6–7.
10. John Corbin, "The Drama of the Slums," *Saturday Evening Post*, March 20, 1909, n.p.
11. Eugene O'Neill, "Letter to Edward Sheldon," February 21, 1925 [1926], *Selected Letters of Eugene O'Neill*, ed. Travis Bogard and Jackson R. Bryer (New Haven: Yale University Press, 1988), 199.
12. Murphy, *American Realism*, 112.
13. Ibid.
14. W. B. Worthen, *Modern Drama and the Rhetoric of Theater* (Berkeley: University of California Press, 1992), 5.
15. Eugene O'Neill, *The Web*, in *Ten "Lost" Plays* (New York: Dover, 1995), 51.
16. Ibid.
17. Ibid.
18. Ibid.
19. Ibid., 52.
20. Ibid., 53.
21. Ibid., 54.
22. Ibid., 55.
23. Ibid., 54–55.
24. Ibid., 59–60.
25. Ibid., 60.
26. Chad Heap, *Slumming: Sexual and Racial Encounters in American Nightlife, 1885–1940* (Chicago: University of Chicago Press, 2009), 113.
27. O'Neill, *The Web*, 60–61.
28. Ibid., 53.
29. Ibid., 60–61.

30. Gavin Jones, *American Hungers: The Problem of Poverty in U.S. Litera-
    ture, 1840–1945* (Princeton: Princeton University Press, 2008), 3.
31. O'Neill, *The Web*, 60.
32. Ibid., 55.
33. Keith Gandal, *The Virtues of the Vicious: Jacob Riis, Stephen Crane, and
    the Spectacle of the Slum* (New York: Oxford University Press, 1997),
    5–6.
34. Zander Brietzke, *The Aesthetics of Failure: Dynamic Structure in the
    Plays of Eugene O'Neill* (Jefferson, NC: McFarland, 2001), 208.
35. John M. Synge's *Riders to the Sea*, in *The Complete Plays of John M.
    Synge* (New York: Vintage Books, 1935), for instance, has remarkably
    complex characters in a one-act play.
36. William Dean Howells, *Impressions and Experiences* (New York:
    Harper, 1909), 186–87.
37. O'Neill, *The Web*, 57.
38. Ibid., 65.
39. Ibid., 61.
40. The Social Gospel movement was centered on religious groups like the
    Salvation Army advancing philanthropy toward the poor in New York
    from the 1890s through the 1920s. For more details see Norris Mag-
    nuson, *Salvation in the Slums: Evangelical Social Work, 1865–1920*,
    1977; and Loren K. Ruff, *Edward Sheldon*, 1982.
41. O'Neill, *The Web*, 60.
42. Howells, *Impressions and Experiences*, 206.
43. Gelb and Gelb, *O'Neill*, 398.
44. Margaret Loftus Ranald, "From Trial to Triumph (1913–1924): The
    Early Plays," in *The Cambridge Companion to Eugene O'Neill*, ed.
    Michael Manheim (Cambridge: Cambridge University Press, 1998),
    51.
45. Jack Patrick Diggins, *Eugene O'Neill's America: Desire Under Democ-
    racy* (Chicago: University of Chicago Press, 2007), 22.
46. Murphy uses them to contextualize O'Neill's early period, while
    Watermeier oddly erases them altogether with the erroneous claim
    that "all of O'Neill's early plays were staged by the Provincetown Play-
    ers" (Daniel J. Watermeier, "O'Neill and the Theatre of His Time," in
    The Cambridge Companion to Eugene O'Neill, ed. Michael Manheim
    [Cambridge: Cambridge University Press, 1998], 38).
47. Charles Fish, "Beginnings: O'Neill's 'The Web,'" *Princeton Library
    Chronicle* 27 (1965): 3.
48. Less explicit, this concept is nevertheless evident in Gelb and Gelb,
    O'Neill; Ranald's work on the early plays; Diggins, *Eugene O'Neill's
    America*; among others.

Works Cited

Brietzke, Zander. *The Aesthetics of Failure: Dynamic Structure in the Plays of Eugene O'Neill*. Jefferson: McFarland, 2001. Print.

Corbin, John. "The Drama of the Slums." *Saturday Evening Post* 20 Mar. 1909: n. page. Print.

Davis, Hartley. "The Slum Invades the Theatre." *Everybody's Magazine* April 1909: n. page. Print.

Diggins, John Patrick. *Eugene O'Neill's America: Desire under Democracy*. Chicago: U of Chicago P, 2007. Print.

Dowling, Robert M. *Slumming in New York: From the Waterfront to Mythic Harlem*. Urbana: U of Illinois P, 2007. Print.

Fish, Charles. "Beginnings: O'Neill's '*The Web*.'" *Princeton Library Chronicle* 27 (1965): 3–20. Print.

Gandal, Keith. *The Virtues of the Vicious: Jacob Riis, Stephen Crane, and the Spectacle of the Slum*. New York: Oxford UP, 1997. Print.

Gelb, Arthur, and Barbara Gelb. *O'Neill: Life with Monte Cristo*. New York: Applause, 2000. Print.

Heap, Chad. *Slumming: Sexual and Racial Encounters in American Nightlife, 1885–1940*. Chicago: U of Chicago P, 2009. Print.

Howells, William Dean. *Impressions and Experiences*. New York: Harper, 1909. Print.

Jones, Gavin. *American Hungers: The Problem of Poverty in U.S. Literature, 1840–1945*. Princeton: Princeton UP, 2008. Print.

Magnuson, Norris. *Salvation in the Slums: Evangelical Social Work, 1865–1920*. Metuchen: The Scarecrow P, 1977. Print.

Murphy, Brenda. *American Realism and American Drama, 1880–1940*. Cambridge: Cambridge UP, 1987. Print.

O'Neill, Eugene. Letter to Edward Sheldon. 21 February 1925 [1926]. *Selected Letters of Eugene O'Neill*. Ed. Travis Bogard and Jackson R. Bryer. New Haven: Yale UP, 1988. 199. Print.

———. *The Web. Ten "Lost" Plays*. New York: Dover, 1995. Print.

———. "From Trial to Triumph (1913–1924): The Early Plays." *The Cambridge Companion to Eugene O'Neill*. Ed. Michael Manheim. Cambridge: Cambridge UP, 1998. 51–68. Print.

Ruff, Loren K. *Edward Sheldon*, Twayne's United States Authors Series. Boston: Twayne P, 1982. Print.

Recchiuti, John Louis. *Civic Engagement: Social Science and Progressive-Era Reform in New York City*. Philadelphia: U of Pennsylvania P, 2007. Print.

Synge, John M. *Riders to the Sea*. In *The Complete Plays of John M. Synge*. New York: Vintage Books, 1935. Print.

Watermeier, Daniel J. "O'Neill and the Theatre of His Time." *The Cambridge Companion to Eugene O'Neill*. Ed. Michael Manheim. Cambridge: Cambridge UP, 1998. 33–50. Print.

Worthen, W. B. *Modern Drama and the Rhetoric of Theater*. Berkeley: U of California P, 1992. Print.

CHAPTER 3

Eugene O'Neill's *Abortion*
and Standard Family Roles
The Economics of Terminating
a Romance and a Pregnancy

Lesley Broder

Abortion made its stage debut in New York in 1959, six years after Eugene O'Neill's death. It was not a critical success. Arthur Gelb, who would go on to coauthor O'Neill's biography with his wife Barbara Gelb, reported in *The New York Times*, "There are several good reasons why the so-called 'Lost Works' of Eugene O'Neill have never been done before in New York. The production of three of them at the Key Theatre last night does not invalidate any of these reasons."[1] The Key Theatre production eliminated the suicide of the hero Jack Townsend, prompting Gelb to complain, "What was needed was more shooting, not less."[2] This response matched those of critics nearly a decade earlier. When New Fathoms Press revived a collection of O'Neill's one-act plays, including *Abortion*, in 1950, reviewers regretted that O'Neill's wishes to let the plays fall into obscurity were not respected.[3] One reviewer thought it would be an understatement to call its publication "reprehensible and shameful"[4] while another commented, "I feel sorry for anyone who thinks he has a treat in store for him."[5]

Gelb could not decide whether the performance or the newly reprinted edition of these "Lost Plays" was worse and believed that only scholars could find any interest in them.[6] In the intervening years, however, *Abortion* has received little attention, much of it trivializing, in the volumes of criticism produced about the playwright each year. Few critics have taken the play as the subject of their work, instead using *Abortion* to highlight stylistic development or biographical connections across O'Neill's plays.[7]

Though frequently dismissed by theater critics, academics, and producers,[8] *Abortion* is an artifact of its time, revealing tensions regarding class and gender that emerged in the early twentieth century. The subject of abortion began to appear as a recurring theme as modernist writers interpreted and represented a rapidly evolving world. Christina Hauck connects modernism to abortion in her article "Abortion and the Individual Talent," an analysis of T. S. Eliot's "The Waste Land." Hauck details how "reproductive failure" was a tremendous "crisis" for British and American culture.[9] She writes, "Abortion can be understood as revealing a momentous interpretive conflict at the site of maternity. For the culture at large, maternity constituted the epitome of femininity, the physiological, psychic, and social fulfillment of every woman."[10] In O'Neill's play, abortion is unsuccessfully used as a way to reduce the threat to the family unit. The single procedure provides Jack with the illusion that he can protect his honor, his future wife's purity, and his family's reputation. With one payment to the doctor, all his sins seem to be expunged. Access to abortion is dependent on economic power and is used as a means to preserve the nuclear family. Rather than protecting the characters, however, abortion has consequences for Jack, his family, and the community. The play's working-class Nellie—who only has access to a questionable doctor—is silenced before the curtain even rises and is as disposable as her male lover, Jack, who kills himself at the end. The grotesque and unnecessary nature of the deaths that frame the play is magnified by the celebrations in Jack's honor occurring as the plot unfolds, the praise heaped upon him by his family, and the grief of Nellie's brother. This pattern conforms to Judith Wilt's (1990) suggestion that writers provide "some kind of aftermath" as a price for having an abortion.[11]

Even though it was not produced for decades, and thus has no measurable social impact in the early twentieth century, the play highlights O'Neill's impression of how abortion could impact family units. Four years prior to writing the play, O'Neill had a child with Kathleen Jenkins, whom he soon abandoned. Rather than end the relationship with Jenkins, O'Neill secretly married her and then, with his father James's assistance, fled to Honduras without his bride.[12] He did not manage to keep the relationship a secret. An article ran in the *New York World* reporting the birth of their son, much to James O'Neill's displeasure. The scandal escalated when the paper eagerly revealed that Eugene O'Neill had returned to the United States but had never contacted his wife.[13] O'Neill was motivated to maintain his distance because of his father's reaction, but there are conflicting reports about his real feelings about his son. Arthur Gelb says that O'Neill's mother, Ella, confided to a friend that "Eugene had wept when they talked of his situation."[14] On the other hand, not only did he boast about leaving Jenkins when he discovered she was pregnant, he also claimed not to miss the boy since he was "just an accident of nature."[15] This sentiment seems parallel to Jack Townsend's flip comment that he was merely "the male beast who ran gibbering through the forest after its female thousands of years ago."[16]

The playwright's relationship with Jenkins is often a starting point for critical considerations of the text, though these interpretations vary widely. Louis Sheaffer calls Nellie's death "unconscious wish-fulfillment" only atoned for by Jack Townsend's suicide.[17] Travis Bogard says even though the play "possibly reflects some of his concern" over his first wife's pregnancy, "it is not, however, an autobiographical play."[18] In contrast, Virginia Floyd goes so far as to call Jack Townsend a "self-portrait."[19] Though it is impossible to know whether O'Neill thought of abortion as a possibility in his personal life, it is clear that the topic, used as a plot device, served him well as a dramatic element.

While *Abortion* was not a success in the twentieth century and may seem like melodrama to twenty-first-century sensibilities, it was quite a radical piece for its time. *Abortion* was written in 1914—long before O'Neill received the Nobel Prize for literature and multiple Pulitzer Prizes for drama—but he could not find a producer for it, even when his father agreed to take a part in the play.[20] *Abortion* may lack the nuances of his later work, but it is also possible that its subject matter made it undesirable at the time. Kristin Luker explains that in the United States, antiabortion efforts meant the operation evolved from being generally accepted by common law at the turn of the nineteenth century to being outlawed in every state at the turn of the twentieth century, with exceptions made for the pregnant woman's health. As was the case for Great Britain, the procedure was a felony for the abortionist and, depending on the state, for the pregnant woman as well.[21] Private decisions regarding abortion suddenly required a new kind of expertise and intervention.

Behind much of these changes was Anthony Comstock, a political force from the mid-nineteenth century into the twentieth century. The United States actively began to police both contraceptive and abortion activities in the 1860s; laws eventually sought to censor any

discussion of reproduction, contraception, or abortion. Such legisla-
tion, codified in the 1873 Comstock Law, served to make the very
word "abortion" a profanity. Comstock had a long career defending
the purity of the nation, staying active until the end of his life when,
as special agent of the US Post Office, he seized birth control activist
Margaret Sanger's publication *The Woman Rebel* in 1914 and then
shut down a birth control clinic in New York in 1916.[22] While wom-
en's magazine advertisements often used covert language to subvert
these laws, access to information about family planning was curtailed.

The late activity in Comstock's career coincides with the composition
of *Abortion*. Though abortion appears in some early twentieth-century
texts, this play's title and open discussion of sex and human desires
would have made it indecent under Comstock's laws. State control
over the practice and discussion of abortion impacted literary representations that maintained propriety by discussing it in veiled terms.
Despite the resistance to Margaret Sanger's birth control campaign,
the Comstock Law, and legal prohibitions on abortion, women still
sought to terminate pregnancies—plays like *Abortion* reveal that state
regulation of birth control did not stop couples from having sex, getting pregnant, or seeking abortions.

This was the climate in the United States when O'Neill enrolled
in English 47, a playwriting class at Harvard University taught by
George Pierce Baker, shortly after completing *Abortion*. As he considered writing about controversial subject matter, probably regarding
his play *The Personal Equation*, he wrote to his girlfriend Beatrice
Ashe that if staged, "the authorities will cast [him] into the deepest dungeon of the jail and throw away the key" but that he would
continue work on it since, "one writes what one *must*, what one *feels*.
All else is piffle. [He] will be [an] artist or nothing."[23] Nevertheless,
O'Neill's desire to have a published play overtook his desire to be an
"artist." By early 1915, he seems to have returned to *Abortion*, and he
considers its prospects in another letter to Ashe:

> You know I told you a few weeks ago about my giving one scenario for
> a long play to Baker. It was on the subject of abortion and was written
> with my peculiar mental twists in plain evidence. He said he thought
> it would make a very powerful play but advised me not to write it for
> this course. It would stand no chance of production in this country or
> England, he said—only on the Continent. But he told me to write it by
> all means as the idea was great, but to lay it aside for the nonce, so t.s.[24]

While O'Neill could write about abortion without apprehension, he needed to cast the topic aside to further his own career. Even if the play would never be considered as central among O'Neill's works, his ability to discuss the forbidden subject at all indicates the risks and innovations he would later bring to the stage.

Abortion is the story of a college hero who is admired for his ethics and his tremendous potential. Upper-class Jack's relationship with working-class Nellie serves as an invisible emotional life underneath the surface of his rarefied world of college rallies and baseball games. He finds his lover pregnant and must deal with the consequences of her death after her abortion. Despite the title, abortion is referred to in hushed euphemisms and is cast as a shameful reality that cannot be addressed openly, threaded through the story as representative of the larger issue of women's submission to men. Even the 1958 introduction to the play seems to circumvent its subject. Lawrence Gellert describes the plot while delaying reference to the title, calling it initially "the first play in the volume."[25]

Women's status as a commodity to be traded and exchanged winds through the discussion that Jack and his father John have about abortion; the sanctity of their economic and social position and Nellie's lower-class status preoccupy them. After determining that the abortion was complete, John vocalizes traditional fears about paternity: "Are you sure—you know one's vanity blinds one in such cases—are you sure, absolutely sure, you were the father of this child which would have been born to her?"[26] Jack immediately defends Nellie's purity and claims they would have married had he not been in love with his fiancée Evelyn. Despite Jack's proclamations of affection, Nellie seems sordid in comparison to his public life. When he remembers Evelyn, "the other affair seem[s] so horrible and loathsome," and this disgust justifies his decision to break off contact with the woman once the abortion is secured.[27] He adapts his father's worldview since social class stifles his feelings for Nellie and casts a negative light on their time together.

Jack attempts all manner of sloughing off responsibility for the act onto an outside source. He cites his father's dalliances in college, invoking a hereditary flaw; he claims he did not have the affair—it was the prehistoric man inside him, not the one who loves Evelyn; he blames society's ethics, "which are unnatural and monstrously distorted," viewing evil where it doesn't exist and forcing him "into evasions." Finally, Jack decides "the whole thing seemed just a pleasant game."[28] The meeting becomes a moment for father and son to bond, comparing experiences and reaffirming their status as moral, upright, and superior. Jack is reassured by their conversation and proclaims that now he can be a better man for all that *he* has suffered. His economic position and gender allows for an easy resolution to the troubling situation. "I have had my glance into the abyss. In loss of confidence and self-respect, in bitter self-abasement I have paid."[29] Significantly, Nellie's "glance into the abyss" will never be represented since her life ends before the play begins. Economic powerlessness eradicates her voice; for Nellie, this choice turns out to be no choice at all.

Economic considerations determine John's perception of the affair since he is less distressed by the abortion than by his son's choice of women. He chastises his son, wondering, "What I cannot understand is how you happened to get in with this young woman in the first place. You'll pardon me, Jack, but it seems to me to show a lack of judgment on your part, and—er—good taste."[30] The whole debacle would be more understandable if he chose someone of his own class, though Jack's attraction to Nellie may stem from the thrill of interacting outside his expected circle. Here again, class differences evoke suspicion from his father. After asserting that the woman "was hardly of the class [Jack had] been accustomed to associate with," he becomes even more disappointed when he hears of the family's precarious financial situation, as they are supported by Nellie, who is a stenographer, and her brother, a machinist.[31] Considering the possible long-term implication of the affair, John ensures that no one in her family could learn about the abortion.

What remains unspoken is what her refusal to abort would have meant. "And she and her brother support the others?" And Jack, "*avoiding his father's eyes*," admits that they do. John's "*expression stern and accusing, starts to say something but restrains himself*"; all he can say is "Ah."[32] This interaction can be read in two ways: Either Jack has taken advantage of a woman of little means who could not resist his advances; or perhaps more alarming for father and son, her refusal to have an abortion would have linked the two families, forever sullying their reputation and making them financially responsible for an unwanted child and, perhaps, Nellie's family.

The abortion seems to relieve all these troubles and is obtained easily once Jack acquires the $200.00 needed from his father. Jack admits that without asking his dad, he "couldn't get it in any other way very well. Two hundred dollars is quite a sum for a college student to raise at a moment's notice."[33] The jest returns the father to his place of pride as he declares, "The wages of sin are rather exorbitant."[34] Father and son shake hands, and though Jack wants to pay him back, John insists they put the whole affair behind them. For this family, economic power has allowed them to easily discard the emotional consequences of the end of the relationship and the pregnancy.

Jack attempts to use his financial power once again when Nellie's brother, Murray, returns to exact vengeance. In order to preserve the respect of his family, particularly of his mother and his girlfriend, Jack begs Murray to remain quiet about the affair; these are the innocent whom he cannot bear to disappoint. "You say the doctor gave you money? I'll give you ten times as much as he did . . . I'll see that you get so much a year for the rest of your life. My father is rich. We'll get you a good position, do everything you wish."[35] Here, Jack has misread his adversary. Money cannot return Murray's beloved sister and he draws a gun and exclaims, "You want—to pay me—for Nellie!"[36] Murray ultimately decides to get the police, and Jack, unable to face the disappointment of his family and peers, shoots himself. The play doles out punishment to the unformed nuclear family unit on two fronts: if Jack has prevented its honest formation with the working girl, he will not have the luxury of establishing one with his fiancée.

The disconnect between his reputation and his actions forces him to acknowledge his callous behavior, but Murray easily perceives the commitment to class that has been the root of Jack's actions: "Yuh think yuh c'n get away with that stuff and then marry some goil of your own kind, I s'pose—. . . . Yuh come here to school and yuh think yuh c'n do as yuh please with us town people. Yuh treat us like servants, an' what are *you*, I'd like to know?—a lot of lazy no-good dudes spongin' on your old men."[37] Behind the anger about his sister is a lifetime of resentment against the social system that divides the "townies" from the university students. Too ashamed to let the purity of his external life be crushed by his involvement in the young woman's death, Jack takes refuge in suicide. Quelling his affection for Nellie has allowed him to maintain membership in his own social class and in the attachments that have helped form the core of his identity; when these are threatened, life is no longer worth living.

O'Neill overtly states the play's subject in the title, *Abortion*, yet the word is never once uttered by the characters throughout the action of the play, even by the brother who returns to seek revenge. O'Neill can break a taboo with his title, but he cannot put the word into the mouths of his characters. The father refers to it clinically as an "operation." Yet abortion has the power to disturb even when it is not mentioned. When Murray comes to confront Jack, their conversation

actively avoids mentioning the procedure. Jack pretends to not understand what Murray is talking about:

> **Murray**: "Don't give me any of that. Yuh know what I mean. Yuh
> know how she died." (*Fiercely*) "Yuh know who killed her."
> **Jack**: (*His voice trembling—not looking at Murray*) "How she died?
> Killed her? I don't understand—"
> **Murray**: "Yuh lie! She was murdered and yuh know it."
> **Jack**: (*Horror-struck*) "Murdered?"
> **Murray**: "Yes, and *you* murdered her."
> **Jack**: (*Shuddering*) "I? What? I murdered?—Are you crazy?"[38]

In this short exchange, abortion becomes synonymous with Nellie's
death, revealing the powerful taboo placed on the act. The justifications
that Jack built up with his father collapse; her demise is an unintended
consequence he had not even considered as he rationalized his actions.

While the slow realization of the scope of his actions sinks in,
abortion is linked to the death of the mother and the father. As the
twentieth century progressed, the play began to reflect the growing
tension the subject inspired in the culture at large. In "Child Murder
and Incest in American Drama," Peter L. Hays conflates infanticide
and abortion as he traces how infanticide functions in modern drama
and is often accompanied by incest plots. Within his analysis, he clas-
sifies abortion as "child murder":

> O'Neill's first use of child murder in *Abortion*, written in 1914, is largely
> for shock effect and melodramatic subject material . . . The abortion of
> the child here has no large symbolic meaning except to foreshadow the
> death of both of its parents. It is certainly not a sacrifice of the future
> for the sake of the present, since Nellie and Jack are not to have a future
> together: Jack has made that clear and is trying to protect his future
> with his fiancée. The child's death comments, as does O'Neill, on sex
> versus love, and on social reasons for not marrying beneath one's class
> in presumably egalitarian America. But primarily, the multiple deaths
> are no more than shrill and colorful markers in O'Neill's melodramatic
> portrait of the ironies of life.[39]

Hays makes apt observations about the way that abortion functions in
the text of this play, but equating the fetus with an infant or deeming
it "child murder" is in itself a political statement. He must have been
aware that he was treading on controversial ground as he justifies the
slippage between infanticide and abortion in a brief footnote, claiming, "Three of the infanticides to which I refer are abortions. I do not

want to enter the controversy of whether a fetus ought to be regarded as a living being, or any legal or ethical argument in this essay. For these plays, abortion results in the death of a child as surely as does the murder of a live-born infant, and the symbolic result for the plays is identical."[40] This justification undermines the author's argument since there is no need to broach ethics or philosophical debate about the fetus. It seems that the umbrella term "infanticide" simply serves to build his point of view. E. Ann Kaplan comments that in the late twentieth century, the fetus "is discursively constructed as if it already were a *subject*, and one which once again supersedes the *mother*'s subjectivity."[41] In this instance, Hays's point of view frames the fetus as a subject, simply by grouping different terms into one category.

Chester Clayton Long makes a different kind of social statement as he considers Jack's lack of adequate information. "He thinks an abortion will solve the threat of society's Nemesis; but since it must be performed in secret under improper conditions, it involves the risk of death for the woman. That even death must be risked to avoid exposure is monstrous; that Jack's training apparently had deprived him of the knowledge of contraceptives is probably the final absurdity."[42] It does seem unlikely, moreover, that a male in Jack's position would understand the danger that abortion presented to Nellie. As far as he could tell, he secured the best available doctor that money could buy, the only one he "could find who would do that sort of thing."[43] Jack's faith in institutions and economic solutions leads him to believe she has adequate medical care once he makes his payment. And as soon as his role is complete, he severs his relationship.

Abortion gives insight into the limited options available to women who found themselves unmarried and pregnant. Bound to a stenography job that supports her family, Nellie must agree to Jack's desire to abort the pregnancy since he does not offer marriage and its attendant economic benefits. Without his support, she can only passively comply with his wishes, and as a result, she nullifies her threat to Jack and his family. Her voice is never heard on stage throughout the course of the short drama; her only strength comes in the form of a male protector, her brother, who seeks to right the situation for her. According to Murray's description of Nellie's love, she would have continued the pregnancy if she had Jack's support. Further, since she has no capital, she cannot choose the person to perform the abortion and must rely on Jack's choice of doctor. Bringing her pregnancy to term alone would have been impossible because of her family's dependence on her income. Pregnancy wrests away Nellie's control of her own body and passes it to men: her lover, her brother, and her doctor. Her death

seems to preserve Jack's potential family unit, but O'Neill cannot let
Jack move on without retribution, punishing, in turn, his immediate
family and the larger college community. The implication is that the
consequences of abortion extend through all socioeconomic levels.

The tragedy of the play lies in class structures that govern decision making. Nellie is compelled to abort because of external pressure
as well as her inability to live outside the nuclear-family norm. The
reader is led to believe that the she opposes the abortion but submits
to male desire, expediency, and convention, thus becoming a victim of
her domestic decisions. Jack, too, is a prisoner of his class and cannot
imagine a life that transcends social bounds. While he has affection for
Nellie, it is not a relationship that he could seriously consider beyond
making a payment to dispose of the uncomfortable situation.

The melodrama of this early O'Neill play reflects abortion's function as a means to keep the nuclear family intact, where a woman's
inability to make decisions in the public sphere was mirrored in her
private decisions. The first well-known texts to hint at or feature abortion at this time were plays. In addition to O'Neill's *Abortion*, there
was Elizabeth Robins's *Votes for Women!* (1907) and Harley Granville
Barker's *Waste* (1907). The implication in each portrayal is that the
characters that have abortions long to be, in some way, mothers in a
stable family relationship. When these relationships are unavailable,
abortion solves the problem of how to resolve pregnancy outside the
nuclear family, with awful consequences, and it therefore becomes the
tool to hold onto standard family roles.

In discussing his characters' motives while directing *The Iceman
Cometh*, O'Neill once said, "In all my plays sin is punished and
redemption takes place."[44] This oft-quoted phrase neatly applies to
dramas throughout his oeuvre, but the rest of his thoughts are just
as revealing: "Vice and virtue cannot live side by side. It's the humili-
ation of a loving kiss that destroys evil."[45] In this one-act play, sin
certainly is punished, but no one is redeemed, as there is no opportunity for that "loving kiss." O'Neill's sense of morality is apparent in
this early work—he cannot allow Jack's pretense of virtue to endure
and so exacts a price. There is no chance at redemption in *Abortion*;
the real cost of putting reputation before love is death, grief, and the
dissolution of family bonds.

NOTES

1. Arthur Gelb, "O'Neill's 'Lost Works,'" review of Eugene O'Neill's "Lost Works," including *Abortion*, directed by Nils L. Cruz, Key Theatre, *New York Times*, October 28, 1959, 40.
2. Ibid.
3. O'Neill did not realize that the typescript of *Abortion* and other early plays would be available in the Library of Congress Copyright Office once he let his 1914 copyright lapse. Travis Bogard, ed., *Eugene O'Neill: Complete Plays 1913–1920* (New York: Library of America, 1988), 1088.
4. John Mason Brown, "Finders Keepers Losers Weepers," review of *Lost Plays of Eugene O'Neill*, by Eugene O'Neill, *Saturday Review of Literature*, June 17, 1950, 31.
5. Barrett H. Clark, "*Lost Plays of Eugene O'Neill*. New Fathoms Press, Ltd. $3.00," review of *Lost Plays of Eugene O'Neill*, by Eugene O'Neill, *Theatre Arts* 34 (July 1950): 7–8.
6. Gelb, "O'Neill's 'Lost Works,'" 40.
7. Timo Tiusanen discusses the technical aspects of the play, particularly how the climax of Jack's suicide is made compelling by the fusion of stage elements like lighting and the crescendo of the crowd, the latter of which O'Neill would use in later works. Timo Tiusanen, *O'Neill's Scenic Images* (Princeton: Princeton University Press, 1968), 44.

   In her chapter about small-town characters in O'Neill's works, Ima Herron also notes elements of the dramatist's later style by examining the dualisms present in Jack's character. Ima H. Herron, "O'Neill's Lost Townsmen," in *The Small Town in American Drama* (Dallas: Southern Methodist University Press, 1968), 280–81.

   Robert J. Higgs posits that Jack's character type lives on in *Strange Interlude*, a later O'Neill drama that includes a college athlete-hero from New England who dies, in this case, before the action of the play. Robert J. Higgs, "Apollo" in *Laurel and Thorn: The Athlete in American Literature* (Lexington: University Press of Kentucky, 1981), 56.

   For Thierry Dubost's catalog of the interpersonal relationships and inner worlds of O'Neill's characters, it is not necessary to privilege the more accomplished late plays since "there is a direct continuity between *Abortion* and *The Iceman Cometh*." Thierry Dubost, *Struggle, Defeat or Rebirth: Eugene O'Neill's Vision of Humanity* (Jefferson, NC: McFarland, 1997), 4.

   In his analysis of the play's characterization, structure, and organization, Chester Clayton Long observes that abortion creates an underlying tension, since "the society presented in the play (imitated in it) makes no provision for the darker side of the nature of the characters that inhabit it. Appetency simply is not accorded any public recognition either in law or custom. But as a matter of fact it exists in this imitated social milieu, as it did in the actual society which was the object of the imitation of the dramatic milieu." The abortion becomes a tangible symbol of the appetites Jack should have transcended in his status as an upper-class, white college hero. Chester Clayton Long, "Abortion, Thirst, and the Moon of the Caribbees," in *The Role of Nemesis in the Structure of Selected Plays by Eugene O'Neill* (The Hague: Mouton, 1968), 39. This overview of critical treatment emphasizes how *Abortion* is most often considered in relation to O'Neill's better-known works rather than as its own entity. Further, this outline represents the bulk of decades of criticism regarding this play.

8. The play did not even generate much response when it was revived in 1999 as part of an ongoing festival featuring every one of O'Neill's plays, which was staged to celebrate the reopening of The Provincetown Playhouse. Praise did come from the online review site CurtainUp, which claimed "The stunning surprise is 'Abortion,' an emotional roller coaster of a play that in less time than any single act of *A Long Day's Journey Into Night* demonstrates that O'Neill already had his hand on the devastating playwriting throttle that served him, and his audiences, so well." Les Gutman, "Playwrights Theater Festival of O'Neill II *'Bound East for Cardiff,' 'Abortion' and 'The Movie Man,'*" review of The Birth of an Artist play series, including *Abortion*, Playwrights Theater, *Curtain Up: The Internet Theater Magazine of Reviews, Features, Annotated Listings*, last modified August 1999, http://www .curtainup.com/oneillreport.html.

9. Christina Hauck, "Abortion and the Individual Talent," *English Literary History* 70, no. 1 (Spring 2003): 225.

10. Ibid., 232.

11. Judith Wilt, *Abortion, Choice, and Contemporary Fiction: The Armageddon of the Maternal Instinct* (Chicago: University of Chicago Press, 1990), 4.

12. Arthur Gelb and Barbara Gelb, *O'Neill: Life with Monte Cristo* (New York: Applause, 2000), 253–56.

13. Ibid., 271–73.

14. Ibid., 264.

15. Louis Sheaffer, *O'Neill: Son and Playwright*, vol. 1 (New York: Cooper Square, 2002), 263.

16. Eugene O'Neill, *Abortion*, in *The Lost Plays of Eugene O'Neill*, ed. Lawrence Gellert (New York: Citadel, 1958), 24.

17. Sheaffer, *O'Neill: Son and Playwright*, 149.

18. Travis Bogard, *Contour in Time: The Plays of Eugene O'Neill*, 2nd ed. (New York: Oxford University Press, 1988), 23.

19. Virginia Floyd, "Abortion," in *The Plays of Eugene O'Neill: A New Assessment* (New York: Frederick Ungar, 1985), 71.

20. Robert M. Dowling, "Abortion: A Play in One Act (completed, 1914; first produced, 1959)," in *Critical Companion to Eugene O'Neill: A*

Literary Reference to his Life and Work, 2 vols. (New York: Facts on File-Infobase, 2009), 23.

21. Kristin Luker, *Abortion and the Politics of Motherhood* (Berkeley: University of California Press, 1984), 13–15. Luker says that doctors used abortion to professionalize their work and to raise their status as medical experts. To achieve this goal, they had to convince the public of a contradictory assertion. Luker explains that "ironically, what the physicians did, in effect, was to simultaneously claim both an *absolute* right to life for the embryo (by claiming that abortion is always murder) and a *conditional* one (by claiming that doctors have a right to declare some abortions 'necessary')" (32).

22. Michael Grossberg and Christopher Tomlins, eds., *The Cambridge History of Law in America: The Twentieth Century and After (1920–)*, vol. 3. (Cambridge: Cambridge University Press, 2008), 243.

23. Travis Bogard and Jackson R. Bryer, eds., *Selected Letters of Eugene O'Neill* (New Haven: Yale University Press, 1988), 36.

24. Ibid., 52.

25. Lawrence Gellert, introduction to *Lost Plays of Eugene O'Neill*, by Eugene O'Neill (New York: Citadel, 1958), 8.

26. O'Neill, *Abortion*, 23.

27. Ibid., 23.

28. Ibid., 24–26.

29. Ibid., 26.

30. Ibid., 25.

31. Ibid., 25.

32. Ibid., 25.

33. Ibid., 26.

34. Ibid., 26.

35. Ibid., 32.

36. Ibid., 32.

37. Ibid., 30.

38. Ibid., 29.

39. Peter L. Hays, "Child Murder and Incest in American Drama," *Twentieth Century Literature* 36, no. 4 (Winter 1990): 435–36.

40. Ibid., 447.

41. E. Ann Kaplan, *Motherhood and Representation: The Mother in Popular Culture and Melodrama* (London: Routledge, 1992), 14.

42. Long, *The Role of Nemesis*, 40.

43. O'Neill, *Abortion*, 26.

44. Croswell Bowen, *The Curse of the Misbegotten: A Tale of the House of O'Neill* (New York: McGraw-Hill, 1959), 309.

45. Ibid.

WORKS CITED

Bogard, Travis. *Contour in Time: The Plays of Eugene O'Neill*. Rev. ed. New York: Oxford UP, 1988. Print.

———, ed. *Eugene O'Neill: Complete Plays 1913–1920*. New York: Library of America, 1988. Print.

———, and Jackson R. Bryer, eds. *Selected Letters of Eugene O'Neill*. New Haven: Yale UP, 1988. Print.

Bowen, Croswell. *The Curse of the Misbegotten: A Tale of the House of O'Neill*. New York: McGraw, 1959. Print.

Brown, John Mason. "Finders Keepers Losers Weepers." Rev. of *Lost Plays of Eugene O'Neill*, by Eugene O'Neill. *Saturday Review of Literature* 17 June 1950: 28, 30–31. Print.

Clark, Barrett H. "*Lost Plays of Eugene O'Neill*. New Fathoms Press, Ltd. $3.00." Rev. of *Lost Plays of Eugene O'Neill*, by Eugene O'Neill. *Theatre Arts* 34 (July 1950): 7–8. Print.

Dowling, Robert M. *Abortion: A Play in One Act (completed, 1914; first produced, 1959)*. *Critical Companion to Eugene O'Neill: A Literary Reference to his Life and Work*. Vol. 1. New York: Facts on File-Infobase, 2009. 23–27. Print.

Dubost, Thierry. *Struggle, Defeat or Rebirth: Eugene O'Neill's Vision of Humanity*. Jefferson: McFarland, 1997. Print.

Floyd, Virginia. "Abortion." *The Plays of Eugene O'Neill: A New Assessment*. New York: Ungar, 1985. 71–75. Print.

Gelb, Arthur. "O'Neill's 'Lost Works.'" Rev. of Eugene O'Neill's "Lost Works," including *Abortion*, dir. Nils L. Cruz. Key Theatre. *New York Times* 28 Oct. 1959: 40. Print.

———, and Barbara Gelb. *O'Neill: Life with Monte Cristo*. New York: Applause, 2000. Print.

Gellert, Lawrence. Introduction. *Lost Plays of Eugene O'Neill*. By Eugene O'Neill. New York: Citadel, 1958. 7–10. Print.

Grossberg, Michael, and Christopher Tomlins, eds. *The Cambridge History of Law in America: The Twentieth Century and After (1920–)*. Vol. 3. Cambridge: Cambridge UP, 2008. Print.

Gutman, Les. "Playwrights Theater Festival of O'Neill II: 'Bound East for Cardiff,' 'Abortion' and 'The Movie Man.'" Rev. of the Birth of an Artist play series, including *Abortion*. Playwrights Theater. *Curtain Up: The Internet Theater Magazine of Reviews, Features, Annotated Listings*, August 1999. Web. Accessed 18 February 2009. http://www.curtainup.com/oneillreport.html.

Hauck, Christina. "Abortion and the Individual Talent." *English Literary History* 70.1 (Spring 2003): 223–66. Print.

Hays, Peter L. "Child Murder and Incest in American Drama." *Twentieth Century Literature* 36.4 (Winter 1990): 434–48. Print.

Herron, Ima H. "O'Neill's Lost Townsmen." *The Small Town in American Drama*. Dallas: Southern Methodist UP, 1968. 273–337. Print.

Higgs, Robert J. "Apollo." *Laurel and Thorn: The Athlete in American Literature*. Lexington: UP of Kentucky, 1981. 22-90. Print.

Kaplan, E. Ann. *Motherhood and Representation: The Mother in Popular Culture and Melodrama*. London: Routledge, 1992. Print.

Long, Chester Clayton. "Abortion, Thirst, and the Moon of the Caribbees." *The Role of Nemesis in the Structure of Selected Plays by Eugene O'Neill*. The Hague: Mouton, 1968. 27–74. Print.

Luker, Kristin. *Abortion and the Politics of Motherhood*. Berkeley: U of California P, 1984. Print.

O'Neill, Eugene. *Abortion*. *The Lost Plays of Eugene O'Neill*. Ed. Lawrence Gellert. New York: Citadel, 1958. 11–34. Print.

Sheaffer, Louis. *O'Neill: Son and Playwright*. Vol. 1. 1968. New York: Cooper Square, 2002. Print.

Tiusanen, Timo. *O'Neill's Scenic Images*. Princeton: Princeton UP, 1968. Print.

Wilt, Judith. *Abortion, Choice, and Contemporary Fiction: The Armageddon of the Maternal Instinct*. Chicago: U of Chicago P, 1990. Print.

CHAPTER 4

THE MOVIE MAN
THE FAILURE OF AESTHETICS?

Thierry Dubost

If one wished to establish a hit parade of Eugene O'Neill's plays, one might argue that *The Movie Man* could reasonably compete with a few others for the last place. However, stating that this early dramatic work can be viewed as a clumsy attempt by a young playwright does not sum it all up.[1] In spite of its flaws, like many early works, *The Movie Man* deserves some critical attention because it exposes a series of threads that O'Neill later wove in different shapes, both thematically and aesthetically. The purpose of this essay, then, is to analyze the causes—past and present—for this failure, contrasting some thematic or aesthetic aspects with O'Neill's future writing modes. Highlighting how the young playwright failed will be the first step to explain why this one-act play led to a dramatic dead end. Still, this initial failure will not merely serve to explain why, contrary to some early plays, *The Movie Man* can be ignored by directors. It will also show why it remains interesting for critics, as a crossroads of genres, a possible starting point to define a new aesthetic frame within which, however, the playwright never included his future works.

In O'Neill's early plays, especially his one-acters, one notes that the coherence of his works often results from the characters' inability to escape their tragic fate and avoid the consequences of a lethal environment (see for instance *Thirst*, *The Web*, or *Fog*). The restricted length of these early attempts helped the young playwright focus on a single issue, making it easier for the audience to understand the play.

In *Servitude*, his first three-act play, O'Neill wrote a longer script but, following the rules of the time, he provided a global perspective that spectators could follow. He remained consistent, and the audience never wondered what the stakes were, when he depicted various stages of a betrayed husband's revenge stratagem. Although *The Movie Man* is only a one-act play, one could argue that O'Neill tried to extend the scope of its plot by merging what could be viewed as two different scenarios—a love story and a war story.[2]

The title—*The Movie Man*—leaves no doubt about O'Neill's major perspective, but this one-sided outlook does not erase the other side of the story. Staging Mexican warriors who surrender to the power of the media and agree to perform like ordinary actors (almost puppets), the playwright wrote a political play—albeit a weak one—but a political play nonetheless.[3] In this respect, one may consider that the Mexican Revolution is more than mere background. Thus even if O'Neill gives prominence to the story of a "movie man" who falls in love with a help- less Mexican girl, spectators also discover the dark side of a civil war.

In earlier works, O'Neill had dealt with the themes of war and love separately. In *The Movie Man*, the combination of war and love was a new challenge for the young playwright, which may explain why he resorted to melodrama and used the tropes of a genre he despised. "In melodrama, man is pitted against another man, or against certain other men, or a social group or order, or a condition, or even against events and phenomena. In melodrama, one attacks or is attacked; it is always a kind of war."[4] In *The Movie Man*, Rogers is expected to remain an outsider, but O'Neill followed the rules of melodrama, and Rogers is eventually "pitted against another man." The film director gets involved in the conflict, not for political motives but because he wants to save a young woman about to give herself to a General in order to save her father's life.

> **Rogers**: (*Disgustedly*) What you can see in these skirts has got me beat.
>   They're so homely the mules shy at them.[5]

In the opening scene, Rogers had condemned any male involvement with Mexican women, but he quickly changes his mind when he finds himself in a position to rescue an innocent victim. If *The Movie Man* were a tragedy, his early statement would amount to *hamartia*, since in the course of this short play, Rogers falls in love with a Mexican girl, Anita, and defends her honor by competing in a trial of strength with a Mexican general. Rogers eventually triumphs, and all's well that ends well—a rather surprising feature considering O'Neill's early works.[6]

The issue of happy versus unhappy endings needs to be addressed in view of the young playwright's repeated wish to redefine American drama. Although O'Neill had often expressed his intention to break from the hackneyed features of melodrama, *The Movie Man* blatantly reveals that he proved unable to do so. One of the reasons for his failure to adopt new aesthetics might be that shared love between characters seemed to call for the traditional staging modes of his father's theatre, hence the tropes of melodrama with Boucicault's Irish melodramas serving as models.

In *The Movie Man*, the ethnic background proves essential. Ungrammatical English gives an alien touch to characters' speeches and adds to Anita's frailty: "my mothair—die and I must come home to the house of my fathair becose I have more years—I am older than my sisters."[7] On the other hand, the rough language of the military men (the Spanish translation for "soldier") reinforces their unrefined portrayal. Their inadequate speech modes add to O'Neill's primitive—some might view it as racist[8]—portrait of the seemingly dangerous Mexicans.

Anita's situation reminds one of Boucicault's Irish plays, where the playwright staged the meeting of opposite cultures and had English soldiers behave like protective gentlemen when faced with a frail native young woman. In spite of the "primitive" aspect of the Irish people they wanted to tame, English warriors respected some of them and were attracted to charming "lassies."[9] In *The Movie Man*, as is generally the case in melodrama, when a young woman is threatened, evil powers are eventually counterbalanced by positive forces, with which the audience delightfully sides.

> Rogers: (*Decisively*) I'll save your old man if I have to start a revolution of my own to do it.
> Anita: (*Her eyes shining with gratitude*) Ah, thank you, señor—but if you should fail?
> Rogers: (*Emphatically*) I won't fail. You just watch me start something![10]

For a contemporary reader, Roger's assurance and behavior no longer resonate. Eventually, justice prevails and he saves Anita's father. This reassuring staging mode corresponded to the expectations of a nineteenth-century public, but even in 1914, such aesthetics no longer met the standards of the time, in particular that of the Provincetown Players. This initial discrepancy has increased with the passing of time, and probably explains why most critics reject the play nowadays. In view of the initial melodramatic frame that O'Neill used, one could view *The Movie Man* in opposition to O'Neill's future dramatic choices since he later abandoned the optimistic perspectives expected of happy endings. Indeed, the play's concluding dialogue amounts to a first step toward a happy future, when Anita tells Rogers that, from then on, he will be part of their family:

> **Anita**: As a brother, my father's son, shall you be to us!
> **Rogers**: (*Holding her hand and looking into her eyes*) Only—a brother?
> **Anita**: (*Drawing her hand away in confusion, she runs to the door; then turns*) Quién sabe, señor? Who knows?[11]

Verbal and gestural clichés reveal that O'Neill knew only too well what traditional producers required: entertaining and unchallenging dramatic works for self-satisfied spectators. In light of the young playwright's admiration for August Strindberg or Henrik Ibsen, however, and especially if one thinks of *Before Breakfast*, it seems paradoxical that he should associate an impending wedding with a picture of happiness.

Before reaching a concluding verdict, one needs to ponder the significance of Rogers's transformation. A common feature of melodrama is love at first sight. As a result, it might be tempting to consider that O'Neill's use of melodramatic tropes reveals his acceptance of the genre. However, although Rogers is suddenly overwhelmed by Anita, one should tread softly on those dangerous grounds. In other words, should this episode be restricted to a compulsory item of melodrama or should it be viewed as a genuine O'Neillian questioning of the nature of love and its amazing powers? Undoubtedly, Anita's arrival brings to light Rogers's true personality when he suddenly commits himself to protect her, as expected in melodramas. All things considered, however, the genre may not explain everything. Anita and Rogers's meeting reminds one of Yank and Mildred's in *The Hairy Ape*. In both cases, a man is overwhelmed by a woman whose sole presence calls into question the founding ground of their lives.

Even if O'Neill's true questioning of love is masked by the outer frames of melodrama, it remains that Anita's behavior shows she belongs in an outdated romantic universe. Anita's willingness to rely on the kindness of a stranger illustrates that O'Neill still adhered to his father's sham theatre traditions, and that his stereotypical views of male/female relations were closer to Alexandre Dumas's perspectives than to those of his female Provincetown friends of the time. Indeed, even at the beginning of the twentieth century, the image of a frail woman in need of man's protection—as the essence of femininity—was sometimes challenged or even rejected. Alluding to Susan Glaspell's *Woman's Honor*,[12] Joel Pfister writes, "Shielded One protests the interpretation of female honor as chastity, asking her fellow volunteers: 'Aren't we something more than things to be noble about?'"[13] O'Neill's answer to such a question will remain unknown, but it's doubtful whether he would have shared all of Glaspell's views as far as gender issues were concerned. Obviously, *The Movie Man* no longer resonates today, and the melodramatic frame that O'Neill used may not solely account for this; his global view of gender relationships may actually be the decisive factor.

The other major feature characterizing *The Movie Man* is O'Neill's treatment of the Mexican Revolution, even if it only provides the background for this romantic story. At the time, people would probably have rejected the depiction of the conflict as irrelevant.[14] Nowadays, paradoxically, in contrast to O'Neill's views on love and gender relationships, his characterization of war has gained credibility. Indeed, the connection between war and film—rather unrealistic during the early 1910s—has now become part of any major conflict. It would be wrong to view O'Neill as a soothsayer predicting the future rapports between armies and the media, and the vital difference lies in his global verdict on the whole adventure. To the seriousness of contemporary conflicts shown in films or in the media, he opposed a distanced point of view, highlighting the almost absurd aspect of the war. The sentry's comment about the two Americans, "Muy loco!" (very crazy), amounts to an authorial comment that characterizes the whole conquering venture. This scathing verdict shows that although O'Neill failed in his attempt at defining new aesthetics in *The Movie Man*, he tried to use the dramatic tools of classical theatre as well as those of melodrama to write this love and war play. Here, the soldier plays the part of a Greek chorus. His insistence on the shared madness of the two men reflects the whole situation and, as a result, partly explains the genre of the play. Moreover, the soldier's speech echoes the condescending remarks of the two Americans who agree with him, but with respect to Mexicans at war, whom they consider to be crazy. This shared outlook on the Other as a mad individual acting in crazy ways could be viewed as the touchstone of this war comedy.

> **Delvin**: You remember the other day when they were going after that fort on the outskirts?
> **Rogers**: Sure—good stuff—plenty of real live action that day.
> **Delvin**: (*indignantly*) It was good stuff all right, but I missed all the first part of it on account of the simp General Virella. He was just

waving his sword and ordering 'em to charge when I came up. "Here, you!" I said to him. "Wait a minute. Can't you see I'm not ready for you yet? And what do you think the greaser said to me? You know he speaks good English. He says: "Shall my glorious soldiers be massacred waiting for your machine?" And away he runs with all his yellow-bellies after him.[15]

The combination of Delvin's lack of empathy for the soldiers and his anger at the Mexican general who refuses to abide by the rules of the film company provides potential amusement. The use of "greaser" illustrates the cameraman's racist attitude, which implies that the fate of primitive individuals is none of the movie men's concern.

A similar tone is set away from the battlefield. Immediately after their conversation about the incident, Rogers tells his friend that Anita's father will be executed. Although both men admit they like him as a person, Rogers's verdict (before he meets Anita) is that it will "make a great picture."[16] Their only concern is changing the time of execution so that Delvin has enough light to film the shot.

This episode stages an American outlook on a war of supposedly primitive people, which could explain the rather negative point of view on the fighting parties. Still, when O'Neill changes sides and has a Mexican general speak, for the audience, the image of the conflict remains far from flattering:

> **Gomez**: The plan is fine, the town will be ours, my soldiers will steal and no more grumble against Gomez. Tomorrow I will shoot all the prisoners for your picture, I promise eet.[17]

Neither the movie men nor the Mexican general pay much attention to sacrificed lives; the sole motives for the war seem to be power and money. In another war play, *The Sniper*, O'Neill hints at the almost absurd nature of conflicts that cause the unacceptable death of innocent victims. In *The Movie Man*, however, the philosophical and aesthetic stakes are more complex, since tragedy is combined with comedy. Starting from such premises (tragedy, comedy, and absurdity), O'Neill might have explored the new aesthetics of absurdist drama, which had not yet been conceptualized but triumphed in the 1950s. Indeed, Ionesco's thoughts on comedy and tragedy could apply here: "As for me, I have never managed to understand the difference people make between the comic and the tragic. The comic, which foreshadows the absurd, seems more depressing than the tragic. With the comic, there is no way out. I say 'depressing,' but it is actually beyond despair or hope."[18] As mentioned earlier, although O'Neill mixed comedy and tragedy, the young playwright included his war depiction within the classical frame of melodrama. For him, another more contemporary model could then have been Alfred Jarry's *Ubu Roi*, which was first performed in 1896. The mixture of tragedy and comedy in a universe where human beings are mainly viewed as primitive grossly corresponded to what O'Neill had in mind. Resorting to a grotesque dramatic mode, he could have set his work within a new aesthetic frame, but failed to do so. The first reason for this may have been ignorance, but another explanation for his failed attempt was probably his lack of proficiency in dramatic construction. Faced with the need to unite love and war in a comedy, it's likely he chose the easier route of melodrama.

The basic explanation for his choice may also lie elsewhere. When looking at the final encounter between General Gomez and Rogers, it's possible to argue that O'Neill's lack of formal investigation may actually find its roots in a philosophical stance. After accepting to save Anita's father and, as a result, gaining the right to launch a night attack, Gomez takes his leave in the following way:

> **Gomez**: And now I must prepare the attack. (*He goes to the door, then turns and remarks grandiloquently*) Should anyone wish me, señor, tell them that een the hour of battle, *Pancho Gomez*, like the immortal Juarez, will ever be found at the head of his brave soldiers. *Adiós!*
> (*He makes a sweeping bow and goes out past the saluting sentry*)
> **Rogers**: (*With a long whistle of amusement—turning to Anita*) Some bull! Honest, you've got to hand it to that guy, at that.[19]

In spite of Rogers's condescending views on Mexicans, and his rather distant outlook on the conflict, he cannot help admiring the general's bravery. This final encounter leading to a revised appraisal of the other man's behavior proves vital to our understanding of the play. Despite his previous insistence on the brutal, vulgar, and primitive attitudes of the Mexican soldiers, Rogers can't help but respect their courage. His change of heart recalls the similarities between his initial negative judgment about Mexican girls and his immediate attraction to Anita.

In view of the modified perspectives on the conflict that Rogers's new perception provides, one might question the coherence of the play and wonder whether Rogers's change of attitude results from the compulsory structural need of a happy ending. Another of O'Neill's early plays contradicts this proposal. In *The Emperor Jones*, Smithers,

a white man, finds himself in a similar situation. In spite of his hatred
for an extravagant and overbearing Jones, he cannot help but respect
his unabated courage, a feeling that O'Neill characterizes as "puzzled
admiration."[20] In *The Movie Man*, through Rogers's remark, O'Neill
conveys the same kind of judgment on Gomez, which comes across
as a rather surprising ideological perspective, even in pre–World War
I times. A few years later, in *Ah, Wilderness!*, O'Neill draws his own
portrait of the artist as an anarchist, looking back fondly on the par-
rotlike and extreme political outbursts of a young man. By 1914,
although O'Neill had matured, *The Movie Man* shows that there was
room for improvement both politically and aesthetically. Regarding his somewhat naïve and extreme views, it should be noted that
O'Neill biographers highlight the influence of Nietzsche's writings
on the future Nobel Prize winner. Therefore, it's possible to imagine
that his unexpected outlook on men about to wage a battle probably
finds its source in the German philosopher's point of view on wars,
summarized as follows in *Human, All Too Human*: "People will discover many other such surrogates for war, but perhaps that will make
them understand ever more clearly that such a highly cultivated, and
therefore necessarily weary humanity as that of present-day Europe,
needs not only wars but the greatest and most terrible wars (that
is, occasional relapses into barbarism) in order not to forfeit to the
means of culture its culture and its very existence."[21] In O'Neill's
mind, the situation described in *The Movie Man* likely corresponded
to one of these "occasional relapses into barbarism." It follows that,
for the Nietzschean playwright, the combination of inhuman violence with the depiction of rather grotesque characters does not lead
to a tragic reading of the world, but remains acceptable in a comedy
framed by melodrama.

This analysis of *The Movie Man* reveals the complexity of O'Neill's
early aesthetics, a mixture of tradition and innovation, with various
striking aspects. First, in the field of comedy, remember that the play
reveals two roads not taken by O'Neill. Indeed, in *The Movie Man*,
O'Neill neither investigated the absurd aspects of wars nor explored
grotesque comedy as a way of highlighting differently the tragic
aspects of life. Important as it may be for *The Movie Man*, his initial
failure to investigate these dramatic fields proves even more interesting in view of his theatrical output, especially for a playwright who
tried so many dramatic forms in his plays, but never trod on the paths
of absurd drama or grotesque comedy.

The second point has to do with the dialogue between form and
content in this play about love and war: "All great dramatists have used

the dialogue between form and content to create the theatre experience, emphasizing continually that the event is happening now, that the theatrical action is real, takes place in the audience's imagination, in the moment of performance, in what I have called 'the theatrical metaphor.'"[22] Today, it would be difficult to praise O'Neill for his dialogue between form and content in *The Movie Man*. When he wrote it, he probably used the old fashioned tools of melodrama because he thought they could still work. For a contemporary reader—or spectator—and contrary to some early works, like *Bound East for Cardiff*, *The Movie Man* no longer resonates. Obviously, the all's-well-that-ends-well frame of melodrama has become strikingly obsolete. Thematically, however, old-fashioned and romantic visions of love—even if they prove challenging in terms of gender relationships—could still appeal to a twenty-first-century audience precisely because they no longer correspond to contemporary views and would be deemed harmless because of their disconnect with today's life. Regarding the war, unfortunately, the issue is far from obsolete, as the daily succession of conflicts shows. Like romantic love, the war background, with its series of primitive versus civilized innuendos, belongs in an outdated vision, but with opposite results. One may actually argue that the war issue is the breaking point, when the failure of aesthetics meets that of the themes used by the playwright. Complete disrespect for human lives, and insistence on the atrocious aspects of war can still be staged today, but within a different aesthetic frame. Grotesque comedy, or very violent works—both of which eventually highlight the tragic essence of conflicts and their terrifying aspects—are acceptable because of the implicit allusion to the horror of twentieth-century conflicts. Conversely, today, a light treatment of wars might amount to breaking a taboo. Consequently, the failure of aesthetics in *The Movie Man* cannot be restricted to form; it springs from an inadequate dialogue between form and content, within a very different social frame. The verdict may be harsh, but the moral weight of the crimes perpetrated during the twentieth century is so heavy that the ethics of most contemporary spectators imply a refusal of nineteenth-century aesthetics, in particular melodrama, for a dramatic staging of devastating wars.

NOTES

1. "*The Movie Man* (1914), a ham-fisted attempt at a romanticofarci-cal treatment of Pancho Villa's Mexican revolution and the financial involvement in it of the United States, here represented by the Earth Motion Picture Company. Pancho, renamed Gomez, has signed a con-tract with the American company, agreeing to stage raids and execu-tions only when the light is right for documentary filming. But Henry Rogers, an Earth representative, falls for the buxom charms of the dis-traught Anita Fernandez, whose father, one of Gomez' subordinate generals, has been sentenced to execution the next morning. Rogers agrees to permit Gomez one night raid if he will free her father, and the General complies, permitting the play a happy ending . . . *The Movie Man*, I fear, should return to a well-deserved oblivion." Frederick C. Wilkins, review of "Three Lost Plays of Eugene O'Neill" (*A Wife for a Life, The Movie Man* and *The Web*), dir. Michael Fields, Lotus Theatre Group, Playhouse 46, New York City, November 4–20, 1982, *Eugene O'Neill Newsletter* 6, no. 3 (Winter 1982).

2. See, for instance, *The Web, A Wife for a Life, The Sniper, In the Zone,* and *Shell Shock.*

3. "Despite all that has been written about Reed and O'Neill, however, the academic community has remained relatively quiet on their impor-tant literary exchange beyond the fact that O'Neill's *Movie Man*, a 1914 play about Hollywood's filming of the Mexican War, was inspired by his auspicious meeting with Reed in the winter of 1913." John S. Bak, "Eugene O'Neill and John Reed: Recording the Body Poli-tic, 1913–1922." *Eugene O'Neill Review* 20, nos. 1–2 (Spring/Fall 1996): 18.

4. J. L. Styan, *Drama, Stage and Audience* (London: Cambridge Univer-sity Press, 1973), 72.

5. O'Neill, Eugene. *The Movie Man*, in *Ten "Lost" Plays of Eugene O'Neill* Bennett Cerf, ed. (New York: Random House, 1964), 174.

6. Even if *The Movie Man* is not quite exceptional in this respect. See also *A Wife for a Life.*

7. O'Neill, *The Movie Man*, 176.

8. In view of Leveratto's perspective, the American characters' outlook on the Mexican warriors may also explain why contemporary readers (and spectators) would find it hard to relate to this work, and this ethi-cal stance goes beyond political correctness: "This confirms the need of spectators to defend their personal dignity by gauging the social acceptability of the show they attend by what people deem accept-able. This principle makes that a contemporary spectator will not allow himself to participate in a racist show, or in a show that is shocking for a religious or ethnic community" (my translation). « Nous confirme le souci du spectateur de défendre sa dignité personnelle, en mesur-ant l'acceptabilité sociale du spectacle auquel il participe à l'aune de

l'opinion publique. C'est ce principe qui fait que le spectateur contemporain s'interdira de participer à un spectacle raciste, ou à un spectacle qui choque les opinions d'une communauté ethnique ou religieuse. », Jean-Marc Leveratto, *Introduction à l'anthropologie du spectacle* (Paris: La Dispute, 2006), 79.

9. See, for instance, Dion Boucicault's *The Shaughraun*.

> **Molineux** (a young English officer) I know a dairymaid that was intended for me.
>
> **Claire.** That speech only wanted a taste of the brogue to be worthy of an Irishman.
>
> **Molineux.** (kissing her). Now I'm perfect.

Boucicault, The Shaughraun, 264.

10. O'Neill, *The Movie Man*, 178.
11. Ibid., 184.
12. Produced in New York City by the Provincetown Players during the 1917–18 season.
13. Joel Pfister, *Staging Depth: Eugene O'Neill and the Politics of Psychological Discourse* (Chapel Hill: University of North Carolina Press, 1995), 198.
14. Unlikely though the story may seem, it is based on fact; indeed, the reality was more ludicrous than the playwright's fiction. Shortly before he wrote his one-act play in 1914, the American newspapers ran front-page stories about Pancho Villa, the Mexican revolutionary, signing a contract with a New York movie company to wage his war only in daytime and under other circumstances favorable to the photographers. Since the movie men were dissatisfied with his appearance—ragged civilian clothes and a slouchy hat—Villa meekly submitted to being outfitted with a smart-looking uniform. Faithful to his contract, he delayed an attack on Ojinaga—besieged by his forces—until the cameramen arrived. Not to be outdone, a general on the other side deployed his army for a large scenic shot. (For a full account of the matter, see Terry Ramsaye, *A Million and One Nights*, 1926, 670–73.) Louis Sheaffer, "Correcting some Errors in Annals of O'Neill," *Eugene O'Neill Newsletter* 8, no. 1 (Spring 1984).
15. O'Neill, *The Movie Man*, 17.
16. Ibid., 173.
17. Ibid., 183.
18. Eugene Ionesco, *Notes, contre-notes* (Paris: Gallimard, 1966), 60. "Pour ma part, je n'ai jamais bien compris la différence que l'on fait entre comique et tragique. Le comique étant intuition de l'absurde, il me semble plus désespérant que le tragique. Le comique n'offre pas d'issue. Je dis «désespérant» mais en réalité il est au-delà du désespoir ou de l'espoir."
19. O'Neill, *The Movie Man*, 183.

20. 187 SMITHERS. (Then with a grin) Silver bullets! Gawd blimey, but
    yer died in the 'eight o' style, any'ow! 204.
21. Friedrich Nietzsche, *Human, All Too Human* (1878; Great Literature
    Online, n.d.), 477, accessed March 12, 2011, http://www.classicauthors
    .net/Nietzsche/Human/Human9.html.
22. Gordon McDougall, "Revolution and Recreation," in *The Routledge
    Reader in Politics and Performance,* ed. Lizbeth Goodman and Jane de
    Gay (London: Routledge, 2000), 126.

WORKS CITED

Bak, John S. "Eugene O'Neill and John Reed: Recording the Body Politic,
    1913–1922." *Eugene O'Neill Review* 20.1-2 (1996). 17-35. Print.
Boucicault, Dion. The Shaughraun. Selected Plays of Dion Boucicault. Ed
    Andrew Parkin. Gerrards Cross: Colin Smythe, 1987. 257-329.
Ionesco Eugene. *Notes, contre-notes.* Paris: Gallimard, 1966. Print.
Leveratto, Jean-Marc. *Introduction à l'anthropologie du spectacle.* Paris: La
    Dispute, 2006. Print.
McDougall, Gordon. "Revolution and Recreation" *The Routledge Reader in
    Politics and Performance.* Ed. Lizbeth Goodman and Jane de Gay. Lon-
    don: Routledge, 2000. 123-129. Print.
Nietzsche, Friedrich. *Human, All Too Human. Great Literature Online.* Great
    Literature Online, n.d. Web. 12 Mar. 2011. 477. http://www.classicauthors
    .net/Nietzsche/Human/Human9.html.
O'Neill, Eugene. *The Movie Man. Ten "Lost" Plays of Eugene O'Neill.* Bennett
    Cerf, ed. New York: Random House, 1964. 167-185. Print.
———. *The Web. Ten "Lost" Plays of Eugene O'Neill.* Bennett Cerf, ed. New
    York: Random House, 1964. 33–54. Print.
———. *Servitude. Ten "Lost" Plays of Eugene O'Neill.* Bennett Cerf. New
    York: Random House, 1964. 225–303. Print.
———. *A Wife for a Life. Ten "Lost" Plays of Eugene O'Neill.* Bennett Cerf,
    ed. New York: Random House, 1964. 209–223. Print.
———. *The Sniper. Ten "Lost" Plays of Eugene O'Neill.* Bennett Cerf, ed. New
    York: Random House, 1964. 187–207. Print.
———. *Shell Shock.* Children of the Sea and Three Other Unpublished Plays
    by Eugene O'Neill. Jennifer McCabe Atkinson, ed. Washington: Micro-
    card Editions, 1972. 191–209. Print.
———. *In the Zone. The Plays of Eugene O'Neill,* Vol III. Jennifer McCabe
    Atkinson, ed. New York: Random House, 1982. 513–532. Print.
———. *The Emperor Jones. The Plays of Eugene O'Neill,* Vol I. Jennifer
    McCabe Atkinson, ed. New York: Random House, 1982. 171–204. Print.
Pfister, Joel. *Staging Depth: Eugene O'Neill and the Politics of Psychological
    Discourse.* Chapel Hill: U of North Carolina P, 1995. Print.

Sheaffer, Louis. "Correcting some Errors in Annals of O'Neill." *Eugene O'Neill Newsletter* 8.1 (Spring 1984). *http://www.eoneill.com/library/newsletter/viii_1/viii-1a.htm*. Accessed April 1, 2012.

Styan, J. L. *Drama, Stage and Audience*. London: Cambridge UP, 1973. Print.

Wilkins, Frederick C. Rev. of "Three Lost Plays of Eugene O'Neill" (*A Wife for a Life, The Movie Man* and *The Web*), dir. Michael Fields. Lotus Theatre Group. Playhouse 46, New York City. 4–20 November 1982. *Eugene O'Neill Newsletter* 6.3 (Winter 1982). Print.

CHAPTER 5

"GOD STIFFEN US"
QUEERING O'NEILL'S SEA PLAYS

Phillip Barnhart

Richard B. Sewall's essay, "Eugene O'Neill and the Sense of the Tragic," sets the tone for the centenary celebration of Eugene O'Neill's work, *Eugene O'Neill's Century*. In it he suggests that the playwright was quite fully vested in his "tragic set of his mind" by the time he began his writing career.[1] Sewall argues that one of O'Neill's greatest influences, alongside August Strindberg, Henrik Ibsen, and Friedrich Nietzsche, was the great émigré novelist, Joseph Conrad, whose works repeatedly used both the jungle and the sea as settings for often tragic examinations of social anxiety. Several scholarly examinations have been made of the role of homosexuality in the works of Joseph Conrad, notably among them Richard Ruppel's 2008 monograph, *Love Between the Lines*. To date, there are no such works that investigate fully the possible homosexual themes in O'Neill's work.

Thematically, the early O'Neill one-act plays pay tribute to intimate relationships between men, occasionally pushing the lines between the idealized friendship and the romantic friendship, though never allowing this possibility outright. From his very early one-act play "A Wife for a Life"—really nothing more than a sketch in which he considers the relationship between two men who have lived solitarily as gold-mining partners—to his first sea play *In the Zone*, which highlights the deep commitment of two men to one another, and culminating with his final sea play, which may be seen as an illustration of the sometimes violent end result of sexual panic, O'Neill frames the relationship of men brought together, by choice, in closed and intimate spaces, simultaneously surrounded by the great expanse of nature. In all these illustrations the men fail to make the connection for which they seem to desperately be searching; the connection to something that will complete them, ground them, and make them whole. I am suggesting, in this essay, that on one level it is the inability to make the leap from the homosocial to the homosexual that causes anxiety and indicates, as one of the fundamental possibilities, O'Neill's tragic mind set.

Tragedy wears several masks, one being the arousal of pity in the audience when, through the complications of the plot, the protagonist fails to get what he or she desires, and by this, or by the mere desire itself, the protagonist is unraveled.[2] O'Neill said of his first sea play, *Bound East for Cardiff*, that within the short work, which should be noted helped to establish O'Neill as a playwright, "can be seen, or felt, the germ of the spirit, life-attitude, etc., of all my more important future work."[3] Taking O'Neill at his word, then, this play holds a key to understanding O'Neill and his particular sense of tragedy, helping us to read, perhaps, what is not explicitly stated. Before delving into *Bound East for Cardiff*, though, it will be helpful to take a closer look at O'Neill's first play, the one-act titled *A Wife for a Life*, which mirrors at least one of the main themes in the sea plays

In all these early plays, O'Neill experiments with the tension between the small enclosed spaces inhabited by the characters against the vast expanse of nature in which they are located. In this first play O'Neill uses the desert, a landscape he will not return to again but one that mirrors the sea. Both the desert and the sea reflect expansive desolation, both are fraught with potential danger, and both envelop the encampment or the sea vessel. This close and intimate space, created in a largely unknown territory, allows a type of repository to be developed, a place of secrets. The desert and the ocean are opposites from a geographic standpoint; what they do have in common, though, is that both places suggest an environment in which things can remain hidden. Both can appear to be unending and both are, at this point in history, nearly void of population. In this work, O'Neill's first extant play, two men travel together in the desert for five years, alone but for themselves. This scene seems to be as much a private place as can possibly be construed. Notice O'Neill's stage directions for *A Wife for a Life*: "The edge of the Arizona desert; a plain dotted in the foreground with clumps of sagebrush. On the horizon a lonely butte is outlined, black and sinister against the lighter darkness of a sky with stars. The time is in the early hours of the night. In the foreground stands a ragged tent the flap of which is open. Leaning against it are some shovels and pick or two. Two saddles are on the ground nearby."[4]

In this play the men are unwittingly in love with the same woman. The given circumstance is quite extraordinary since this woman is always at least a continent away. O'Neill will come back to the theme of "sharing" the same women repeatedly in his work—perhaps suggesting that this is the only acceptable conduit for physical intimacy between men. As the brief play unfolds, we find that the older man has left the woman because of his alcoholism and that the younger man has been waiting for a message from her announcing the legal dissolve of her marriage (to the older man). The end comes when the older man intercepts this letter and rather than destroying it, gives it to his young companion without the explanation of his role as that of the first husband. What is telling about this play is that the story has taken place over a five-year time frame in which these two men have wandered about the desert, sleeping in the same small tent, in search of gold. At the end the older man confesses to himself that the only two people he had ever truly loved had been his wife and his young friend: the wife in a traditional marriage in Buenos Aires, and this young man, his companion in the vast Arizona desert made smaller by the shared tent that brings them closer together. As the younger man leaves the exclusively masculine world of the itinerant mining camp to meet his soon-to-be wife in New York, the audience cannot help but feel pity for the older man, who, without either of his only loves, must travel on alone, left to take comfort in their happiness.

This is the only time that O'Neill will focus on the desert as a setting for a play—for shortly thereafter he sets his dramas in the geological opposite of the desert: the sea. In mid-1913, after writing *A Wife for a Life*, O'Neill wrote a play titled *Thirst*, which takes place on a life raft adrift at sea. Later that year he writes *Warnings*, which takes place, in part, aboard a steamer much like the SS *Glencairn* of his sea plays; early the next year he writes *Fog*, which depicts the action taking place aboard a life boat about to be picked up by a steamer. That same year he also writes *Bound East for Cardiff*, revisiting the themes of death and loss and the sea he had developed in his earlier attempts. It is with this play that O'Neill established himself as a maturing playwright, and as mentioned, it is within this play that we are given clues to the foundational drives of his later work.

O'Neill's turn to the sea as a prominent setting for his early works is based on his own experiences as a sailor beginning in 1909. In October of that year, O'Neill, who had become involved in what he felt to be an untenable relationship with Kathleen Jenkins, married her under pressure from his father and from her family. Two weeks later, upon turning 21, he set sail for Honduras—mostly, according to his biographers, to escape life with her.[5] He resists marriage and domestic life for the life at sea, spurred on by Conrad's stories of conflict and adventure. What resulted was a relatively short time at sea, and though accounts vary, O'Neill could not have been at sea for more than a couple years in total. Regardless of the exact length of time spent at sail, he would return to those experiences again and again, resurfacing them as a recurring theme throughout his prolific career.

Bound East for Cardiff is important for several reasons. Not only did the play establish O'Neill as an upcoming new playwright, but it brought attention to the newly formed Provincetown Playhouse, a venue that was, in effect, to have an enormous influence on American drama in the twentieth century. The notion of a "little theater" was, at the premier of this play on July 28, 1916, unheard of, and through the critical success of this play and others like it, the monolithic influence of the Broadway syndicate was diminished. When the Provincetown Playhouse moved to New York, theatre impresarios like the powerful David Belasco disdained these new small venues, but nevertheless these "little theaters" could produce plays that addressed social issues in a way that the giant theaters on Broadway refused.[6]

The play's action occurs aboard the tramp steamer the *Glencairn*. The sailors onboard the SS *Glencairn* live in their own confined space. The close proximity of their bunks, somewhere down below far from the captain and first mates, places them in a dark, shady territory. They are always in various states of undress and one imagines, over time, the developing intimacy of this exclusively male environment. This private space is surrounded by the vastness of the ocean, in isolation, without the advanced communications capabilities of the mid-twentieth century.

O'Neill uses a heightened poetic language to describe these intimate spaces—in lengthy stage directions that are really only matched by Tennessee Williams in terms of lyricism and poetic coloring:

> The seamen's forecastle of the British tramp steamer Glencairn on a foggy night midway on the voyage between New York and Cardiff. An irregular shaped compartment, the sides of which almost meet at the far end to form a triangle. Sleeping bunks about six feet long, ranged three deep with a space of three sides . . .
>
> Five men are sitting on the benches talking. They are dressed in dirty patched suits of dungaree, flannel shirts, and all are in their stocking feet. Four of the men are pulling on pipes and the air is heavy with

rancid tobacco smoke. Sitting on the top bunk in the left foreground, a Norwegian, Paul, is softly playing some old song on a battered accordion. He stops from time to time to listen to the conversation

In the lower bunk in the rear a dark-haired, hard featured man is lying apparently asleep. One of his arms is stretched limply over the side of the bunk. His face is very pale, and drops of clammy perspiration glisten on his forehead.[7]

These stage directions serve as a platform for O'Neill's continuing romance with the male figure, culminating in a major work such as *The Hairy Ape* in which the hypermasculinized eroticization of the male form all but dominates the play. That the sailors are in stocking feet suggests a comfortable intimacy and the character of Yank, who is the figure at the back lying in the bunk, is highly suggestive of the famous Roman replica of the Greek sculpture known as *The Dying Gaul*, a classical depiction of a captured slave who embodies the beauty of the strength of the male form, rendered tragic by its enslavement, or in the case of Yank, by his wound and impending death.

The dynamic between the good-looking American, Yank, and the strong Irishman, Driscoll, is established in this first play and resurfaces in the other plays, though the American's name changes occasionally from Yank to Jack. In *Bound East for Cardiff*, the character Yank has been hurt in an accident and is dying. His friend and soul mate, Driscoll, is trying to comfort him as Yank faces the end of his life and both begin to muse tragically on their time together.

> **Driscoll**: Twas just such a night as this the auld Doer wint down. Just about this toime ut was, too, and we all sittin' round in the fo'c'stle, Yank beside me, whin all av a suddint we heard a great sliterin' crash, and the ship heeled over till we was all in a heap on wan side. What come afther I disremember exactly, except 'twas a hard shirt to get the boats over the side before the auld teakettle sank. Yank was in the same boat wid me, and sivin morthal days we drifted wid scarcely a drop of wather or a bite to chew on. 'Twas Yank here that held me down whin I wanted to jump into the ocean, roarin' mad wid the thirst. Picked up we were on the same day wid only Yank in his senses, and him steerin' the boat . . . *(Yank groans and stirs uneasily, opening his eyes. Driscoll hurries to his side.)* . . .
>
> **Yank**: *(peevishly)* What're yeh all lyin' fur? D'yah think I'm sacred to— *(He hesitates as if frightened by the word he is about to say.)*
>
> **Driscoll**: Don't be thinkin' such things! *(The ship's bell is heard heavily sounding eight times. From the forecastle head above the voice of the*

lookout rises in a long wail: Aaall's welll. The men look uncertainly
at Yank as if undecided whether to say good-by or not.)
Yank: (*in an agony of fear*) Don't leave me, Drisc! I'm dyin', I tell yuh.
I won't stay here alone with everyone snorin'. I'll go out on deck.
(*He makes a feeble attempt to rise, but sinds back with a sharp groan.*
His breath comes in wheezy gasps.) Don't leave me, Drisc! (*His face*
grows white and his head falls back with a jerk.)
Driscoll: Don't be worryin', Yank. I'll not move a step out av
here— . . .[8]

As Yank reflects on his life, it is only the time spent with Driscoll that
he recalls. It is Driscoll who has comprised his family and who was the
sole consolation for choosing the wretched life of a sailor rather than,
as Yank bitterly reflects, a farmer with a wife and children. In effect,
Driscoll was Yank's life partner, sharing brawls and jails, dreams and
booze, rescuing one another and in the end consoling one another. In
a crucial moment of the play, Yank confesses to his Driscoll that he had
a foreboding feeling about this particular voyage. He had vowed it to
be his last, and he nearly didn't sign up for it, preferring rather to cash
in his earnings and buy a farm in South America where he and Driscoll
could spend the rest of their lives as ranchers. Poignantly, Driscoll had
the same idea, but rather than share it, he too signed up for what would
accurately be Yank's final voyage. What is keeping these men from finding a woman to marry, settling down, and having children? What would
drive Yank to plan his remaining years with Driscoll, ranching rather
than at least attempting a conventional domestic life?

When Yank dies Driscoll sobs, and this action, heartfelt and ten-
der, is not exactly the stoic ideal of manhood that is often projected
throughout the nineteenth and twentieth centuries. O'Neill certainly
knew this and is playing with these roles as he dips back into bits of
melodrama, throwbacks to his father's theatre, a trope he will manipu-
late and utilize throughout his career. Just beneath the surface this
action speaks of a relationship between two men, *normal* and *masculine* by all social standards, who have very deep feelings for one
another and who have spent their lives together by choice.

The figure of the effeminate man, on the other hand, has also had
strong models throughout theatre history. Aristophanes peppered
his comedies with jokes about homosexuals being sissies and similar
evidence can be found down through the Renaissance and in Enlightenment dramas as well. Not much had changed by the nineteenth
century, however in the later part of that century the societal view of
the effeminate man was embedded with a graver significance. During

this time the fop, the dandy, and the bachelor began to be seen, increasingly, as representations of the homosexual lifestyle and therefore a threat. The dandy was exemplified by Oscar Wilde, who, when travelling in the late 1880s in the United States, was celebrated and adored by men across the country, miners and cowboys alike. But by the time of his infamous trial at the end of the century, his persona had become the manifestation of decadence and corrupt sexual inversion. That Wilde himself failed to recognize the term *homosexual* speaks to a changing time in which the formation of the identity surprised even those who were its most famous adherents. The effeminate man was characterized by his preponderance for fancy clothes, his aristocratic bearing, his aversion to athletic activities, his immersion into the arts, and his general love of rather young men. In the United States the model of the effeminate man was already an established literary trope and was nearly always a city dweller and nearly always English. O'Neill was to continue this characterization in his sea plays.

Oscar Wilde's trial at the end of the nineteenth century brought the issue of homosexuality into the public discourse and caused a panic that shook England to its core. In response to this building crisis, the identity of the hypermasculinized man began to form throughout the Victorian Era. Hero worship developed around men who represented idealized versions of a masculine identity, probably in response to the increasing industrialization of men and women and the further remove from traditional agrarian-based skills, such as hunting and land stewardship. Crises mounted, though, when several hypermasculine war heroes were then brought before the court for gross indecency, and their threatened exposure resulted in the suicides of several men who had been valorized for their military prowess. By the early part of the twentieth century, British sensational journalist and member of Parliament Noel Pemberton Billing published an article in his magazine, *The Vigilante*, charging that the German Secret Service possessed a list of 47,000 prominent English men and women who were active homosexuals. Ripples of fear spread throughout England, probably based on the likelihood that there was, in fact, rampant homosexuality among the aristocracy. That some of the aristocracy had used its power or wealth to gain sexual favors with working class men was a theme in the Wilde trial and was sensationalized in the newspapers in England and United States.[9] This alleged list strengthened the imagined relationship between homosexuality and threats to national security, laying the groundwork for a common theme that continued throughout the twentieth century, especially during World War II and the McCarthyism of the Cold War, right up to the dispute over gays in the military and "Don't Ask, Don't Tell."

What O'Neill might have been suggesting, though the time period and topic of these sea plays was that as times were changing, the simple innocent relationships between men, so common in the past, were under greater scrutiny and took on new meaning as a way in which security was being threatened. Or what he may have been suggesting was that relationships are never really simple and never really innocent, and that the closer and more intimate two people become, the greater the threat of exposure. The latter would certainly be more in line with O'Neill's biography, but it is also a recurring theme throughout his later, more mature works as well.

Another recurring theme, which figures prominently in the next sea play, *The Moon of the Caribees*, is the escape hatch known as alcohol. Alcohol and what we would now call alcoholism are staples in O'Neill's oeuvre. In O'Neill's work, the bottle is the place where the fearful always return. In play after play, his characters crawl into the bottle to escape the possibility of living to their fullest potential. They drink to hide from the weight of their dreams, their tragic pasts, or their terrible futures. The figure of Smitty is one such character. He appears in each of the sea plays as the refined Englishman who is out of place in the hold of the steamer. In *The Moon of the Caribees*, he drinks to avoid the painful memories of his failed love affair, which ended, quite cyclically, because of his drinking. Alcoholism as a clinical and treatable problem is a relatively new concept, and so on one level Smitty's drinking can be taken at face value for the underpinning of his tragedy, but on a different level O'Neill's character development throughout the arc of these sea plays suggests something more. Notice the way in which these characters are depicted. Smitty is *aristocratic*, with fine features and a blond mustache, relatively feminine compared to big brawny Irishmen, such as Driscoll, the stocky Swedes, and roguishly good-looking Americans, like Yank or Jack. In O'Neill the Irish and the Americans are always the powerfully built, good-looking ones, and the English are the effeminate, suspicious ones.

Note the various descriptions of these three characters in the sea plays:

Driscoll: (*a brawny Irishman with the battered features of a prizefighter*)[10]
Driscoll: (*a powerfully built Irishman who is sitting on the edge of the hatch, front—irritably*)[11]
Smitty: (*a young Englishman with a blond mustache. He is sitting on the forecastle head looking out over the water with his chin supported on his hands.*)[12]

Yank: (*a rather good-looking rough who is sitting beside Driscoll*)[13]
Jack: (*Jack enters. He is a young American with a tough, good-natured face. He wears dungarees and a heavy jersey.*)[14]

In *The Moon of the Caribees*, we find Smitty as a bitter alcoholic whose aristocratic demeanor has earned him the moniker "The Duke." In this short play he and Yank are pals, and after a young prostitute boards the ship Yank is willing to share her with his English friend. When the good-looking prostitute, who has her pick of the sailors, shows a particular interest in him, for the same refined and effeminate manners that set him apart from the other sailors, he spurns her, much to her anger and vitriol.

In this particular play, the enclosed male space is more elaborately detailed and romanticized, if not outright eroticized: "Most of the seamen and firemen are reclining or sitting on the hatch. Paul is leaning against the port bulwark, the upper part of his stocky figure outlined against the sky. Smitty and Cocky are sitting on the edge of the forecastle head with their legs dangling over. Nearly all are smoking pipes or cigarettes. The majority are dressed in patched suits of dungaree. Quite a few are in their bare feet and some of them, especially the firemen, have nothing on but a pair of pants and an undershirt. A good many wear caps."[15] The sensuality of this play is in keeping with the tropical scene: the hot warmth of the night; the full moon; the torpor; the eroticized women, large, swaying, and ripe like the fruit and booze they bring aboard the *Glencairn*. Every character succumbs to this erotic tableau, every character but Smitty,who rejects the offer of sexual companionship for a drunk—a deeper return to his private escape, and a continuation of his self-imposed exile in a world almost exclusively made up of men.

It would be foolish to suggest that these plays are so heavily inscribed with homosexual subtext that they are gay plays. That said, it is worth considering the time in which O'Neill wrote and the potential complexity of sexuality for O'Neill and his peers. His third wife, Carlotta Monterey, claims that a temporary estrangement late in their marriage was precipitated by a homosexual incident, in which she discovered O'Neill and an old friend in bed together one afternoon.[16] It is a fact that O'Neill was very close friends with both Charles Demuth and Marsden Hartley, important early twentieth-century American painters, both of whom were "out" homosexuals. In fact, the homosexual character in O'Neill's long surrealist play *Strange Interlude*, Charles Marsden, takes his name from an amalgamation of these two friends. O'Neill himself said of his character Marsden, "I like Marsden . . .

I've known many Marsdens on many different levels of life and it has always seemed to me that they've never been done in literature with any sympathy or real insight."[17] It is striking that O'Neill would acknowledge knowing gay men on "many different levels" and this, along with Monterey's story, suggest that O'Neill may have had a broader sexual appetite than has been documented by his biographers.

What does seem rather certain is that there was a type of homosexual man who was seen, clearly, as a homosexual. He was effeminate, lost, formed and manipulated by dominant women, and increasingly seen as a threat to middle-class values; he was the fop, the dandy, the pansy, the molly—and his position vacillated between the comical and the reprobate. This effeminate man must be paralleled with another type of man that may also be homosexual, yet deeply hidden in the closet: the hypermasculine man who prefers the world of men, travel, fighting, and isolation with other men like him. As Andrew Sofer suggests in his essay on the possible homosexual themes in *Ah, Wilderness!*: "Since the eighteenth century, the paths to male entitlement in both England and America require intense male bonds that could not readily be distinguished from the most reprobate bonds. As a result 'male homosexual panic became the normal condition of male heterosexual entitlement.'"[18] With this we examine the final sea play, *In the Zone*. The play begins with a scene that has become familiar to us by now, men together, sleeping, waking, packed into a tight space but apparently quite comfortable and at ease:

> Davis enters the forecastle, places the coffee-pot beside the lantern, and goes from one to the other of the sleepers and shakes them vigorously, saying to each in a low voice: Near eight bells, Scotty. Arise and shine, Swanson. Eight bells, Ivan. Smitty yawns loudly with a great pretense of having been dead asleep. All of the rest of the men tumble out of their bunks, stretching and gaping, and commence to pull on their shoes. They go one by one to the cupboard near the open door, take out their cups and spoons, and sit down together on the benches. The coffee-pot is passed around. They munch their biscuits and sip their coffee in dull silence.[19]

The sea plays have, by this point, established Smitty as an other in terms of his background and, in a practical sense, by his lack of skills as a sailor. In *Bound East for Cardiff*, Smitty appears briefly, his character simply a sketch of a blond Englishman. In *The Moon of the Caribees*, he is the central character in the play, a man who has turned to the bottle and to the sea to try, ostensibly, to forget his lost love. I am arguing that this escape into the bottle can be construed as movement back into the place where secrets are kept, paralleling with the escape to sea—and though I do not suggest that O'Neill is calling attention to the possibility of sex occurring between the men aboard the steamers, it is certainly reasonable to assume that it may have occurred—and on many levels the occurrence of sex, or at least the threat of it, becomes a problem to be solved through a reordering of the established social expectations.

In the Zone, written in 1917, uses World War I as a background to tell its brief but powerful story. The SS *Glencairn*, loaded with ammunition, has entered the war zone somewhere in the North Atlantic. The ship has entered the zone while the sailors were asleep and therefore only those on active duty have realized this by the beginning of the play. Tension builds immediately as two sailors have witnessed Smitty, out of his bunk and in his footlocker, retrieving a small black box while the others slept. Apparently this is suspicious enough and indicates to a great extent the real intimacy these men must have experienced, living on top of one another for so long a stretch. At the beginning of the play someone has left the porthole window, which we assume is opaque, opened, and thus the light emanated from the cabin exposes the ship to potential attack as it sails over enemy waters. On the surface the incredible tension is caused by the fear of being blown up by a German submarine while transporting ammunition to the Allied Forces. Underneath the surface, though, is a story of men compressed into a small space together, living in a subterranean and submerged environment (the bowels of a ship), and regulating their established order, which includes their belongings, nutrition, hygiene, and sexuality. As Eve Kosofsy Sedgewick indicates in her landmark study, *The Epistemology of the Closet*, these types of environments—the army, a ship at sea, boarding schools, lumber camps—result in a double bind, by which the very nature of the men together may cross the line from homosocial to homosexual, creating a need for a stopgap to what one assumes must be the threat of an all-out homosexual condition:

> The result of men's accession to this double bind [whereby homosocial bonds are enforced even as homosexual desire is proscribed] is, first, the acute *manipulability*, through the fear of one's own "homosexuality," of acculturated men; and second, a reservoir of potential for *violence* caused by the self-ignorance that this regime constitutively enforces. The historical emphasis on enforcement of homophobic rules in the armed services in, for instance, England and the United States supports

this analysis. In these institutions, where both men's manipulability and their potential for violence are at the highest possible premium, the *pre*scription of the most intimate male bonding and the *pro*scription of (the remarkable cognate) "homosexuality" are both stronger than in civilian society—are, in fact, close to absolute.[20]

In the play, as the sailors begin to wake up and realize that they have entered the war zone, and as the suspicious, though perfectly innocent activities of Smitty are spread around the gossipy breakfast table, tension mounts. The general assumption is that Smitty is not an Englishman at all (though they have lived with him for two years) but, in fact, a German spy. The sailors take the small box Smitty has exhumed from his trunk and examine it for its potentiality as a bomb. Into the mix comes Jack, the American, whose name is changed in this play, but for all intents is the same character as Yank in the other sea plays. Jack assumes the role of the authority and in a very telling exchange offers the following to his shipmates in reference to Smitty, whom he refers to by his nickname, the Duke:

> Jack: . . . (*Jack looks after him [Smitty] with a frown.*) He's a queer guy. I can't figger him out.
> Davis: Nor anyone else. (*lowering his voice—meaningly*) An' he's liable to turn out queerer than any of us think if we ain't careful.[21]

The semantic shift in meaning of the word *queer*, from something not straight (in the physical sense) to an effeminate homosexual man appears to have occurred in the very late nineteenth century and, in fact, in the infamous Queensbury versus Oscar Wilde trials there is evidence that the ninth Marquess of Queensbury uses this term (with the homosexual meaning) in a letter to his son, Lord Alfred Douglas, in reference to Oscar Wilde.[22] I'm not suggesting that O'Neill is using *queer* with so overt a meaning, however, I am suggesting that O'Neill would be aware of the semantic shift occurring and that he may, in fact, be guiding the reader or viewer to a deeper meaning of the exchange taking place between the sailors. Note the next use of the term in the play as Davis attempts to convince Jack that Smitty is up to no good:

> Davis: Listen! He was standin' right there—(*pointing again*) in his stockin' feet—no shoes on, mind, so he wouldn't make no noise!
> Jack: (*spitting disgustedly*) Aw!

Davis: (*not heeding the interruption*) I seen right away something queer was up so I slides back in the alley-way where I kin see him but he can't see me.[23]

Again O'Neill uses references to sailors in states of undress, which underscores an intimate environment and, in this case, secrecy and *queer* behavior.

The case against Smitty escalates rapidly and by the time Smitty returns to the cabin, all the sailors have convinced themselves that Smitty is a danger to their safety and that something needs to be done about it. When Smitty enters back into the cabin the sailors bind him and begin their interrogation, which centers on the contents of the box. Bound and furious, Smitty refuses to tell his shipmates the contents of the box, pointedly accusing them of cowardice. The audience may wonder, "Cowardice of what?" Is it a fear of examining the truth of their chosen existences? In a time before the creation of *lifestyle choices*, an exclusively male environment like the sea could, and was, a place where men who loved men could live without, at the very least, the societal pressure to perform heteronormatively.

Rather than taking the matter to their superiors, the sailors take the matter into their own hands. This is also an interesting indication of the self-regulating that would have been needed in regard to possible intercabin sex; if it did occur in discreet amounts it would have needed to be kept from the authority of the captain or first mates since it would have been a punishable offense.

Eventually the box is examined. In the box is a bundle of letters from Smitty's former girlfriend—who has spurned him due, at least on the surface, to his continued alcoholism. It is worth examining the language O'Neill uses to suggest this. In a letter leading up to her rejection of him, the girl writes (as recited by Driscoll), "But b'fore I can agree to live out my life wid you, you must prove to me that the black shadow—I won't menshun uts hateful name but you know what I mean—which might wreck both our lives, does not exist for you. You can do that, can't you, dear? Don't you see you must for my sake?"[24] On the surface that thing that she refuses to name is alcoholism. But underneath this she may well mean another drive, also known as the "love that dare not speak its name"—a turn of the century euphemism for homosexuality, which would keep the two of them from enjoying a married life together.

The sailors refuse, at first, to believe that these letters are real—still convinced that Smitty is a German spy and that these letters are in code. Eventually, however, the reality of the situation surfaces, Smitty's given name is read aloud, and the sailors begin to realize that the man whom they have bound, who now sobs in anguish, is no spy but one of them. Rather than make reparation, though, the tension has been excised and the lives of the sailors return to *normal*, as if nothing had happened.

These sea plays are often viewed collectively. Since the setting and characters are predominantly alike in all three, they do work as a sort of triptych in which the audience can see clearly and deeply into the relationships between these men confined in this intimate space. This space is private and holds secrets, some of which can be acknowledged and some of which remain unknown, perhaps even to those who possess them. The possibility of secret homosexual desire may, in fact, figure into later more well-developed O'Neill plays. *The Great God Brown, Strange Interlude,* and *Ah, Wilderness!* all have male characters who fall short of the heteronormative ideal. *Mourning Becomes Electra* is based on a type of sexual inversion that may be read in a queer light, and *The Iceman Cometh* deals with issues of men comforting men in a closed and private environment. Given that we have benefited recently from a great deal of scholarship in queer studies, it is probably time for a more in-depth investigation of O'Neill through this lens. The tragic element often associated with homosexuality in the pre-Stonewall era should be examined for its relative meaning then, as well as how and if, in fact, these sea plays contain clues pointing us toward this particular tragedy. It would be best to take O'Neill at his word when he tell us that *Bound East for Cardiff* functions as a nascent touchstone.

NOTES

1. Richard B. Sewell, "Eugene O'Neill and the Sense of the Tragic," in *Eugene O'Neill's Century* ed. Richard F. Moorton, Jr. (Westport, CT: Greenwood, 1991), 5.

2. Aristotle, *Poetics,* trans. Francis Fergusson (New York: Hill and Wang, 1961), part XIV, p. 78 & part XVIII, pp. 90–91.

3. Arthur Gelb and Barbara Gelb, *O'Neill* (New York: Harper and Row, 1962), 233.

4. Eugene O'Neill, *Complete Plays 1913–1920,* ed. Travis Bogard (New York: Library of America, 1988), 3.

5. Louis Sheaffer, ed., *O'Neill: Son and Playwright,* vol. 1 (New York: Cooper Square, 1968), 147–56.

6. Ibid., 372.

7. O'Neill, *Complete Plays,* 187.

8. Ibid., 191–92.

9. For further discussion of this see Neil Miller's excellent history *Out of the Past* (New York: Alyson Books, 2006), particularly Chapter 7, "England During the Great War."

10. O'Neill, *Complete Plays.*
11. Ibid *Complete Plays,* 188.
12. Ibid. *Complete Plays,* 527–28.
13. Ibid. *Complete Plays,* 528.
14. Ibid. *Complete Plays,* 473.
15. Ibid. *Complete Plays,* 527.
16. Sheaffer, *O'Neill: Son and Artist,* vol. 2 (New York: Cooper Square, 1968), 579.
17. Sheaffer, *O'Neill: Son and Artist,* vol 2., 242.
18. Andrew Sofer, "Something Cloudy, Something Queer: Eugene O'Neill's *Ah, Wilderness!* and Tennessee William's *Period of Adjustment* as Problem Comedies," *Journal of Dramatic Theory and Criticism* vol. XIX, No. 1: Fall 2004, 49.
19. O'Neill, *Complete Plays,* 471.
20. Eve Kosofsky Sedgwick, *Epistemology of the Closet* (Berkeley: University of California Press 2008), 186.
21. O'Neill, *Complete Plays,* 474.
22. Miller, *Out of the Past,* 45.
23. O'Neill, *Complete Plays,* 476.
24. Ibid. *Complete Plays,* 486.

Works Cited

Aristotle. *Poetics.* Trans. Francis Fergusson. New York: Hill, 1961. Print.

Gelb, Arthur, and Barbara Gelb. *O'Neill.* New York: Harper, 1962. Print.

Kosofsky Sedgwick, Eve. *Epistemology of the Closet.* Berkeley: U of California P, 2008. Print.

Miller, Neil. *Out of the Past.* New York: Alyson, 2006. Print.

O'Neill, Eugene. *Complete Plays 1913–1920.* Ed. Travis Bogard. New York: Library of America, 1988. Print.

Sewell, Richard B. "Eugene O'Neill and the Sense of the Tragic." *Eugene O'Neill's Century.* Ed. Richard F. Moorton Jr. Westport: Greenwood, 1991. Print.

Sheaffer, Louis, ed. *O'Neill: Son and Playwright.* 2 vols. New York: Cooper Square, 1968. Print.

Sofer, Andrew. "Something Cloudy, Something Queer: Eugene O'Neill's *Ah, Wilderness!* and Tennessee William's *Period of Adjustment* as Problem Comedies." *Journal of Dramatic Theory and Criticism* Vol. XIX, No. 1, (Fall 2004): 204. Print.

CHAPTER 6

EPISTEMOLOGICAL CRISES IN O'NEILL'S SS *GLENCAIRN* PLAYS

Michael Y. Bennett

Michael D'Alessandro, in his essay "Shifting Perceptions, Precarious Perspectives in Two of O'Neill's Early Sea Plays," discusses the intentional shifts Eugene O'Neill makes in some of his early sea plays in order to present different versions of reality to the audience: "O'Neill introduces one vision of reality, one center of the plot, but then supersedes the given dominant thread with another. More than his other novice one-acts, the sea plays display O'Neill's remarkable attention to atmospheric detail . . . these works' undeniable moods exist for more than mere effect."[1] D'Alessandro continues, "O'Neill introduces such sea illusionism, among other reasons, to contrast the objective and the subjective, to juxtapose real and imagined perceptions . . . O'Neill expresses a consistent impatience with a single perspective, using the sea's tempting enchantment to distort supposedly dependable observations."[2]

I admire this line of thought begun by D'Alessandro through his examination of *Fog* and *Where the Cross Is Made*; I would like to extend and delve deeper into the perspectives of reality that O'Neill generates by looking at the sea plays of the SS *Glencairn* cycle. I argue, instead, that the sea plays play out what Alasdair Macintyre has called in *The Tasks of Philosophy*, an "epistemological crisis." Macintyre suggests that one suffers from an epistemological crisis when one's personal "schemata" is either contradicted or made self-aware of its limitations. I suggest that the sea plays display a generic tension between, respectively, realism and naturalism: on one hand, the sailors—neither good nor bad—act as solitary and free individuals, yet, on the other hand, O'Neill seems to suggest that they are bound by the harsh realities of the world. Each perspective destroys the foundations of the other perspective. This becomes a twofold epistemological crisis: one for the sailors themselves and one for the audience. Ultimately, in the tension between naturalism and realism in the sea plays, O'Neill anticipates Bertolt Brecht's notion of alienation effect. This alienation effect is achieved by subtly forcing the audience to oscillate between accepting the worldviews of naturalism and realism, thereby destroying the stability of either worldview.

THE SITUATION ABOARD THE SS *GLENCAIRN*

In his agonizing march to death after a fall in O'Neill's *Bound East for Cardiff* (1914), Yank is fully aware of the plight of the sailor: "This sailor's life ain't much to cry about leavin'—just one ship after another, hard work, small pay, and bum grub; and when we git into port, just a drunk endin' up in a fight, and all your money gone, and then ship away again. Never meetin' no nice people; never gittin' outa sailor town, hardly, in any port; travelin' all over the world and never seein' none of it; without no one to care whether you're alive or dead. (*with a bitter smile*) There ain't much in all that that'd make yuh sorry to lose it, Drisc."[3] Yank continues, "It must be great to stay on dry land all your life and have a farm with a house of your own with cows and pigs and chickens, 'way in the middle of the land where yuh'd never smell the sea or see a ship. It musht be great to have a wife, and kids to play with at night after supper when your work was done. It must be great to have a home of your own, Drisc."[4]

The *situation* of the merchant marines of the SS *Glencairn* is paradoxical. While the life of the sailors on the *Glencairn* is as open and free as the sea that they sail on, they are trapped not only by the physical confines of the ship but by the life of the merchant marine. This is not a secret to the sailors themselves though. While we ascertain that many if not most of the sailors began this life to escape their life on land, they know that the impermanence of living life port to port has them yearning for land, especially a plot of land that they can call their own.

The desire for land is the strongest for Olson in *The Long Voyage Home* (1917). His dreams echo Yank's, but it appears not to just be a pipe dream, but something Olson has been actively working toward:

> You know, Miss Freda, I don't see my mother or my brother in—let me tank—(*he counts laboriously on his fingers*) must be more than ten year. I

write once in a while and she write many time; and my brother he write me, too. My mother say in all letter I should come home right away. My brother he write same ting, too. He want me to help him on farm. I write back always I come soon; and I mean all time to go back home at end of voyage. But I come ashore, I take one drink, I take many drinks, I get drunk, I spend all money, I have to ship away for other voyage. So dis time I say to myself: Don't drink one drink, Ollie, or, sure, you don't get home. And I want to go home dis time. I feel homesick for farm and to see my people again.[5]

Of course, what Olson says is prophetic and pathetically true: Olson's ginger beer is spiked by the "*proprietor of a dive*"[6] and he is eventually robbed of the money that he has been saving for the long voyage home. Yank's words, spoken earlier in *Bound East for Cardiff*, ring particularly true and are worthy of being mentioned again: "when we git into port, just a drunk endin' up in a fight, and all your money gone, and then ship away again." In a sense, *The Long Voyage Home* and *The Moon of the Caribbees* dramatize the reoccurring narrative of hope-filled futility.

These plays aboard the SS *Glencairn* examine the quashed dreams of a lower class of sailors who struggle to stay afloat. But it is not just their pipe dreams about land that keep these merchant marines going. O'Neill shows that human contact and companionship, whether real or imagined, also sustains them. In *Bound East for Cardiff*, while dying, Yank sees little to nothing in the sailor's life to live for, except one thing: "I don't like to leave you, Drisc, but—that's all."[7] Simple friendship, not even quite acknowledged as such, provides Yank, at least, with *some* reason to live. Similarly, in 1917's *In the Zone*, Smitty—who, it is revealed, has by the estimation of his lover, run away to sea and chosen drunkenness over the woman that he loves— still finds some solace in the numerous love letters from Edith that he keeps under his mattress. Despite the fact that it comes out at the end of the play, in one of the love letters, that Edith has decided to leave Smitty, we can guess that in his "*muffled sobbing*,"[8] Smitty is publically confronted with the reality of the last letter, which he has probably suppressed in order to feed off of the hope and warmth of the other, earlier letters. It appears that Smitty, up until this point, knew in Viktor E. Frankl's words, that "the salvation of man is through love and in love."[9] In *Man's Search for Meaning*, Frankl writes, "*The salvation of man is through love and in love.* I understood how a man who has nothing left in this world still may know bliss, be it only for a brief moment, in the contemplation of his beloved. In a position of utter desolation, when man cannot express himself in positive action, when his only achievement may consist in enduring his sufferings in the right way—an honorable way—in such a position man can, through loving contemplation of the image he carries of his beloved, achieve fulfillment."[10] It was not only through Edith's letters that Smitty was able to continue through the "contemplation of his beloved" but through the "dried-up flower"[11] that metonymically provides an "image" of his and Edith's love. However, by others knowing that Edith left Smitty, it becomes impossible for Smitty to continue what we perceive was his psychological suppression of this fact.

Though, for many aboard the SS *Glencairn*, there is a wishful light at the end of the tunnel, O'Neill argues, not that the dream is pointless, but that it will simply just not happen. In *Bound East for Cardiff*, Yank dies at sea, despite his dream of owning land and having a family. In *In the Zone*, Smitty, through the public revelation of Edith leaving him, is more alone at sea than he ever was. In *The Long Voyage Home*, having lost all of his money and not being able to return to the farm and his family, Olson is back where he started numerous times before. And in *The Moon of the Caribbees*, there's just another port call and another time to get drunk and spend their money. Despite the glimpses of dreams that enable their will to go on, the four sea plays aboard the SS *Glencairn* ultimately suggest the futility of leaving the sailor's life and actually being able to pursue their hopes of living on land and/or love.[12]

THE EPISTEMOLOGICAL CRISIS IN THE SEA PLAYS

In *The Tasks of Philosophy*, Alasdair MacIntyre argues that the relationship of *seems* to *is* is what constitutes an epistemological crisis.[13] The "rational justification of inferences from premises about the behavior of other people to conclusions about their thoughts, feelings, and attitudes," is the very thing that comes into conflict for the person experiencing an epistemological crisis.[14] Our reason is informed by past experiences; in an epistemological crisis, then, these experiences and our reason are destroyed by reflecting upon what we understand and experience in a particular situation.

For MacIntyre, culture plays a huge role in developing our "schemata": each culture shares a particular "schemata" of how to act, why to act, and how to interpret those actions.[15] The ability of members of a society to make inferences about things based on premises about past behavior is determined by that society's schemata. These schemata, however, are not empirical generalizations, but are "prescriptions for interpretation."[16] The schemata of a particular culture provide a coherent narrative for its members to *read* reality. When this coherent narrative is revealed as implausible—that is, either the situation makes the schemata self-apparent or the present narrative questions the possibility that the other narratives at his or her disposal can provide the truth—one experiences an epistemological crisis.[17] When the epistemological crisis gets resolved, this resolution forces the creation of an entirely new narrative that allows the person to understand both how he/she held the beliefs that he/she did prior to his/her epistemological crisis and how he/she was misled by past beliefs.[18] Ultimately, undergoing an epistemological crisis leads a person to reformulate the criteria for truth and understanding. Understanding itself, then, reveals itself to be an iffy proposition, as schemata can be put into question at any time and a person can never possess the truth or be fully rational.[19]

Many of the sailors aboard the SS *Glencairn* experience these epistemological crises, particularly the main characters of each play. In some sense, it may be argued that this is actually the criterion for establishing the protagonist of O'Neill's sea plays. Unlike in traditional drama (some form of Aristotelian drama)—where the protagonist undergoes a change of fortune (*peripeteia*), suffers (*pathos*), and then reaches some form of understanding (*anagnorisis*)—a protagonist in one of O'Neill's sea plays is the character whose worldview (schemata) is shown to be in conflict with his or her reality. In *Bound East for Cardiff*, Yank and Driscoll both realize that their desire to live out their lives on land is impossible in the face of Yank's all-too-true statement: "Just one ship after another, hard work, small pay, and bum grub; and when we git into port, just a drunk endin' up in a fight, and all your money gone, and then ship away again." The death of Yank on the ship only reinforces this truth for Driscoll. Smitty, in *In the Zone*, is publically confronted with the truth of his past with Edith and, therefore, has to reconcile his lonely reality with the dream that he did not allow himself to admit. In *The Long Voyage Home*, Olson, despite being sure that he is going home and leaving the seafaring life this time, is going to wake up to reality that he is back where he started: he is not going home and must rely on seafaring in order to dream again of going home.

THE SEA PLAYS AND THE AUDIENCE: RIDING THE WAVES BETWEEN NATURALISM AND REALISM

In light of the protagonist of each sea play undergoing an epistemo-logical crisis, the audience experiences one as well. Because O'Neill creates such human characters, we long to see their desires fulfilled. Therefore, when we see the characters long for land—and the audience sees living on land as the norm—we naturally ask the question, "Why don't they just leave the ship?" And this is the central tug of the play: not the wrenching losses of the characters aboard the SS *Glencairn*, but the difficulty of the audience to continue to believe in their own stability while being confronted with the realities facing these merchant marines. This is where the lines of naturalism and real-ism start to blur.

Travis Bogard discusses the impact that August Strindberg's naturalistic works must have had on O'Neill when he was reading Strindberg's plays in 1913.[20] Bogard argues that O'Neill had set "aside Strindbergian novelties" when he took up, again, writing about the crew of the SS *Glencairn*.[21] Bogard does not fully connect these two statements and certainly does not delve deeply into the naturalism of the sea plays. Since the sea functions as a key naturalistic element, by extending Bogard's previous two assertions there is a clear tension between naturalistic and realistic elements in these plays.

In naturalism, there is something so weighty about culture, society, and nature that its uncompromising pull and heft are left unques-tioned. And in realism, the focus on the individual, who is generally portrayed as neither all good nor all bad, gives the character some sort of agency (or responsibility), the ability to affect his or her future (which is the exact opposite in naturalism). But here, in the sea plays, the audience experiences the characters in a difficult situation. But aren't these individuals free? These merchant marines are not tied down to family or a normal job: they have the freedom of the open seas. And that is what is so puzzling to the audience, which has to wade through this paradox. How can these same characters who *seem* to be the freest individuals also *be* the most confined? Though each sea play takes the audience on the protagonist's journey to the full under-standing of their situation, in the end the main characters understand the paradox of their life better than the audience. This moves further than D'Alessandro's observation that "O'Neill's innovation lies thus in his relegating the audience to the same blindness as the figures onstage."[22]

From Didacticism to Alienation Effect

D'Alessandro turns to Travis Bogard's suggestion that a particular dialogue in O'Neill's *Fog* is "oddly Shavian in its subject, if not its tone"[23]: "While Travis Bogard correctly points out the mishmash of narratives onstage—'Against the haunted background and in the midst of the miraculous action, the dialogue of the two men sounds out-of-key. It is oddly Shavian' (27)—he fails to credit O'Neill with intentionally undermining his own dramatic structure. In a play so concerned with not allowing anyone too clear a perspective, O'Neill presents a certain 'type' or genre of play only to replace it moments later."[24] Here I agree with D'Alessandro's notion of O'Neill's intentionality. However, while it may have been a passing remark, I think Bogard's "Shavian" assertion is too important not to receive some proper attention. Whereas Bogard appears to be referring particularly to the similarity in George Bernard Shaw and O'Neill's vehement distaste of poverty (stemming from a capitalistic society), lurking behind the two playwrights (and Bogard's statement) is the notion of theatrical *didacticism*. And thus, we can begin to trace an unconscious line from Shaw to O'Neill to Brecht. O'Neill's innovation, I argue, in the sea plays is his anticipation of the didacticism of Bertolt Brecht's alienation effect[25] by portraying an epistemological crisis, while forcing the audience to experience a similar epistemological crisis as well. This undeveloped alienation effect (as opposed to the fully developed theatrical methods that Brecht employs to enact his version of the alienation effect on the audience) still has a similar effect on the audience as Brecht's epic theatre by distancing the audience from the emotional ride of the play in order to turn the audience into an observer of the world who can respond to the play through analysis rather than just pure emotion.

However, while Shaw's didacticism is overtly moralistic and Brecht's didacticism is overtly metatheatrical and metasocial/political, O'Neill's didacticism is subtly couched in the tension between the subtly warring dramatic genres of naturalism and realism. In a sense, the audience is forced to reckon with the worldviews, not necessarily of the characters but with the worldviews of naturalism and realism. Thus as the sea plays tug the audience back and forth between the worldviews of naturalism and realism, the audience feels just as unstable as the lives of the crewmembers aboard the SS *Glencairn*. This instability forces the audience member to reassess his/her *own* worldview and, taking his/her newfound knowledge into account, he/she must develop a new narrative in order to modify his/her personal schemata.

THE NARRATIVES OF NATURALISM
AND REALISM ABOARD THE SS *GLENCAIRN*

Returning to MacIntyre, a particular schemata is narrativistic. This idea that narrative shapes the audience's schemata is what, I argue, gives the sea plays their tension. Each of the four plays aboard the SS *Glencairn* has two narratives (i.e., a naturalistic narrative and a realistic narrative). What O'Neill appears to do in these sea plays is to create an overarching naturalistic plot with characters in the mode of realism.

In *Bound East for Cardiff*, the naturalistic narrative is maybe the most clear of the four plays. Having sustained a great fall, Yank is literally and metaphorically quashed by nature and is dying at sea. And while the audience sympathizes with Yank, his explanations of the hard life at sea (as quoted earlier) suggest that the only escape from the sea is death. O'Neill creates a narrative of a realistic life of an individual who is neither a hero nor a villain, who, while not deserving his fate, is not entirely an innocent victim of nature and society. For one, the fall was, for all intents and purposes, due to Yank's own carelessness: "He puts his leg over careless-like and misses the ladder and plumps straight down to the bottom."[26] And second, Yank was certainly no saint: "Fights we've had, God help us, but 'twas only when we'd a bit av drink taken"[27] Drinking creates both fault and an excuse. After all, Yank got drunk, but at the same time, he supposedly only fought because he was drunk; he was both himself and not himself. Furthermore, Yank (with Driscoll) "was both locked up in Sydney for fightin'" and in Cape Town Yank stabbed a "skulkin' swine" in self-defense.[28] The fighting is highlighted, but the violence associated with individuals who regularly brawl is mitigated by the story of Yank defending himself (suggesting that maybe Yank did not generally instigate the fights but fought out of self-defense). A flawed character, but clearly a good friend, Yank and the audience flounder over the question that Yank asked Driscoll: "D'yuh think [God]'ll hold it up against me?"[29]

O'Neill views not only nature as harsh but also fellow humankind. Society, in *The Long Voyage Home*, is the oppressive force in this naturalistic plot. Olson is a realistic character who is good (he gave up drinking, would possibly like to get married "if [he] find a nice girl,"[30] and he writes to his mother and brother), and although he is not without faults, he has supposedly learned from his past (as suggested by his decision to abstain from alcohol while ashore. However, Freda, Nick, and Joe are not seen as realistic characters and are portrayed as a greedy mob that is out to get Olson. What Freda, Nick, and Joe do to Olson (spike his drink and rob him of his money), who is not in a position of power, represents how the poor and innocent are trampled by those more powerful, vicious, and cunning. In short, your average person (though not a saint), as represented by Olson, has no chance in a world full of people like this.

In the Zone has an interesting twist to the tension O'Neill creates between naturalism and realism. In this play, the naturalistic element is not external to Smitty, but internal. In other words, it is not society or nature, per se, that keep him forever bound to the sea, but his own drunkenness. In a sense, and we see this throughout much of O'Neill's oeuvre, the *disease* of alcoholism[31] is an inescapable force. While O'Neill examines some of the psychology behind an alcoholic (particularly if one thinks of *Long Day's Journey into Night*)—and, thus, we see the realistic side of human nature that goes into the disease—drinking, as in all the sea plays, is much more a *way of life* for these sailors, particularly in the harsh world that O'Neill depicts, than it is a choice. While Edith suggests that Smitty has "chosen" his "drunkenness," there appears to be little *choice* in the matter. Both his *disease* and his *situation* determine his fate of loneliness.

Of *The Moon of the Caribbees* (O'Neill's favorite one-act)—which Arthur and Barbara Gelb call "a small poetic gem"[32]—O'Neill said that it was "his first real break with theatrical conditions." The break came from his disregard of plot and action and focused, instead, on poetic mood.[33] Being much closer to his slightly later form of expressionism, Smitty's "*sigh that is half a sob*," after listening intently to "*the melancholy song of the negros*," is a realization that all bottles of rum come to an end with "*the flash of a knife held high in the moonlight and a loud yell of pain.*"[34] The tragedy is that the Donkeyman's statement, "there'll likely be more drink," suggests that one of their sole pleasures (i.e., drinking) is also the very thing that will get you knifed or produce the most amount of pain.[35] In a sense, the world offers them what they want, but in enjoying it, they are doomed to a dangerous cycle of fights and empty bottles.

CONCLUSION I:
THE CHARACTERS AND THE AUDIENCE

Brecht's epic theatre operates through historical adaptation, where the audience sees characters in an unfamiliar situation and asks: how would I act if I were in their situation? By being estranged from the setting in Brecht's theatre, the audience has trouble making an emotional journey with the characters, thus allowing the audience to react analytically to the social and political circumstances and reality that engenders the grim situation of each of Brecht's plays.

While O'Neill does not focus at all on the political world and very little even about the social world (preferring to focus on character and individual action and desire), the sea plays have a very similar effect on the audience as Brecht's historical adaptations. While the (typical) audience, despite the sailors' poor English and seemingly rough life, can connect with these realistic characters (for the audience can relate to both their good qualities and their flaws, even if their flaws are not the same as his or her own), the way that O'Neill portrays (via naturalism) the inescapable doomed fate of the sailors is presumably something the audience either cannot or does not want to understand in relation to his or her own life. Therefore, in the sea plays, O'Neill estranges the audience from the setting, making the audience member ponder the same question as Brecht: what would (or could) I have done in that situation?

Once O'Neill enters his final and longest stage of his career with realism, the *situation* of the characters becomes totally relatable to the audience. Consider the setting of O'Neill's two most iconic and written-about plays—a bar (*The Iceman Cometh*) and a home (*Long Day's Journey into Night*). Here, the bar and the home are not inescapable settings. They may not bring consolation and may further and/or even be the cause of the characters' unhappiness, but unlike the sea for these sailors, escape now becomes much more of a choice (albeit, a difficult one).[36]

CONCLUSION II:
THREE STATEMENTS ON SIGNIFICANCE

Drawing my reading to its natural conclusions, I hope that I can legitimately make the following three statements. First, the sea plays aboard the SS *Glencairn* demonstrate an important pivotal moment in O'Neill's writing career. Thinking about his oeuvre and his tendency and aptitude for experimentation, these plays—with their oscillation between realism and naturalism—show how O'Neill was tinkering and playing around with genre and worldviews. We should be able to situate these plays the crucial turning point in O'Neill's career where he moves away from melodrama and toward realism. In terms of seeing O'Neill's oeuvre as a whole, my reading suggests these sea plays are essential to understanding O'Neill's entire arc as a playwright. Second, through O'Neill as a prime example, we witness a lag in the influence, one can say, of Strindberg on both O'Neill and American theatre. Like Strindberg, but at least a decade behind, O'Neill and American theatre first went through a relatively brief period of naturalism (which—in keeping with Strindberg's competitor, Henrik Ibsen—naturally wrestled with realism) and was then followed by a relatively brief period of expressionism. We witness this change play out through the microcosm of O'Neill's sea plays. And third, given that there are very few, if any, real scholarly discussions of O'Neill with regards to philosophy, O'Neill criticism can be enlightened by philosophical conversations. On a somewhat related note, much of O'Neill scholarship has tended to avoid theory. And while this has been helpful for avoiding jargon-filled essays about the popular critical theory of the day, I hope that my reading demonstrates that analytical paradigms can, as long as the plays remain the focus (as opposed to the theory), be useful in unlocking some meaning that more traditional literary readings cannot achieve. I also think that engaging with, for example, philosophy, demonstrates that O'Neill was not just a tremendously talented playwright who had "a touch of the poet," but he was a very serious thinker, as well.

NOTES

1. Michael D'Alessandro, "Shifting Perceptions, Precarious Perspectives in Two of O'Neill's Early Sea Plays," *The Eugene O'Neill Review* 29 (2007): 21.

2. Ibid., 22.

3. Eugene O'Neill, *Bound East for Cardiff*, in *Eugene O'Neill: Complete Plays 1913–1920*, ed. Travis Bogard (New York: Library of America, 1988), 195.

4. Ibid.

5. Eugene O'Neill, *The Long Voyage Home*, in *Eugene O'Neill: Complete Plays 1913–1920*, ed. Travis Bogard (New York: Library of America, 1988), 520–521.

6. Ibid., 508.

7. O'Neill, *Bound East*, 195.

8. Eugene O'Neill, *In the Zone*, in *Eugene O'Neill: Complete Plays 1913–1920*, ed. Travis Bogard (New York: Library of America, 1988), 488.

9. Viktor E. Frankl, *Man's Search for Meaning: An Introduction to Logotherapy* (New York: Pocket Books, 1972), 59.

10. Ibid.

11. O'Neill, *In the Zone*, 488.

12. In 1924, O'Neill wrote *Desire Under the Elms*. Already a two-time Pulitzer Prize winner, O'Neill was no longer an aspiring playwright under the weighty influence of his financially successful actor-father. Though, of course, O'Neill's genre was always and continued to be

dramatic tragedy, there is a slight shift—one that may be a signal of
O'Neill's shift in personal success—from the admixture of the harsh
realities of naturalism and the mirror cast upon the audience by realism
to the mixed bag of realism.

The farm is everything that the sailors in the sea plays dream of,
but in *Desire Under the Elms*, it is not something unilaterally desir-
able. As Peter, one of Eben's step-brothers says, "Here—it's stones
atop o' the ground—stones atop o' stones—makin' stone walls—year
atop o' year—him 'n' yew 'n' me 'n' then Eben—makin' stone walls
fur him to fence us in!" (Eugene O'Neill, *Desire Under the Elms*, in
Eugene O'Neill: Complete Plays 1920–1931, ed. Travis Bogard [New
York: Library of America, 1988], 320). Similarly to the SS *Glencairn*
on the open sea, the farm is on the wild open land, yet it is still as suf-
focating as being confined to the ship. Yank's desire for a family and
Olson's desire for returning to his family is replaced by family itself (in
the form of the father, Ephraim), being the very cause of their misery.
What should be home is more like prison. The farm is too stable and
stifling and the step-brothers desire is to flee the confines of the farm
in search of gold—which brings stability in terms of wealth, but was
the most liquid and moveable of all forms of wealth in 1850, when this
play takes place. Therefore, the step-brothers, who have experienced
living at home on a farm, desire something even more freeing and
less-stable (in the sense of the stability of land and a home) than the
merchant marines in the "Sea Plays."

Eben, however, sees the farm not only as a connection to his mother
(and thus, his "home"), but as something that he can possess, that can
be all his own: It's Maw's farm agen! It's my farm! Them's my cows!
I'll mild my durn fingers off fur cows o' mine! . . . It's purty! It's
damned purty! It's mine . . . Mine, d'ye hear? Mine!" (331)

Yet even for Eben, who hopes to inherit the farm, the narrative of
the play suggests that land is not the answer. Eben, time and again,
experiences what I call landed homelessness. Eben lives on land, but it
is not a home for him. Eben hates his father, who still technically owns
the farm, and Abbie, for much of the play, is a constant outside threat,
threatening not just the prospects of owning the farm, but the idea of
their family and taking Eben's beloved mother's place. In short, at the
beginning of the play, Eben more or less, just wants his mother back—
just wants to feel at home—and the farm is his way to psychologically
accomplish that.

It is only when Eben and Abbie acknowledge their love that Eben
finds joy and, in a sense, a home. Abbie represents not just a stable
present but a loving future. And what is more, Abbie's love literally
and figuratively silences the ghost of Eben's mother, both for Eben's
mother's and Eben's sake. Even further, their baby is a physical manifestation of the permanence of their love and the creation of a family

and home. But, of course, given that neither Eben (at least since his mother died) nor Abbie seem to have experienced a stable loving home and family life, the two lovers have no practical knowhow or good models of a loving relationship to make their love transform into a stable home.

Though there is hope at the end of the play, O'Neill presents a mixed message. Whereas Eben early in the play said—"Love! I don't take no stock in sech slop!" (328)—Eben, in the very name of love, is willing to go to jail and maybe even be hanged for a crime he did not commit. While we fully expect Eben and Abbie to bear the suffering of their sentence by doing what Frankl suggests—through the loving contemplation of the image they carry of their beloved, they will achieve fulfillment—the irony and tragedy of the play is that, much like Yank's dying admission that he does not want to leave Driscoll, in Eben and Abbie's moment of recognition they simultaneously lose the farm and, for all practical purposes, their relationship and, ultimately, maybe even their lives.

Here, *Desire under the Elms* contradicts the desire or desirability of land/farm/home found in O'Neill's "Sea Plays." In a sense, land brings the characters no satisfaction and becomes just as isolating and impermanent as the sea. O'Neill suggests that neither land nor sea offer characters a feeling of home or permanence. In *Desire Under the Elms*, O'Neill argues that only love, which is almost equally unstable and complex in its own right in the play, counteracts the metaphorically inevitable sense of homelessness.

13. Alasdair MacIntyre, *The Tasks of Philosophy: Volume 1: Selected Essays* (Cambridge: Cambridge University Press, 2006), 3.

14. Ibid.

15. Ibid., 4.

16. Ibid.

17. Ibid.

18. Ibid., 5.

19. Ibid.

20. Travis Bogard, *Contour in Time: The Plays of Eugene O'Neill*, rev. ed. (New York: Oxford University Press, 1988), 76–77.

21. Ibid., 80

22. D'Alessandro, "Shifting Perceptions," 23.

23. Bogard, *Contour in Time*, 28. Note that D'Alessandro does not include the entire quote, which does potentially suggest a different reading (i.e., the reading that I suggest in a moment).

24. D'Alessandro, "Shifting Perceptions," 24–25.

25. In a sense, this statement suggests that Brechtian theatre is a particular type of theatre that forces the audience to experience an epistemological crisis. Though this equation cannot be expanded upon here (and is

far out of the reach of this essay), I would not disagree with the general notion that I am implying.

26. O'Neill, *Bound East*, 189.
27. Ibid.
28. Ibid., 197.
29. Ibid.
30. O'Neill, *Long Voyage*, 518.
31. See especially the work of Steven F. Bloom and George F. Wedge: Steven F. Bloom, "Alcoholism and Intoxication in *A Touch of the Poet*," *Dionysos* 2, no. 3 (Winter 1991): 31–39; Bloom, "Denial as Tragedy: The Dynamics of Addiction in O'Neill's *The Iceman Cometh* and *Long Day's Journey into Night*," *Dionysos* 1, no. 2 (1989): 3–18; Bloom, "Empty Bottles, Empty Dreams: O'Neill's Use of Drinking and Alcoholism in *Long Day's Journey into Night*," in *Critical Essays on Eugene O'Neill*, ed. James J. Martine (Boston: Hall, 1984), 159–77; Bloom, "The Role of Drinking and Alcoholism in O'Neill's Late Plays." *Eugene O'Neill Newsletter* 8, no. 1 (Spring 1984): 22–28; and George F Wedge, "Mixing Memory with Desire: The Family of the Alcoholic in Three Mid-Century Plays," *Dionysos* 1, no. 1 (1989): 10–18.
32. Arthur Gelb and Barbara Gelb, *O'Neill: Life with Monte Cristo* (New York: Applause, 2002), 605.
33. Ibid., 611.
34. Eugene O'Neill, *The Moon of the Caribbees*, in *Eugene O'Neill: Complete Plays 1913–1920*, ed. Travis Bogard (New York: Library of America, 1988), 542–43.
35. Ibid., 544.
36. And even think about O'Neill's work very shortly after, as in the 1924 *Desire Under the Elms* (see the earlier endnote for a reading of this play in light of the sea plays). While land (the farm) might not be the answer for finding a satisfying life, the farm is not as inescapable as the sea in the "Sea Plays"; after all, the play begins with Eben's two step-brothers leaving to find their fortune in California.

WORKS CITED

Bloom, Steven F. "Alcoholism and Intoxication in *A Touch of the Poet*." *Dionysos* 2.3 (Winter 1991): 31–39. Print.

———. "Denial as Tragedy: The Dynamics of Addiction in O'Neill's *The Iceman Cometh* and *Long Day's Journey into Night*." *Dionysos* 1.2 (1989): 3–18. Print.

———. "Empty Bottles, Empty Dreams: O'Neill's Use of Drinking and Alcoholism in *Long Day's Journey into Night*." *Critical Essays on Eugene O'Neill*. Ed. James J. Martine. Boston: Hall, 1984. 159–77. Print.

———. "The Role of Drinking and Alcoholism in O'Neill's Late Plays." *Eugene O'Neill Newsletter* 8.1 (Spring 1984): 22–28. Print.

Bogard, Travis. *Contour in Time: The Plays of Eugene O'Neill.* Rev. ed. New York: Oxford UP, 1988. Print.

D'Alessandro, Michael. "Shifting Perceptions, Precarious Perspectives in Two of O'Neill's Early Sea Plays." *Eugene O'Neill Review* 29 (2007): 21–35. Print.

Frankl, Viktor E. *Man's Search for Meaning: An Introduction to Logotherapy.* New York: Pocket, 1972. Print.

Gelb, Arthur, and Barbara Gelb. *O'Neill: Life with Monte Cristo.* New York: Applause, 2002. Print.

MacIntyre, Alasdair. *The Tasks of Philosophy: Volume 1: Selected Essays.* Cambridge: Cambridge UP, 2006. Print.

O'Neill, Eugene. *Bound East for Cardiff. Complete Plays 1913–1920.* Ed. Travis Bogard. New York: Library of America, 1988. 185–99. Print.

———. *Desire Under the Elms. Complete Plays 1920–1931.* Ed. Travis Bogard. New York: Library of America, 1988. 317–78. Print.

———. *In the Zone. Complete Plays 1913–1920.* Ed. Travis Bogard. New York: Library of America, 1988. 469–88. Print.

———. *The Long Voyage Home. Complete Plays 1913–1920.* Ed. Travis Bogard. New York: Library of America, 1988. 507–23. Print.

———. *The Moon of the Caribbees. Complete Plays 1913–1920.* Ed. Travis Bogard. New York: Library of America, 1988. 525–44. Print.

Wedge, George F. "Mixing Memory with Desire: The Family of the Alcoholic in Three Mid-Century Plays." *Dionysos* 1.1 (1989): 10–18. Print.

CHAPTER 7

"THE CURTAIN IS LOWERED"

SELF-REVELATION AND THE
PROBLEM OF FORM IN *EXORCISM*

Kurt Eisen

On Easter Sunday in 1920, *New York Times* drama critic Alexander Woollcott published the review of *Exorcism* that would serve for the next 91 years as the main source of plot information for Eugene O'Neill's one-act play. O'Neill would soon pull this directly autobiographical work from its run on a three-play bill at the Provincetown Playhouse and try to kill it completely by destroying all copies of the script. From the hints in Woollcott's review and the opening stage directions recorded in O'Neill's notebook, scholars have long speculated on what *Exorcism* might reveal about O'Neill's desperate state in 1912 when, while rooming in New York at the rundown hotel-barroom known as Jimmy the Priest's, he swallowed a stash of barbiturates and awaited his death. The play was thought forever lost until 2011 when Faith Yordan, widow of writer Philip Yordan, discovered a yellowed envelope among her late husband's papers with a note from Agnes Boulton, O'Neill's second wife, and confirmed that the document it contained was the missing script.[1] Purchased by the Beinecke Library, *Exorcism* had its first publication in the October 17, 2011, issue of *The New Yorker* under the heading, "Found Pages," followed in February 2012 by an edition from Yale University Press.[2] For O'Neill scholars, this recovery of a famously lost play, based so closely on a crucial event in the playwright's life, seems a kind of miraculous resurrection.

In his preface to *The New Yorker* printing, critic John Lahr affirms scholars' high expectations and calls *Exorcism* "the tipping point—the moment in O'Neill's tortured life when he gave up the romance of death for the romance of art," observing that it "may be the most accurate account both of his death wish . . . and of the rebirth that follows."[3] Indeed, shortly after this attempt at self-annihilation, which followed his shameful divorce from his first wife Kathleen Jenkins, O'Neill made a commitment to writing plays and to becoming, as he said in his 1914 letter to George Pierce Baker as a fledgling play-wright, "an artist or nothing,"[4] implicitly rejecting the commercial theater of his father, the actor James O'Neill. Beyond the personal crisis of 1912, which marks the beginning of his personal rebirth, the writing of *Exorcism* in 1919, the last one-act play he would complete before writing the masterful and elegiac *Hughie* in 1941, was also itself a creative turning point for O'Neill. By 1919 he was thinking beyond the one-act form on which he had made his early reputation with *Bound East for Cardiff*, *The Rope*, and *The Long Voyage Home* and that suited the collective spirit and limited resources of the Provincetown Players.

In giving *Exorcism* the subtitle "A Play of Anti-Climax," O'Neill suggests ambivalence about the formal shortcomings of a work that so directly explores his own personal trauma and a plot that begins as tragedy and concludes in a kind of comic regeneration. Having already written *The Straw* and *Beyond the Horizon* by 1920, he would soon undertake the longer, more mature and ambitious works of the 1920s and early 1930s. In retrospect *Exorcism* seems a premature glimpse of the later masterpieces that he began to write in 1939, *The Iceman Cometh* and the even more starkly self-revealing *Long Day's Journey into Night*, the productions of which he delayed while carefully preserving the scripts. Though one can never fully separate O'Neill's personal life from his art, with the recovered text we can see *Exorcism* more in terms of its place in his development as an artist rather than primarily as a window into his personal life during the crucial year of 1912. Reliving his guilt over the sordid brothel scene that was arranged to legitimize his divorce from his first wife Kathleen Jenkins, O'Neill created a surrogate self in *Exorcism* who attempts to confront his own darkness, sketching out the existential dilemma of the "pipe dream" that dominates *Iceman* and the confessional rigor of *A Moon for the Misbegotten*. Though Ned Malloy survives his suicide attempt and looks forward to a new life, the play's title itself suggests that in writing it, O'Neill was more determined to clear away his past than to come to terms with it, an artistic challenge he would become truly equal to only after many more years of formal experimentation and growth.

Robert M. Dowling's account of the play in his 2009 *Critical Companion to Eugene O'Neill*, offers an excellent summary of its scholarly status shortly before its discovery, drawing from known facts and scholarly inferences to create a snapshot of *Exorcism* on the shadowy fringes of the O'Neill canon. Dowling helpfully situates the episode from O'Neill's life that it depicts as coming just before the experiences on which *Long Day's Journey* and *The Straw* are based, and just after the period portrayed somewhat less directly in *Iceman*; we can see more clearly now that we have the script how strongly *Exorcism* is linked thematically to all three of those works. Calling the destruction of the play "a terrific loss for O'Neill scholars,"[5] Dowling repeats the assumption that the script would offer the most accurate picture of the playwright's psyche at the time of his suicide attempt, and endorses the argument of Stephen A. Black that O'Neill destroyed the play not because it was artistically bad or too self-revealing, but because it would have hurt his parents to see it in print or on stage,[6] something he may have realized when reviews appeared in the *Times*, the *New York Tribune*, and *Variety*. Dowling also cites Black's important insight that the suicide attempt shaped O'Neill's view of mortality and thus his tragic sensibility for the rest of his life,[7] and Travis Bogard's observation that Ned Malloy is O'Neill's "first Lazarus," linking him to the title character of the unwieldy biblical stage epic that O'Neill wrote in 1926, *Lazarus Laughed*, based on a figure synonymous with transcending death.[8]

Most helpfully, Dowling attempts to shift critical attention from "why O'Neill destroyed the play" to "why he would have written it in the first place,"[9] a question that becomes especially compelling now that we can read the text and thus more accurately judge its significance within O'Neill's early artistic development. Dowling notes the playwright's contrary impulses to confess and to conceal, described by biographer Louis Sheaffer as "the duality in his nature" that compelled him "to bare himself, to tell all" in spite of his intensely private nature.[10] In writing *Exorcism*, O'Neill was trying to explore his own experience of rebirth, but in the second half of the play, as we can now see in the recovered text, he deviates from the hard path of self-examination toward what seems a willful hybrid of tragic and comic elements. His restless experimentation in the years that follow may be seen as a way to try to reconcile the duality noted by Sheaffer, to create dramatic techniques that allow for self-revelation that is masked by art. In *The Straw* and *Lazarus Laughed*, we can see the impulse toward self-revelation and the theme of rebirth managed very differently; though neither was successful on stage, they are nonetheless important in his search for a sufficient form.

Though not produced until 1921, after *Exorcism* and his breakout successes with *Beyond the Horizon* and *The Emperor Jones*, *The Straw* draws directly on O'Neill's other brush with death very soon after the botched suicide, the bout with tuberculosis that put him in Gaylord Sanatorium in 1913. The primary male character is a fledgling fiction writer, Stephen Murray, an early version of the young dreamer whom O'Neill would continue to attempt to draw more or less oblique as a self-portrait throughout his career. His notebook suggests O'Neill's early struggle with autobiographical material with two full pages of initial ideas evidently erased, as Virginia Floyd observes, with the original name of the lead male character, "Eugene," still legible.[11] Clearly, however, in the final version Stephen's appearance remains modeled after himself, "a tall, slender unusual-looking fellow with a pale face, sunken under high cheek bones, lined about the eyes and mouth," whose eyes "have a tired, dispirited expression in repose, but can quicken instantly with a concealment mechanism of mocking, careless humor whenever his inner privacy is threatened."[12]

This self-concealing instinct in Stephen is compatible with O'Neill's decision not to make him the play's central character, but to focus instead on the tragic fate of Eileen Carmody, whom O'Neill based on a young patient at Gaylord who did not survive her illness. O'Neill himself remarked many years later that *The Straw* "is the girl's play absolutely"[13] because it is she and not Stephen who bears the play's primary theme, which he identified while writing the play as "the significance of human hope—even the most hopeless hope," keeping us "convinced in spite of our reason that there must be some spiritual meaning behind our hope which in some 'greener land' will prove it was all justified."[14] Anticipating this major motif of *The Iceman Cometh*, Stephen recognizes "it's that pipe dream keeps us all going,"[15] and the nurse Miss Gilpin expresses the playwright's own hope that "there must be something back of it—some promise of fulfillment—somehow—somewhere."[16] Eileen herself embodies this hope even on her death bed at the final curtain, dreaming of caring for Stephen as he pursues literary success. As Bogard points out, by making the play about Eileen and not Stephen, "O'Neill treats himself much as he treated the friends of his sailor days [in the *Glencairn* plays, for example], with an objectivity that sought no revelation."[17]

Departing from such overtly autobiographical experience, in *Lazarus Laughed*, O'Neill creates an unwieldy dramatic mythology that expresses his obsession with rebirth through a mix of biblical,

Jungian, and Nietzschean elements, at its center "the man who had been dead for three days," as O'Neill observed in his notes, "and returned to life knowing the secret."[18] Conceived in 1924, completed in 1926, but not produced until 1928 (in Pasadena, not New York), *Lazarus* requires approximately 150 actors to play 420 roles, with an elaborate choral scheme of masked figures intended to represent a full array of human types and ages. The radiant character of Lazarus himself, however, having been liberated from death, "wears no mask."[19] Rather than direct or even indirect self-portraiture, Lazarus embodies a philosophy that O'Neill could not fully explore in so brief a play as *Exorcism*, refashioning the biblical Lazarus, according to Stephen Black, as a "Zarathustra figure whose survival of death placed him psychologically beyond good and evil and made him heedless of the destructive power he held over the mortals around him."[20] His power to subjugate death therefore does not generate tragic awareness, nor does his strange progression from middle age toward youth seem either emotionally or dramatically convincing as an image of rejuvenation. Amid the pageantry, stilted dialogue, and overcrowded spectacle, O'Neill does include some of his more persistent personal concerns, displaced onto historical and biblical figures but identifiably his own. Michael Manheim posits a strong link, for example, between Lazarus and O'Neill's older brother, Jamie, and sees a distorted likeness to the playwright himself in Caligula, but judges the play as a whole to be "a sugar-coating of memories, not an attempt to confront them."[21]

Yet even in *Lazarus* we can discern a mature awareness of his own predicament as a dramatist, as in Lazarus's first exchange with Caligula: "Tragic is the plight of the tragedian whose only audience is himself! Life is for each man a solitary cell whose walls are mirrors. Terrified is Caligula by the faces he makes! But I tell you to laugh in the mirror, that seeing your life gay, your may begin to live as a guest, and not as a condemned one!"[22] The act of laughing in a mirror may be the vision of tragedy that O'Neill aspired to, insofar as it breaks through one's personal fears and offers the possibility of a communal experience, recasting death as something shared and liberating rather than isolating. The symbolic stagecraft of *Lazarus* represents O'Neill's attempt to transcend the confines of mere self-representation, and perhaps to transcend the confessional drive that informs *Exorcism*, but for all its pageantry fails to move beyond its "solitary cell whose walls are mirrors" by drawing a larger audience into its tragic angle of vision.

When asked in 1937 to contribute an explanatory note for *Lazarus Laughed* for an anthology, O'Neill declined but offered this account of the play's origin: "As for what impelled me to write the play, that is a long story starting way back in my boyhood in Catholic schools when I first heard the legend of the dead man brought back from death, and it took a peculiarly deep and fascinated hold upon my imagination. Years later, when I first began writing, I considered as a one-act play the return from death scene. Later, I felt a long play about his second life was the thing I must do."[23] As Virginia Floyd notes, O'Neill would continue in the late 1920s to draft ideas for autobiographical plays that revisit such "return from death" moments, some of them featuring suicide attempts, including a series of plays he called "The Sea-Mother's Son" with the intended subtitle, "The Story of the Birth of a Soul."[24] The plays he actually completed during that period—such as *Dynamo, Mourning Becomes Electra*, and especially *Days Without End*, with its explicit treatment of the lost Catholic faith of his boyhood—obsessively relive "the scars of the past," as Floyd observes, as O'Neill "kept dramatizing ancient battles as though reenacting them would exorcise his ghosts."[25]

This need for a continual confrontation with ghosts points to the problem of finding an adequate form for the revealing self-portraiture that O'Neill was attempting in the writing of *Exorcism*. That Woollcott pronounced it "uncommonly good" in his review should probably be taken as a judgment relative to the rest of the Provincetown bill and the state of American playwriting in 1920.[26] Woollcott could not foretell how such a play might, in O'Neill's own mind, have significantly raised the stakes for self-revelation in his writing, broaching deeply personal issues without a sufficiently mature dramatic form to develop them fully as art. Famously uneven in the quality of his work, O'Neill knew his writing well enough to know when to suppress or even destroy it, including almost all the American history cycle to which he devoted himself in the mid-to-late 1930s, and of which only *A Touch of the Poet* survives as a finished play. Seeing *Exorcism* on stage may have exposed some underlying formal weakness in the play that he had not perceived while writing it, a willful attempt to show himself that the demons of his youth really had been purged, when in fact the continual reenactment of his youthful trauma, as Floyd notes, was the driving force in his art. With the text of *Exorcism* now available, we can see how O'Neill managed its autobiographical elements, particularly the details of his abortive marriage to Kathleen Jenkins and his failed suicide attempt; we can also see more precisely why O'Neill's attempt to refashion these facts from life ultimately seemed to him a premature and ill-advised stab at some kind of resolution that would require, fully two decades later, a dramatic form that was both more technically mature and more nakedly honest.

Exorcism bears the seeds of all three full-length masterpieces that O'Neill completed between 1939 and 1943. Most obviously, it shares with *The Iceman Cometh* the setting of the saloon-hotel on Fulton Street, known as "Jimmy the Priest's," where O'Neill spent his days upon returning from his wanderings at sea in 1911. The characters Jimmy and Major Andrews have slightly modified counterparts in *Iceman*, and the suicide attempt of Ned Malloy anticipates the successful suicide of the even younger Don Parritt near the end of *Iceman*. The encounter between Ned and his father bears some resemblance—though much less developed and with several significant differences—to the dialogues between Edmund and James Tyrone in *Long Day's Journey*, and the unburdening of guilt that Ned declares near the end of the play reveals the same confessional impulse behind Jim Tyrone's monologue at the breast of Josie Hogan in *A Moon for the Misbegotten*. Even *Hughie*, O'Neill's late return to the one-act form in 1941, like *Exorcism* is set in a shabby hotel and features a protagonist losing hope and seemingly near the end of the line. In retrospect, *Exorcism* offers a view of multiple future paths; at the time, it must have seemed to O'Neill a premature attempt at tragic self-understanding for which neither he nor his dramaturgy was ready.

From the scene directions previously available in O'Neill's notebooks, we know the visual and physical details of the play's setting, which are typical of his precise and suggestive realistic style, including the cryptic desperation of walls "spotted with the greasy imprints of groping hands and fingers,"[27] apparently from the residents who had previously occupied that room and sought escape from it. The newly available section of these opening directions begins, "At the rise of the curtain," then describes the cold and dimly lit room, and most important, introduces the two primary characters. Based on a former press agent who roomed with O'Neill on Fulton Street, Jimmy was later portrayed in *Iceman* but had already been featured in 1917 as the main character in O'Neill's only published short story, "Tomorrow," where he ends his life by leaping from a fire escape. Here he is a "stout little man of forty" trying to read his newspaper and keep warm on a cold March day in the dingy and sparsely furnished room that is the play's only setting.[28] In a moment he is joined onstage by Ned Malloy, O'Neill's alter ego and like Stephen Murray in *The Straw*, an early prototype of the young dreamer, a line of characters that leads to explicit self-portraiture in Edmund Tyrone in *Long Day's Journey*.

O'Neill's description of Ned, "a tall slender young fellow of twenty-four," is worth quoting at length: "His mouth is wide, the lips twisted by a bitter, self-mocking irony. His eyes are large and blue, with the peculiar possessed expression of the inveterate dreamer. His forehead, under a thick mass of black hair, is broad and wide, but his chin reveals weakness, indecision. The upper section of his face seems at war with the lower, giving the whole an appearance of conflict, of inner disharmony."[29] Unlike the similar features of Stephen Murray in *The Straw*, these qualities in Ned's appearance are meant to bare his interior life and to reveal its disorder, not to show an instinct for concealment and self-protection. The outward expression of interior "conflict" also anticipates the experiments with masks in such plays as *Lazarus Laughed*, but more directly in *The Great God Brown* (1925) and *Days Without End* (1933) with their masked representations of contrary protagonists who are effectively a single individual psyche divided against itself. Set against Jimmy's resemblance to a "fat but anemic baby" and his way of speaking "with a careful precision" though "the tone of the voice itself is vague,"[30] Ned's visible inward turmoil and grimly foreboding utterances put his fate at the center of the play, starkly in contrast to Art, the first-person narrator of "Tomorrow," a surrogate of the author himself who keeps the focus squarely on Jimmy.

In the opening dialogue, Ned and Jimmy trade observations on the disappointing moral condition of humanity while disagreeing on the promise of spring just a few weeks ahead. Jimmy expresses his characteristic optimism that warmer weather will bring hope and happier times, while Ned hints darkly that there may be no more "later."[31] When Jimmy suggests that Ned should join with Nordstrum, "the big Swede . . . who comes in from the Market" across the street, and head west to Minnesota for the healthier life of a farm, Ned is having none of it, declaring, "There's no fresh air in this world."[32] Just back from a walk in Battery Park, he projects his own inward condition in describing the scene there as "a miserable, soaking strip of mud, the trees dead, and the bay as filthy as an overgrown sewer," reading this as a clear sign that "God's giving us the naked truth today" and not the illusory hope of better times.[33]

Here O'Neill is laying out the terms of an existential dilemma he would explore most fully in *Iceman*: whether one should pursue a sustaining illusion or accept the hard facts of life. As Jimmy begins once more to tell his story of the woman who betrayed him and his own subsequent bad fortune, Ned orders him to stop and vows to make him face "the truth for once"—that Jimmy is happier now living with the story of a faithless woman than he was with the responsibility and risk of loving her.[34] He is now "secure—home at last," Ned insists, "because this place is bedrock. After this there's nothing—but the

Morgue."[35] The only morally defensible way to live, he says, is with unflinching self-knowledge: "To be what you are and face it—that's good."[36] This reads like a preview of the debate between Larry Slade and Hickey in *Iceman*, whose setting Larry dubs the "Bedrock Bar" and remarks, "No one here has to worry about where they're going next, because there is no farther they can go,"[37] while Hickey tries to sell everyone his new formula for happiness: "Just stop lying to yourself and kidding yourself about tomorrows."[38] That young Ned Malloy bears the weight of themes for which O'Neill would later devise two of his greatest characters, Larry and Hickey, conveys some sense of why O'Neill would have found *Exorcism* artistically unsatisfying.

On a more personal level, the play amounts to an attempt by the playwright to follow Ned's advice to Jimmy and confront the truth of his own short-lived marriage to Kathleen Jenkins. The narrator of "Tomorrow" does not flinch from viewing Jimmy's own bloody corpse lying in the mud, leaving the impression that the author's own suicide attempt may have been motivated in part by his friend's suicide, but reveals nothing of the sordid scheme to concoct legal grounds to divorce Kathleen that was most likely the most immediate cause of O'Neill's decision to kill himself.[39] Ned's shame over this scheme drives the plot of *Exorcism*, the story that Ned wants to tell Jimmy "so that things will be understood by someone afterwards"[40] The revelation that follows seems very much a rehearsal for O'Neill's portraits of his dissolute older brother, Jamie, and his self-lacerating confessional monologues as James Tyrone Jr., in *Long Day's Journey* and *A Moon for the Misbegotten*, the latter of which was based partly on events after the writing of *Exorcism* at the time of their mother's death in 1922. Ned recounts with disgust his late-night trip to a brothel to stage an act of infidelity sufficient for divorce under New York state law, describing the prostitute as a "a painted clown with the black on her eyes and the greasy rouge on her lips—like a clown, you understand, a pitiable clown," and an index of his own wretchedness. "How can I go on, eh?" he asks Jimmy. "No! It's over! I'm done! I'm through!—when all the beauty is gone out of the world!"[41] When Jimmy leaves, Ned ingests his "small heap of white tablets," which could be either Veronal (a barbiturate) or morphine, settles into his cot, and announces, "Well, that's over."[42]

At this point, in a kind of inside-out version of Aristotelian temporal unity, "The curtain is lowered to denote the passage of twenty-four hours."[43] Dropping the curtain in the middle of a one-act play may be the clearest signal of O'Neill's difficulty in presenting the transformation he wants to portray in *Exorcism*. If *Long Day's Journey* represents a painful process of tragic self-revelation within the confines of a single day, *Exorcism* offers only before-and-after pictures with minimal attention to process. When the curtain rises again, Ned lies sleeping and his previously tormented face suddenly "has a singularly peaceful and calm expression," and "the strained look of tension is gone."[44] Jimmy reappears, joined by the third roommate, a sodden British ex-officer named Major Andrews who has helped Jimmy to rescue Ned from the near-fatal overdose. As he comes slowly back to consciousness, Ned's apparent inner calm is not reflected in his conscious behavior; his face and manner are described as "startled," "savage," "disgustedly," "impatiently," and "furiously" as he realizes his death has been stymied,[45] but with the passage of 24 hours he is nonetheless a changed man.

The play reaches its anticlimactic climax when Ned's father, Edward, arrives at the rooming house ready to make peace with his son and bring him home. Ned and Edward Malloy bear no close resemblance, but one can assume that since Ned is a common nickname for Edward, the son does bear his father's name; Ned is also sometimes short for Edmund, an intriguing possibility given the name O'Neill gives himself in *Long Day's Journey*, that of his brother who died in infancy. Given the strain between Eugene and James O'Neill Sr., in the years prior to the writing of this play, this scene has a decidedly wish-fulfilling quality. Edward Malloy has "the serene, self-complacent countenance of one who has achieved success in his chosen line," but unlike Tyrone's, that line is not connected with the theater.[46] Nonetheless, O'Neill's decision to bring the father to Ned's room suggests not only a desire for personal reconciliation as he wrote the play in 1919 but a desire to imagine the symbolic presence of his own theatrical father within the theatrical space of the son, as if to grant a tacit blessing to the son's work with its grittier settings and darker themes. The playwright might well have discerned a parallel in Ned's rebirth and imminent departure from his dingy room to the escape of Edmund Dantes from the Chateau d'If to be reborn as the Count of Monte Cristo in a climactic moment in James O'Neill's highly profitable stage vehicle. That Edward Malloy is presented as a somewhat aloof and condescending man of business perhaps implies that as an artist O'Neill could not yet acknowledge his father's theatrical legacy but only his commercialism, a problem he would take up with far greater nuance in *Long Day's Journey*.

Malloy comes not only to help Ned regain his health but also to try to reconcile him to his estranged wife Margaret, who has cancelled her petition for divorce and is now living in the Malloy household with the hope that Ned might return to her. The Gelbs observe that indeed O'Neill's own suicide attempt "elicited the desired remorse and forgiveness" in his father James,[47] but this sentimental image of the faithful wife is nothing like what actually happened in his marriage to Kathleen Jenkins, and Ned's intention never to return to her shows that O'Neill has no interest in conventional happy endings. An even more significant departure from faithful autobiography, however, and one of the key revelations made possible with the discovery of the *Exorcism* text, is the fact that Ned Malloy's mother is deceased. The brief exchange between Ned and his father on this point offers a glimpse ahead to the central situation of *Long Day's Journey*. When Malloy chastises him for shaming the family, speculating particularly on the pain it would have caused "if your poor mother was alive," Ned evades the topic, saying, "If you came to talk about that, it's no use," without elaborating on whatever family trauma may lie behind her death.[48] This angers Malloy for a moment, but he recovers himself and reassures Ned, "The past is past. We'll bury it. But you must see the necessity of leaving this filthy dive as soon as possible."[49] The dead mother and the ready willingness of father and son to "bury" the traumatic past associated with her completely glosses over the tragic presence of O'Neill's mother in his own life and later in the writing of *Long Day's Journey*, where he confronts her morphine habit and the insistence of Mary Tyrone that the family's troubled past is always present. Even if the text of *Exorcism* does not support assertions by Sheaffer and others that the white pills Ned takes are morphine rather than Veronal or some other "poison,"[50] as Woollcott calls it in his review, what is clear is that both Ned and Mary have turned to drugs as an escape from marital disappointments that have stripped life of its beauty.

Ned agrees to leave the rooming house and return home, but only after a rest cure suggested by Malloy at an exclusive, presumably expensive facility in the country—very different from the elder Tyrone's reluctance to spend more money than necessary on Edmund's tuberculosis cure in *Long Day's Journey*. Ned doesn't jump at the offer to return to his old job at his father's firm, but they don't argue over it. He will not follow through on his promise to "have it out face to face" with Margaret, but decides instead to go out to Minnesota with Nordstrum after all, following a month of recuperation and the return of warmer weather. There is no hint of his settling down to conventional domestic life when he declares in perhaps the play's most willful lines:

New leaf be damned. It's a new book without a leaf of the old left in it. The Past is finally cremated. I feel reborn, I tell you! I've had a bath! I've been to confession! My sins are forgiven me! God judges by our intentions, they say, and my intentions last night were of the best. He evidently wants to retain my services here below—for what I don't know yet but I'm going to find out—and I feel of use already! So here's looking forward to the new life, reform or no reform, as long as it's new.[51]

Ned seems more determined to seek new horizons than to take up old burdens or return to old haunts. O'Neill himself did return home after the suicide attempt in 1912, and his divorce from Kathleen Jenkins does not figure in the events depicted from the summer of that year in *Long Day's Journey*. But in 1919, Ned's speech seems to express O'Neill's own modernist determination to leave behind traditional artistic forms and to pursue newer, bolder experiments—not merely turning over a "new leaf" but opening the "new book" of the full-length drama and its larger artistic possibilities.

The almost comic finale that follows recalls the ending of *Iceman*, with its boisterous, cacophonous singing intended to keep up the good spirits. Jimmy's weeping at the final curtain seems to foreshadow the suicide of his real-life counterpart, James Byth, in 1913, soon after O'Neill's own attempt. In any case, it is unlikely that O'Neill was himself fully convinced by the image of resurrection he had created from his own life experience in *Exorcism*. For all the various sacraments and rites that Ned touches on his final monologue—baptism, confession, communion (with drink), funeral, and even divine vocation—the sense of an exorcism is never convincingly realized. The "anticlimax" of the subtitle sounds like an author hedging his bet that he could attain something like the catharsis or deeper recognition of tragedy, a process that would require far more formal latitude than O'Neill could realize in this brief play. The *Tribune* reviewer said of the plot that "its course is unclear and its outlines are blurred,"[52] and Woollcott's review in the *Times* shrewdly discerns the mood of anticlimax: "The suicide comes back to find everything wearisomely the same—everything except himself . . . Slowly it dawns on him that, when a fellow tries hard to kill himself and seems to fail, the effect is quite as though he had succeeded."[53] Perhaps O'Neill himself experienced this realization after his suicide attempt, and it led him to see that the alternative to actual self-annihilation was to reinvent oneself through art, the choice to be "an artist or nothing" as he explained his life's aim to George Pierce Baker in 1914. By 1919 he had recognized that a tragic vision and the possibility of a real transformation would require the breadth and depth of the full-length form.

By 1931, however, after completing what would be his longest play, the trilogy *Mourning Becomes Electra*, O'Neill wrote to Woollcott's successor as *Times* drama critic, Brooks Atkinson, declaring that the whole idea of a cathartic "purging"—and by implication, any prospect of a spiritual exorcism—was not possible in the modern age: "But our tragedy is just that we have only ourselves, that there is nothing to be purged into except a belief in the guts of man, good or evil, who faces unflinchingly the black mystery of his own soul!"[54] As a play, *Exorcism* may not be, as Sheaffer speculated, "the most reliable index of Eugene's frame of mind after his suicide attempt" and his return to his family in 1912,[55] but with its recovery we do have an invaluable glimpse into the growth of a young artist who realized that even in this instance of failing to look without flinching into his own soul, he could see more clearly the ghosts he must face in the long journey that lay before him.

Notes

1. For a brief account of how the script was discovered, see Jo Morello, "O'Neill, Lost and Found," *American Theatre*, December 11, 2011, 14.
2. The Yale edition of Exorcism,published in late February 2012 was not available for citation in this essay.
3. John Lahr, "Found Pages: Introduction," *New Yorker*, October 17, 2011, 73.
4. Eugene O'Neill, *Selected Letters of Eugene O'Neill*, ed. T. Bogard and J. Bryer (New Haven, CT: Yale University Press, 1988), 26.
5. Robert M. Dowling, *A Critical Companion to Eugene O'Neill: A Literary Reference to His Life and Work* (New York: Facts on File, 2009), 155.
6. Ibid.
7. Ibid., 156.
8. Ibid.
9. Ibid.
10. Louis Sheaffer, *O'Neill: Son and Playwright* (Boston: Little, Brown, 1968), 210.
11. Virginia Floyd, *Eugene O'Neill at Work: Newly Released Ideas for Plays* (New York: Ungar, 1981), 9.
12. Eugene O'Neill, *The Straw*, in *Complete Plays 1913–1920*, ed. Travis Bogard (New York: Library of America, 1988), 732.
13. O'Neill, *Selected Letters*, 502.
14. Ibid., 96.
15. O'Neill, *The Straw*, 733.
16. Ibid., 794.

17. Travis Bogard, *Contour in Time: The Plays of Eugene O'Neil*, rev. ed. (New York: Oxford University Press, 1988), 109.

18. Floyd, *Eugene O'Neill at Work*, 92.

19. O'Neill, *Lazarus Laughed*, in *Complete Plays 1920–1931*, ed. Travis Bogard (New York: Library of America, 1988), 542.

20. Stephen A. Black, *Eugene O'Neill: Beyond Mourning and Tragedy* (New Haven, CT: Yale University Press, 1999), 339.

21. Michael Manheim, *Eugene O'Neill's New Language of Kinship* (Syracuse, NY: Syracuse University Press, 1982), 56.

22. O'Neill, *Lazarus Laughed*, 572.

23. O'Neill, *Selected Letters*, 463.

24. Floyd, *Eugene O'Neill at Work*, xxix.

25. Virginia Floyd, *The Plays of Eugene O'Neill: A New Assessment* (New York: Ungar, 1985), 417.

26. Alexander Woollcott, "Second Thoughts on First Nights," *New York Times*, April 4, 1920, X6.

27. Eugene O'Neill, *Exorcism*, *New Yorker*, October 17, 2011, 73.

28. Ibid., 74.

29. Ibid.

30. Ibid.

31. Ibid.

32. Ibid., 76.

33. Ibid., 74.

34. Ibid., 75.

35. Ibid.

36. Ibid.

37. Eugene O'Neill, *The Iceman Cometh*, in *Complete Plays 1932–1943*, ed. Travis Bogard (New York: Library of America, 1988), 577–78.

38. Ibid., 610.

39. Sheaffer speculates that O'Neill created the impression that the suicide of James Byth, the friend on whom he based Jimmy, in "Tomorrow" and in *Iceman*, was a factor in his own suicide attempt; he was really trying to cover up the more proximate cause, his shameful divorce from Kathleen Jenkins; see Sheaffer, "Correcting Some Errors in the Annals of O'Neill (Part One)," *Eugene O'Neill Newsletter* 7, no. 3 (1983), http://www.eoneill.com/library/newsletter/vii_3/vii-3c.htm. Accessed 15 Nov. 2011

40. O'Neill, *Exorcism*, 76.

41. Ibid., 77.

42. Ibid.

43. Ibid.

44. Ibid.

45. Ibid., 77–78.

46. Ibid., 78.

47. Arthur Gelb and Barbara Gelb, *O'Neill: Life with Monte Cristo* (New York: Applause, 2000), 333.

48. O'Neill, *Exorcism*, 78.
49. Ibid.
50. This assumption that Ned takes morphine rather than Veronal is made by Sheaffer (*O'Neill: Son and Playwright*, 210), Bogard (108), Black (257), and Dowling (155), but not by the Gelbs, suggesting that Sheaffer was a direct source for other scholars. In his review, Woollcott refers to the pills Ned takes as "poison," and the *Tribune* review makes no mention of the means of suicide.
51. O'Neill, *Exorcism*, 79.
52. "New Provincetown Plays Display Group's Limitations," *New York Tribune*, April 1, 1920, 13; Jeffery Kennedy identifies the reviewer as Heywood Broun, see *The Artistic Life of the Provincetown Playhouse, 1918–1922* (PhD dissertation, New York University, 2007), 720.
53. Woollcott, "Second Thoughts," X6.
54. O'Neill, *Selected Letters*, 390.
55. Sheaffer, *O'Neill: Son and Playwright*, 214.

Works Cited

Black, Stephen A. *Eugene O'Neill: Beyond Mourning and Tragedy*. New Haven: Yale UP, 1999. Print.

Bogard, Travis. *Contour in Time: The Plays of Eugene O'Neill*. Rev. ed. New York: Oxford UP, 1988. Print.

Dowling, Robert M. *A Critical Companion to Eugene O'Neill: A Literary Reference to His Life and Work*. New York: Facts on File, 2009. Print.

Floyd, Virginia. *Eugene O'Neill at Work: Newly Released Ideas for Plays*. New York: Ungar, 1981. Print.

———. *The Plays of Eugene O'Neill: A New Assessment*. New York: Ungar, 1985. Print.

Gelb, Arthur, and Barbara Gelb. *O'Neill: Life with Monte Cristo*. New York: Applause, 2000. Print.

Kennedy, Jeffery T. *The Artistic Life of the Provincetown Playhouse, 1918–1922*. Diss. New York U, 2007. Print.

Lahr, John. "Found Pages: Introduction." *The New Yorker* 17 Oct. 2011: 73. Print.

Manheim, Michael. *Eugene O'Neill's New Language of Kinship*. Syracuse: Syracuse UP, 1982. Print.

Morello, Jo. "O'Neill, Lost and Found." *American Theatre* 11 Dec. 2011: 14. Print.

"New Provincetown Plays Display Group's Limitations." *New York Tribune* 1 Apr. 1920: 13. Print.

O'Neill, Eugene. *Selected Letters of Eugene O'Neill*. Ed. T. Bogard and J. Bryer. New Haven: Yale UP, 1988. Print.

———. *Exorcism. The New Yorker* 17 Oct. 2011: 72–79. Print.

———. *Lazarus Laughed. Complete Plays 1920–1931*. Ed. Travis Bogard. New York: Library of America, 1988. 537–628. Print.

———. *The Iceman Cometh. Complete Plays 1932–1943*. Ed. Travis Bogard. New York: Library of America, 1988. 561–711. Print.

———. *The Straw. Complete Plays 1913–1920*. Ed. Travis Bogard. New York: Library of America, 1988. 713–94. Print.

Sheaffer, Louis. "Correcting Some Errors in the Annals of O'Neill (Part One)." *Eugene O'Neill Newsletter* 7.3 (1983). *eOneill.com.* n.d. Web. http://www.eoneill.com/library/newsletter/vii_3/vii-3c.htm.

———. *O'Neill: Son and Playwright*. Boston: Little, 1968. Print.

Woollcott, Alexander. "Second Thoughts on First Nights." *The New York Times* 4 April 1920: X6. Print.

CHAPTER 8

"AIN'T NOTHIN' DERE
BUT DE TREES!"

GHOSTS AND THE FOREST
IN *THE EMPEROR JONES*

Paul D. Streufert

*This thing [the ghost] that looks at us, that concerns us, comes to defy
semantics as much as ontology, psychoanalysis as much as philosophy.*

—*Jacques Derrida*

I ain't 'fraid of no ghosts!

—*Ray Parker Jr.*

Eugene O'Neill's *The Emperor Jones* occupies a curious position
in the playwright's extensive catalog. Both wildly popular as well as
theatrically sophisticated, it provided the Provincetown Players their
first and only runaway commercial hit in its initial run, beginning in
November of 1920. O'Neill himself ranked it among his best work,[1]
and its adaptation to film and opera, both in 1933, speaks to its commercial and narrative appeal to audiences and artists. Since its debut,
O'Neill scholars have also approached the text in significant and
intriguing ways, noting its debt to continental expressionism,[2] its use
of Jungian archetypes and Freudian psychology,[3] and its appropria-
tion and portrayal of race.[4] Yet in addition to its complex philosophical and cultural underpinnings, *The Emperor Jones* is also profoundly
theatrical and thrilling, a play that exults in the Aristotelian sense of

spectacle. Fear and terror drive the story, forcing the audience to join Brutus Jones on his journey through his personal and collective past. This essay will look specifically at how O'Neill uses fear and terror in *The Emperor Jones*, focusing on the ghost characters and the medium of the forest, the supernatural place that links Brutus Jones's external and interior realities. O'Neill's use of ghosts and the haunted forest reveals both his debt to the European theatrical tradition of ghost plays, which originated in ancient Athens, as well as his use of the forest as the locus of fear and anxiety found in the early American literary tradition of the Puritans. Through ghosts and the forest, O'Neill manages to create a hybrid place in the play. Though set in the West Indies, a location neither American, nor European, nor African, the setting of *The Emperor Jones* somehow evokes and integrates all three.

By approaching *The Emperor Jones* through close readings of its setting and ghost scenes, I hope to address a significant point left untouched by discussions of the play and playwright to this point. Though *The Emperor Jones* clearly operates as a ghost story and seeks to terrorize its audience, few, if any critics, have approached it as such. Two recent articles in particular bear titles that imply such an approach, yet neither addresses the playwright's choice of genre vis-à-vis ghost characters or setting. Among other things, Carme Manuel's wide-ranging "A Ghost in the Expressionist Jungle of O'Neill's *The Emperor Jones*" provides an excellent history of the responses—both positive and negative—to the play by Anglo and African Americans,[5] yet she focuses more on race than on the ghosts themselves. Another essay, by Noorbakhsh Hooti and Nasser Maleki, includes "terror" in its title, but its authors concentrate on the social aspects of Brutus Jones's ghostly visions and O'Neill's reliance on Aristotelian elements, rather than on terror and its functions per se.[6] O'Neill's use of terror in *The Emperor Jones* roughly follows the example of nineteenth-century writers like Ann Radcliffe, who argues that terror, the anticipation of the bad or the awful, is vastly superior in storytelling to horror, which creates a realization and discovery of something bad or awful. She claims that "terror expands the soul" and that "the great difference between horror and terror [lies] but in the uncertainty and obscurity."[7] The ghosts that visit Brutus Jones on his trek through the woods on his final night inspire his terror and that of the audience as well. Throughout the play, Jones encounters the ghosts, but must also figure them out and deduce why they have appeared and what they want. In some cases, the spirits are linked to Jones personally and terrify him as an individual, as when the ghosts of Jeff and a white prison guard materialize, both of whom were murdered by Jones. The terror builds, though, as the ghosts become more obscure and less personal, when Jones encounters a slave auction, a slave ship, and finally an African witch doctor and a crocodile. These images, which link the protagonist to his collective past, require more interpretive work for both Jones and the audience than the personal ghosts that haunt him. That obscurity, on which Radcliffe insists as a necessary component in terror, marks the play as a complex piece of theater rather than a simple ghost story, and in exploring difficult themes like the Jungian collective unconscious of African Americans, or the expressionistic use of the drumbeat throughout the haunting scenes, O'Neill created one of the most significant plays in the American theater up to that point.[8] The use of ghosts at this early stage in his career also provides a potential hermeneutic for reading his later work, particularly in the exorcism he would perform in writing *Long Day's Journey into Night*.

In staging the spirits that haunt Brutus Jones's island forest and subconscious, O'Neill employed a device as old as the European theatrical tradition itself. The oldest extant play in the West, Aeschylus's *Persians*, performed in Athens in 472 BCE, features the ghost of Darius, a dead king who has returned to learn the fate of his kingdom and son, whom the Athenians had defeated seven years earlier. In the centuries following, the ghosts of Senecan tragedy in Rome inspired a host of playwrights in the Renaissance, including Thomas Kyd, Ben Jonson, and of course William Shakespeare, who used the device to great effect in *Hamlet, Macbeth, Julius Caesar*, and *Richard III*, among others. Though not as popular in European drama after the Renaissance, ghosts return to the stage in the late nineteenth century, due largely to August Strindberg, who directly influenced O'Neill. Playwrights of the twentieth century, particularly in the United States and Britain, make great use of ghosts, and David Edgar rightly calls them "one of the most consistently employed conventional devices in world theatre."[9] Though there are other ghost plays in America before O'Neill's *The Emperor Jones*—for example, African American playwright Angela Gimke's 1916 play *Rachel*[10]—the specters that haunt Brutus Jones helped establish O'Neill as the first American playwright to earn notice at home and abroad.

Scene one offers O'Neill's clearest declaration of *The Emperor Jones* as a story of the supernatural, though it features no ghosts and takes place in broad daylight. This lengthy and expository scene begins with a silent dumb-show sequence that prefigures and foreshadows the events of subsequent scenes, contextualizing the story for the audience as one of fear and terror. The first character to appear on stage enters silently and immediately shows the anxiety of subservience and powerlessness in a ruler's space. O'Neill describes her as "*a native Negro woman*," who is "*very old, dressed in cheap calico*."[11] The verbs he ascribes to her movements evoke terror, as she "*sneaks in cautiously*" to Jones's throne room, and then "*hesitates [. . .], peering back as if in extreme dread.*"[12] As if to mimic the ghosts that will later appear to Brutus Jones in the forest, she "*begins to glide noiselessly [. . .] toward the doorway in the rear.*"[13] The appearance of the Henry Smithers, an unlikable Cockney trader, soon disrupts the ghostly performance of the native woman. After watching her silently for a moment, Smithers "*springs forward and grabs her*," an act that evokes her "*frantic terror.*"[14] This interaction between two minor characters acts as a literal prologue to the play, an overture of sorts that introduces and promises the development of the themes of terror and shock. O'Neill shows the audience that *The Emperor Jones* will tell a ghost story, one where spectral characters will jump out and frighten, all in the interest of terrorizing Brutus Jones as he anticipates his fall from power and death.

The conversation that follows the dumb-show between the native woman and Smithers further forecasts the supernatural and narrative elements of the story to come. He accuses the woman's people of "devilment" and describes Jones's throne room—likely the busiest room in the house, under normal circumstances—as "a bleedin' tomb."[15] The reference to the tomb functions in two ways, by setting up Jones's death at the play's conclusion while also tying the living Jones to a place of death, much like the haunted forest in which he will wander for the next six scenes. In their final moment together, Smithers and the native woman again preview the story's eventual ghosts and Jones's haunting in the woods. When Smithers steps away from her to summon Jones, she "*springs to her feet and runs*"; Smithers in response draws his sidearm and threatens to shoot her.[16] Every ghost scene hereafter, with the exception of scene seven, where he confronts the witch doctor and crocodile, concludes with Jones shooting his gun in a vain attempt to kill a disembodied spirit, followed by his running from the scene. Smithers and the woman then, in their fight and flight, create a template for the protagonist and his negotiation of terror. In spite of its ghostly overtones, this section of *The Emperor Jones*'s first scene has inspired little commentary and explication. Egil Tornqvist even cites one critic who deems the action between the two as "unnecessary."[17] In response, Tornqvist provides a nuanced reading of the scene, claiming, as I do, that it contains an important summary of the play, yet Tornqvist reads the woman's situation in terms of race, as one caught between the violent forces of black and white, represented by Jones and Smithers respectively.[18] To that reading I would add that the scene also foreshadows and mimics the terror and haunting that Brutus Jones will face in the subsequent scenes, when he eventually leaves behind his empty state room for the cluttered and claustrophobic woods.

After the native woman's exit and Jones's subsequent entrance, he and Smithers converse for the remainder of scene one, and while much of their dialogue provides exposition—how Jones came to be self-appointed emperor of the island, his murderous past, and his plans to steal away with the natives' money—they quickly become locked in a duel of words. In search of psychological dominance, each man tries to scare the other by using the sort of anticipatory terror described by Radcliffe. Though the scene contains conventional devices from a variety of supernatural tales, including the silver bullet and full moon from werewolf lore, fear and terror in the scene are most closely aligned with ghosts and ghost stories.[19] O'Neill carefully constructs the remainder of scene one as a power play, picking up the themes of fear and dominance explored between Smithers and the native woman. Once Jones appears and barks orders in his empty room, Smithers "*[shows] himself, in a manner half-afraid and half-defiant.*"[20] With Jones present, Smithers, who tormented the native woman, takes on her fear and sense of domination himself. Clearly Brutus Jones, as his name implies,[21] brutalizes and terrifies the people in his court through the threat of lawless violence. In spite of that, Smithers mentions Jones's first days on the island claiming, "I wasn't afraid to 'ire yer like the rest was—'count of the story about your breakin' jail back in the States."[22] Smithers, in denying the efficacy of Jones's stories about himself, invokes the ghost narrative, as does Jones when he claims, "What I was den is one thing. What I is now's another,"[23] marking himself as mutable and difficult to control but also as an unreliable and potentially harmful entity, not unlike a ghost. As figures of transition, ghosts occupy both, and yet neither, sides of a dichotomy: they are living and dead, present and absent, buried and terrestrial. Ghosts, like Jones, are not now what they were then, and his focus on the transition in his own identity offers another form of ghosting at this moment. As if he had told Smithers a ghost story, Jones hopes to scare him with obscurity and indeterminacy, both key elements in the creation of terror.

Jones goes on to terrorize Smithers further, clarifying his criminal past while threatening him with violence. In a passage particularly reminiscent of the ghost story, they battle for dominance:

Jones: (*sharply*) You ain't 'sinuatin' I'se a liar, is you?

Smithers: (*hastily*) No, Gawd strike me! I was only thinkin' o' the bloody lies you told the blacks 'ere about killin' white men in the States.

Jones: (*angered*) How come dey're lies?

Smithers: You'd 'ave been in jail if you 'ad, wouldn't yer then? (*with venom*) And from what I've 'eard, it ain't 'ealthy for a black to kill a white man in the States. They burns 'em in oil, don't they?

Jones: (*with cool deadliness*) You mean lynchin' 'd scare me? Well, I tells you, Smithers, maybe I does kill one white man back dere. Maybe I does. And maybe I kills another right heah 'fore long if he don't look out.

Smithers: (*trying to force a laugh*) I was on'y spoofin' yer. Can't yer take a joke? And you was just sayin' you'd never been in jail.

Jones: (*in the same tone—slightly boastful*) Maybe I goes to jail dere for gettin' in an argument wid razors ovah a crap game. Maybe I gits twenty years when dat colored man die. Maybe I gits in 'nother argument wid de prison guard was overseer ovah us when we're wukin' de road. Maybe he hits me wid a whip and I splits his head wid a shovel and runs away and files de chain off my leg and gits away safe. Maybe I does all dat an' maybe I don't. It's a story I tells you so's you knows I'se de kind of man dat if you evah repeats one word of it, I ends yo' stealin' on dis yearth mighty damn quick.

Smithers: (*terrified*) Think I'd peach on yer? Not me! Ain't I always been yer friend?[24]

Jones's history, steeped in murder, functions much like a ghost story, and in telling it Jones terrifies Smithers with implied and explicit violence. Jones himself calls it a "story," and, like other stories of the supernatural, it concludes with a cautionary warning.[25] Moreover, Jones's repetition of the word "maybe" keeps Smithers off balance, undercutting the narrative's authority and believability. Just as with a ghost story, the hearer must sort out the truth from the fiction, in this case leaving Smithers to wonder how much of Jones's account of murder and escape from prison is true. Here again, obscurity generates terror, and though Smithers himself raises the specter of racial violence through lynching, an attempt to counterattack Jones's narrative violence, O'Neill's prescriptive line directions leave no doubt as to which man terrifies the other more effectively. Smithers's final plaintive line, delivered in a "terrified" manner, marks him as the submissive player in their game of dominance.

The psychological warfare between the skittish Smithers and the overconfident Jones takes a turn when the Cockney trader mentions the island natives. Tired of abuse and heavy taxation, Lem, the native leader of Jones's subjects, plans to overthrow the "emperor," a fact used by Smithers as a weapon. Jones laughs it off, asking "Does you think I'se scard o' him?,"[26] a rhetorical question that goes unanswered. In spite of his bravado, the first inkling of fear appears in Jones when the natives begin a tom-tom beat, heard by characters and audience, which provokes "*a strange look of apprehension [on] his face for a moment as he listens.*"[27] The terror shown by Jones, in anticipation of losing his power and life, provides Smithers another chance to attack within a supernatural context. He claims, "Ternight when it's pitch black in the forest, they'll 'ave their pet devils and ghosts 'oundin' after you. You'll find yer bloody 'air'll be standin' on end before termorrow mornin'."[28] His vivid description of Jones's fright once again invokes the ghost story, which seeks similar responses from its audience. Intriguingly, Jones scoffs at the idea of fearing the forest and its supernatural inhabitants, turning Smithers's parry into a chance to joke. They continue:

> Jones: (*contemptuously*) You're de frightenedst man evah I see! I tells you I'se safe's 'f I was in New York City. [. . .]
> Smithers: (*maliciously*) Give my regards to any ghosts yer meets up with.
> Jones: (*grinning*) If dat ghost got money, I'll tell him never to ha'nt you less'n he wants to lose it.
> Smithers: (*flattered*) Garn![29]

This exchange predicts and yet downplays the haunting that will begin in the next scene and continue through scene seven, even as it links ghosts and comedy, a connection at least as old as ancient Rome, and very likely reaching back to Greek New Comedy of the third century BCE.[30] In O'Neill's play, the two combatants reach an uneasy peace, with the dominant Jones teasing the weaker man and making light of their fear. In such an instance, juxtaposing a brave man with a terrified one, O'Neill adapts a traditional element in the European haunted house story,[31] wherein a fearless man dispels either a false haunting with logic or a real one by appeasement of the spirits. In *The Emperor Jones*, the brave man is quickly undone while the setting shifts from a house to the wilderness.

The bulk of *The Emperor Jones* takes place in the woods of Jones's unnamed island in the West Indies, and this terrain, encountered by Jones at the start of scene two, functions as the primary agent of terror in the play. The idea, which may have originated during O'Neill's time as a sailor while visiting Honduras,[32] works both thematically—the woods as a place of confusion, isolation, and darkness—and in terms of spectacle for the performance audience. Even in his initial description, O'Neill delineates the space of the cleared land as a place without ghosts, subject to reason and clarity, whereas the forest he calls, "a wall of darkness dividing the world."[33] From this point on, O'Neill utilizes the idea of the woods as a haunted space, an old trope in American literature, one that has appeared since its inception. Whereas an English or European story might locate supernatural activity in a building, a house or castle for example, O'Neill follows the lead of American writers before him and presents the wilderness of *The Emperor Jones* as an uncanny, dangerous, and even hellish place. Of course, American writers too have used the trope of the haunted house to great effect; one need think of Edgar Allen Poe and Roderick Usher's house or Prospero's "castellated abbey" in "The Mask of the Red Death," though the latter is set very specifically in Europe.[34] Yet O'Neill's insistence on setting the ghost scenes in the dark woods shows a deft understanding of his national literature, rather than just an atmospheric or theatrical choice. Though squarely placing *The Emperor Jones* in the company of nineteenth-century writers like Nathaniel Hawthorne and Herman Melville, both of whom used the woods and wilderness of America as symbols of danger and uncertainty,[35] the play looks back even further, to the earliest writings of America's Puritan settlers. One text in particular, Mary Rowlandson's captivity narrative, provides a model for understanding O'Neill's use of the woods in *The Emperor Jones*.

Mary Rowlandson's 1682 text, *The Sovereignty and Goodness of God*, chronicles her captivity by several Native American tribes in colonial Massachusetts. For a three-month period in 1676, Rowlandson and her children lived in the woods of New England with their captors,[36] and her description of these events echoes the terror felt by Puritan settlers of the untamed lands surrounding them. She writes of the "vast and howling *Wilderness*" into which she disappears, and laments the loss of a child, "buried by the Heathen in the *Wilderness* from among all Christians" (emphasis hers).[37] Several years after Rowlandson's captivity, Cotton Mather, infamous for his role in the witchcraft trials at Salem, linked the New England wilderness with hell, as various captivity survivors claimed to have seen the devil in the woods. Only through a return to God and religion could Christians protect themselves from the present hell surrounding them as well as the future hell of the afterlife, he argued.[38]

Though I claim no direct influence by these Puritan authors on O'Neill, certainly he explores and innovates on this trope in the play. Exploration of America's Puritan roots was nothing new to O'Neill, as evidenced most obviously in *Desire under the Elms*,[39] which debuted just four years after *The Emperor Jones*. However, unlike *Elms*, the earlier one-act play focuses much more on setting than character. The first description of the forest, where Jones meets his ghosts in scene two, sounds remarkably like Rowlandson's description of the wilderness of colonial America: "In the rear the forest is a wall of darkness dividing the world. Only when the eye becomes accustomed to the gloom can the outlines of separate trunks of the nearest trees be made out, enormous pillars of deeper blackness. A somber monotone of wind lost in the leaves moans in the air. Yet this sound serves but to intensify the impression of the forest's relentless immobility, to form a background throwing into relief its brooding, implacable silence."[40] Just as Rowlandson spoke of the "vast and howling" wilderness, O'Neill creates a similarly confusing and terrifying natural maze for his protagonist. The woods, like the ghosts that haunt them, function both symbolically—representing Jones's confusion and the power of the natives on the island—and theatrically, as it provides spectacle and atmosphere for the ghost story. Jones's understanding and description of the native other also echoes the Puritan Rowlandson. While she refers to the Native Americans in her text most often as "the Heathen," Jones too uses a list of racist epithets, belittling native religion and civilization. He calls them "bush niggers," "ign'rent black niggers," and most significantly "woods' niggers"[41]—implying a natural relationship between the native people and the woods that will come to haunt him. In scene one, he tells Smithers, "Let dem try deir heathen tricks. De Baptist Church done pertect me and land dem all in hell."[42] His boasts of religious superiority prove nothing more than bravado, as the woods strip away all semblance of Jones's civilized practices, and the heathen tricks—the drums that stir his blood and raise the ghosts of his unconscious—reduce him to easy prey for the silver bullet the natives have prepared for him.

Shortly after entering the woods, Jones finds himself in the sort of wilderness hell described by Mather and Rowlandson, and like those Puritan writers, Jones invokes God and European religion as remedy and protection. Three ghostly encounters in particular terrify Jones into passive reliance on religion. Scene four presents a ghost from his personal past, the white prison guard he murdered as he escaped from a chain gang. Before even seeing the ghosts, he fears them, telling himself, "Ha'nts! You fool nigger, dey ain't no such things! Don't de Baptist parson tell you dat many time? Is you civilized, or is you like dese ign'rent black niggers heah?"[43] Jones turns to religion to makes sense of and order the wilderness, but in so doing he both mimics seventeenth-century thought and couples it with post-Enlightenment disbelief in the spiritual realm. Rowlandson and Mather would have surely believed the wilderness they encountered to be full of malevolent spirits, but Jones tries to deny their very existence, ironically through the words of a Baptist minister. His words reveal his terror that the life he constructed for himself, focused on greed and the abuse of numerous vulnerable people, will be punished. His terror leads to a reenactment of his violent confrontation with the white prison guard, whom Jones attacks with an invisible shovel and then shoots with his real revolver. His last words for the victim—"I kills you, you white debil, if it's de last thing I evah does! Ghost or debil, I kill you agin!"[44]—mimic the Puritan belief that Satan resides in the chaos of the wilderness, and though Jones tries to deny the existence of the supernatural, his stress and anxiety reveal his deepest fears.

The scene that immediately follows contains Jones's longest religious speech, a prayer in which he details his crimes:

> Oh Lawd, Lawd! Oh Lawd, Lawd! (*Suddenly he throws himself on his knees and raises his clasped hands to the sky—in a voice of agonized pleading*) Lawd Jesus, heah my prayer! I'se a po' sinner, a po' sinner! I knows I done wrong, I knows it! When I cotches Jeff cheatin' wid loaded dice my anger overcomes me and I kills him dead! Lawd, I done wrong! When dat guard hits me wid de whip, my anger overcomes me, and I kills him dead. Lawd, I done wrong! And down heah whar dese fool bush niggers raises me up to the seat o' de mighty, I steals all I could grab. Lawd, I done wrong! I knows it! I'se sorry! Forgive me, Lawd! Forgive dis po' sinner! (*then beseeching terrifiedly*) And keep dem away, Lawd! Keep dem away from me! And stop dat drum soundin' in my ears! Dat begin to sound ha'nted, too. (*He gets to his feet, evidently slightly reassured by his prayer—with attempted confidence.*) De Lawd'll preserve me from dem ha'nts after dis.[45]

In this moment, O'Neill shifts the language and imagery of the play from the Puritan fear of ghosts and devils in the haunted woods to a retributive prayer offered by the lapsed Baptist Brutus Jones, who had bragged to Smithers in scene one that he had "[laid] my Jesus on the shelf for the time bein,'" in the interest of stealing from the natives.[46] Here he hopes to return to the Christian God by performing a confession that he thinks will rescue him from the hell of the wilderness, a kind of self-exorcism, which echoes the religious rhetoric of Mather, who believed the first step toward reintegration after captivity in the heathen wilderness to be humility.[47]

As scene five continues, his newfound confidence in divine protection from vengeful spirits proves unfounded, as the ghosts of an 1850s slave auction crowd around him. O'Neill's use of ghosts here, the first of a set from Jones's collective rather than personal past, further evokes Puritan images of wilderness and damnation, both in O'Neill's stage directions and in the language Jones uses in response to them. The ghosts of the slave auction include both Anglo Americans and Africans, and as the sale of slaves begins, an auctioneer includes Jones in the transaction, commodifying his body and its inherent strength. Much like the ghost scene between the native woman and Smithers in scene one, this action takes place silently, and when bidding begins on Jones, O'Neill writes, "*The planters raise their fingers, make their bids. They are apparently all eager to possess Jones.*"[48] The subtly used infinitive, "to possess," works on a historical level, reducing the tyrant Brutus Jones to a subservient slave, yet it also suggests the supernatural claim that a spirit can make on a mortal's body and mind. Indeed, all the ghosts Jones meets, from the "Little Formless Fears" in scene two to the Congo witch doctor, are eager to possess him. Jones's angry response to the white slavers—"And *you* sells me? And *you* buys me? I shows you I'se a free nigger, damn yo' souls!"[49]—ends with a religious curse that again connects the ghosts of these woods with the Puritan wilderness of New England.

The final ghost scene in *The Emperor Jones* amplifies the petitioning rhetoric begun by Jones's prayer in scene five. In scene seven, Jones must confront his collective history in the forms of a Congo witch doctor and an oversized crocodile, ghosts not of his personal crimes but of his ancestral, African past. While critics have explained these images in a variety of ways, little attention has been paid to Jones's terrified, prayer-like response to this encounter. Aside from a brief introductory speech where he claims to remember this site, Jones speaks only four lines in the whole scene. Three of those four lines resemble prayers, exclamations of terror coupled with hope of salvation from the Christian God. The third and final such line, "Lawd, save me! Lawd Jesus, hear my prayer,"[50] leads him to realize that he still has a silver bullet in his gun, which he fires at the crocodile. Though this apotropaic device ostensibly works, as the crocodile and witch doctor disappear, Jones dies shortly thereafter, shot offstage by Lem's men in the play's final scene. It would seem that Christian religion is no match for the magic, the "heathen tricks," as Jones called them, of the natives. This juxtaposition of prayer and violence, the last two acts performed by Jones, once again calls to mind the wilderness hell envisioned by earlier American writers. Though he repents of his sins and asks God for protection, his very last impulse is to return to aggression, an action that implies that Jones's Christian God will not or even cannot save his soul. Jones's passage through the forest of this unnamed island of the West Indies calls to mind other mythic journeys by more successful heroes. As Richard Slotkin describes it, European heroes often left home at a time of crisis to enter "into the realms of dreams, of death, of secret magic, of the unconscious."[51] Brutus Jones's failure to find salvation on his quest marks him as an antihero, one who traverses the terrors of the underworld, but fails to return with any sort of wisdom or help for himself or his people. He's been through the wilderness hell, but unlike Odysseus, Aeneas, or the narrator of Dante Aligheri's *Divine Comedy*, he doesn't return to the world of the living.

Susan Smith, in her article "*The Emperor Jones* and National Trauma," reads this play as distinctly American in its concerns and use of allegory, calling it, "a traumatic confrontation between the audience and the shocking scenes from America's racial history."[52] To her convincing argument, I would add that the play also has deep roots in the American literary tradition and the religious rhetoric of the Puritans. After all, the forest, as described by O'Neill, feels much more like the haunted woods of New England than the rainforests of places like Tobago or the West Indies, the terrain of Jones's unnamed island. While O'Neill's exploration of Jungian archetypes and expressionistic techniques establishes the play as a philosophical puzzle, his use of setting—a composite of America, Africa, and the West Indies—and spirits links it to traditional stories of the supernatural. From its initial image of the gliding native woman to the declaration of Jones's death in scene eight, both of which ironically take place in sunlight, O'Neill provokes that anticipatory terror described by Radcliffe, thus marking the play as an entertaining ghost story, one that hopes to cause "yer bloody 'air [to stand] on end," to use the words of the terrified Smithers.

Despite his deft handling of ghost characters in *The Emperor Jones*, O'Neill used this figure quite sparingly. Actual physically present specters, visible to characters and audience, appear only in one other play, the 1918 one-act, "Where the Cross Is Made." Even in *Gold*, the full-length revision of "Cross" written two years later, O'Neill struck the spirits from the stage, choosing instead to make them visible only to characters driven mad. This transition, from an objective to a subjective ghost, would give way to O'Neill's evolving exploration of the trope of haunting in subsequent decades. Brutus Jones's "ha'nts" would be replaced by the more subtle and symbolic ghosts of family and guilt, as in *Mourning Becomes Electra*. Ghosts haunt the playwright to the very end, as his posthumously published *Long Day's Journey into Night* attests. In his dedication to Carlotta he writes of his resolve "to face my dead at last and write this play—write it with deep pity and understanding and forgiveness for all the four haunted

Tyrones."[53] Like Brutus Jones, whose ghosts predict those of the playwright, O'Neill himself sought a way out of his haunted woods.[54]

Notes

1. Travis Bogard and Jackson R. Bryer, eds., *Selected Letters of Eugene O'Neill* (New Haven, CT: Yale University Press, 1988), 327.

2. Carme Manuel, "A Ghost in the Expressionist Jungle of O'Neill's *The Emperor Jones*," *African American Review* 39, no. 1–2 (2005): 67–85. See also Normand Berlin, *Eugene O'Neill* (New York: Grove, 1982), 56; Virginia Floyd, *The Plays of Eugene O'Neill* (New York: Ungar, 1985), 202; and Horst Frenz, *Eugene O'Neill* (New York: Ungar, 1971), 32–33.

3. C. W. E. Bigsby, *A Critical Introduction to Twentieth-Century American Drama, Volume 1: 1900–1940* (Cambridge: Cambridge University Press, 1982), 56–57. See also Susan H. Smith, "*The Emperor Jones* and National Trauma," *Modern Drama* 52, no. 1 (2009): 57–72; and Leonard Chabrowe, *Ritual and Pathos—The Theater of Eugene O'Neill* (Lewisburg, PA: Bucknell University Press, 1976), 105.

4. Smith, "*Emperor Jones* and National Trauma" 57–72; Manuel, "Ghost" 67–85; and Shannon Steen, "Melancholy Bodies: Racial Subjectivity and Whiteness in O'Neill's 'Emperor Jones,'" *Theatre Journal* 52, no. 3 (2000): 339–59.

5. Manuel, "Ghost," 68–70.

6. Noorbakhsh Hooti and Nasser Maleki, "Terror and Ambivalence of the Human Soul in O'Neill's *The Emperor Jones*, and *The Hairy Ape*," *Global Journal of the Humanities* 7, no. 1–2 (2008): 9–18, accessed August 12, 2011, http://www.globaljournalseries.com/index/index .php/gjh/article/viewfile/188/pdf.

7. Ann Radcliffe, "On the Supernatural in Poetry," in *Gothic Readings: The First Wave 1764–1840*, ed. Rictor Norton (London: Leicester University Press, 2000), 315.

8. Berlin, *Eugene O'Neill*, 56.

9. David Edgar, *How Plays Work* (London: Nick Hern Books, 2009), 188.

10. Anna Andes, "Haunted by Ghosts of Other Mother's Sons: Surrogation and Eugenics in Angela Gimke's *Rachel* and Georgina Douglas Jonson's *Safe*" (paper presented at the Theatre and Ghosts Conference, York, England, July 2, 2011).

11. Eugene O'Neill, *The Emperor Jones*, in *Complete Plays 1913–1920*, ed. Travis Bogard (New York: Library of America, 1988), 1031.

12. Ibid.

13. Ibid.

14. Ibid., 1032.

15. Ibid.

16. Ibid., 1033.
17. Egil Tornqvist, *Drama of Souls: Studies in O'Neill's Super-naturalistic Techniques* (New Haven, CT: Yale University Press, 1969), 233.
18. Ibid.
19. O'Neill, *Emperor Jones*, 1036, 1042.
20. Ibid., 1033.
21. Manuel, "Ghost," 74.
22. O'Neill, *Emperor Jones*, 1034.
23. Ibid.
24. Ibid., 1038.
25. D. Felton, *Haunted Greece and Rome: Ghost Stories from Classical Antiquity* (Austin: University of Texas Press, 1999), 8.
26. O'Neill, *Emperor Jones*, 1040.
27. Ibid., 1041.
28. Ibid., 1041–42.
29. Ibid., 1042–43.
30. Felton, *Haunted Greece*, 50.
31. Ibid., 42.
32. Frenz, *Eugene O'Neill*, 30.
33. O'Neill, *Emperor Jones*, 1044.
34. Edgar Allan Poe, Tam Mossman, ed., *The Unabridged Edgar Allan Poe* (Philadelphia: Running Press, 1983), 532–38, 739–44.
35. Richard Slotkin, *Regeneration through Violence: The Mythology of the American Frontier, 1600–1860* (Middletown, CT: Wesleyan University Press, 1973), 472–77, 538–50.
36. Neal Salisbury, ed., *The Sovereignty and Goodness of God, Together with the Faithfulness of His Promises Displayed, Being a Narrative of the Captivity and Restoration of Mrs. Mary Rowlandson and Related Documents* (Boston: Bedford-St. Martin's, 1997), 5.
37. Ibid., 80, 109.
38. Slotkin, *Regeneration*, 132–33.
39. Floyd, *Plays*, 273–75.
40. O'Neill, *Emperor Jones*, 1044.
41. Ibid., 1035, 1049, 1034.
42. Ibid., 1042.
43. Ibid., 1049.
44. Ibid., 1051.
45. Ibid., 1052.
46. Ibid., 1042.
47. Slotkin, *Regeneration*, 113.
48. O'Neill, *Emperor Jones*, 1053.
49. Ibid., 1054.
50. O'Neill, *Emperor Jones*, 1059.
51. Slotkin, *Regeneration*, 28.
52. "*The Emperor Jones* and National Trauma," 58.

53. Eugene O'Neill, *Long Day's Journey into Night* (New Haven, CT: Yale University Press, 1956), 7.

54. Special thanks are due to Ann Beebe, friend and colleague at UT Tyler, and Spencer Smith, friend and former student. Conversations with them were of great help in developing these ideas. Thanks also go to the family of George F. Hamm, whose endowment helped fund research for this article.

WORKS CITED

Andes, Anna. "Haunted by Ghosts of Other Mother's Sons: Surrogation and Eugenics in Angela Gimke's *Rachel* and Georgina Douglas Jonson's *Safe*." Theatre and Ghosts Conference.University of York, York. 2 July 2011. Lecture.

Berlin, Normand. *Eugene O'Neill*. New York: Grove, 1982. Print.

Bigsby, C. W. E. *A Critical Introduction to Twentieth-Century American Drama, Volume 1: 1900–1940*. Cambridge: Cambridge UP, 1982. Print.

Bogard, Travis, and Jackson R. Bryer, eds. *Selected Letters of Eugene O'Neill*. New Haven: Yale UP, 1988. Print.

Chabrowe, Leonard. *Ritual and Pathos—The Theater of Eugene O'Neill*. Lewisburg: Bucknell UP, 1976. Print.

Edgar, David. *How Plays Work*. London: Hern, 2009. Print.

Felton, D. *Haunted Greece and Rome: Ghost Stories from Classical Antiquity*. Austin: U of Texas P, 1999. Print.

Floyd, Virginia. *The Plays of Eugene O'Neill: A New Assessment*. New York: Ungar, 1985. Print.

Frenz, Horst. *Eugene O'Neill*. New York: Ungar, 1971. Print.

Hooti, Noorbakhsh, and Nasser Maleki. "Terror and Ambivalence of the Human Soul in O'Neill's *The Emperor Jones*, and *The Hairy Ape*." *Global Journal of the Humanities* 7.1–2 (2008): 9–18. Web. 12 Aug. 2011. http://www.globaljournalseries.com/index/index.php/gjh/article/viewfile/188/pdf.

Manuel, Carme. "A Ghost in the Expressionist Jungle of O'Neill's *The Emperor Jones*." *African American Review* 39.1–2 (2005): 67–85.

O'Neill, Eugene. *The Emperor Jones. Complete Plays 1913–1920*. Ed. Travis Bogard. New York: Library of America, 1988. 1029–61. Print.

———. *Long Day's Journey into Night*. New Haven: Yale UP, 1956.

Poe, Edgar Allan. *The Unabridged Edgar Allan Poe*. Ed. Tam Mossman. Philadelphia: Running, 1983. Print.

Radcliffe, Ann. "On the Supernatural in Poetry." *Gothic Readings: The First Wave 1764–1840*. Ed. Rictor Norton. London: Leicester UP, 2000. 311–16. Print.

Salisbury, Neal, ed. *The Sovereignty and Goodness of God, Together with the Faithfulness of His Promises Displayed, Being a Narrative of the Captivity and Restoration of Mrs. Mary Rowlandson and Related Documents*. Boston: Bedford, 1997. Print.

Slotkin, Richard. *Regeneration through Violence: The Mythology of the American Frontier, 1600–1860*. Middletown: Wesleyan UP, 1973. Print.

Smith, Susan H. "*The Emperor Jones* and National Trauma." *Modern Drama* 52.1 (2009): 57–72. Print.

Steen, Shannon, "Melancholy Bodies: Racial Subjectivity and Whiteness in O'Neill's 'Emperor Jones.'" *Theatre Journal* 52.3 (2000): 339–59. Print.

Tornqvist, Egil. *A Drama of Souls: Studies in O'Neill's Super-naturalistic Techniques*. New Haven: Yale UP, 1969. Print.

CHAPTER 9

NEITHER FALLEN ANGEL
NOR RISEN APE

DESENTIMENTALIZING ROBERT SMITH

Thomas F. Connolly

In 1931, the noted German drama critic Julius Bab singled out *The Hairy Ape* as Eugene O'Neill's "most important work." He asserts, "*The Hairy Ape* is the tragedy of the proletariat, seized at the point where it is still tragic—that is to say, before politics enters in."[1] I would amplify Bab's point and assert that the play is not merely social commentary. Yank is not just an exploited worker. Conventional analysis insists that even as the play's staging may be expressionistic, its philosophy is deterministic: Yank is a figure standing for all humanity. Even if he does not understand the universe—or even his part in it—nevertheless, Yank wants to dominate his surroundings. Thus it is interesting that Mildred is able to shatter Yank's confidence effortlessly. Once Yank's own self-confidence is destroyed, once his own image of himself is broken, he is reduced to wandering as an outcast. He becomes freakish—genuinely alien. Considering Yank's successively disastrous encounters, the play can be seen as a transgendered version of the Pygmalion myth with Mildred as Pygmalion and Yank as Galatea. Regarding this point, the play's subtitle, *A Comedy of Ancient and Modern Life*, has attracted too little attention. Thus the concluding scene in which Yank is crushed by the gorilla should be taken not as sad or even pathetic but as the inevitable conclusion to the life of someone who has displaced himself. Traditional criticism of the play offers little more than "biographies" of Robert Smith, the stokehole's "Yank." Such critics are loath to accept Yank as a theatrical character and regard him as a *person* rather than as part of a play. This is, of course, part of the larger problem of the biographical obsession inherent in almost all O'Neill criticism and American drama in particular.[2] It seems all the more limiting to look at Yank as a person rather than as a comic figure, especially as some commentators regard *The Hairy Ape* as only a fitfully expressionistic American play, and almost no one attends to the play's subtitle. Bab's comment about the "tragedy of the proletariat" allows us to cease fixating on Yank as a person; one ought to consider his theatrical function, for example, to consider him as a representation of O'Neill's departure from the pictorial realism of the theatre of his father. Yank's departure from the sociopolitical realities of the stokehole and the play's Manhattan scenes may be viewed as an enactment of O'Neill's modernist aesthetic, but we must also keep in mind that O'Neill is never an "either/or" playwright. Even as he uses expressionism, he allows for melodramatic intensity as well. This is not a flaw; it is the conscious choice of an artist using all the resources available to him. Note that Yank is a brutal and threatening character initially, but he loses all this fearsomeness by the play's final scene. O'Neill does not haphazardly characterize Yank in this way; the playwright places Yank within the convention of the theatrical ape. Let us review some aspects of this convention.

The most important portrayal of the ape (man), before Tarzan,[3] occurs in Gabriel Rochefort's *Jocko; oú, Le singe du Brésil*, a play that was a transatlantic sensation and made Charles-François Mazurier, the original "Jocko," the toast of two continents. Based on an 1824 novel by Charles de Pougens, Rochefort's play is a melodrama about an ape, Jocko, who is captured by a Portuguese traveler in Brazil. Disaster strikes on the voyage back to Europe, and Jocko dies rescuing his captor's child from a shipwreck. Mazurier's performance was so wrenching that audiences demanded the ape live, and the play was subsequently revised to enable the ape's survival. *Jocko* was presented in various adaptations from 1825 through the end of the century.[4] After O'Neill's play, in 1925 a new "Jocko" play, *The Monkey Talks*, was a success in Europe and New York. A film version was made in 1927, but it bears no relation to the original.

In the United States, Jocko the kindhearted ape found his way into all sorts of entertainments, thus embedding the convention of the tenderhearted ape in the popular consciousness. Such stage apes were quite a different matter from living apes on exhibit. The outstanding twentieth-century example and the most (in)famous simian performer of all is "Gargantua the Great," billed as "the largest and fiercest gorilla ever brought before the eyes of civilized man."[5] This gorilla, whose rather tortured life could make a melodrama in its own right, saved the Ringling circus from bankruptcy and was its star attraction from 1937 to 1949. Yet even Ringling attempted to soften the image of "the world's most terrifying living creature"[6] in 1941 through the publicity stunt of presenting a mate to him who was offered to the public as "Mrs. Gargantua." The couple was soon used in advertisements for war bonds. Not unlike other such celebrity unions, the gorillas were indifferent to each other and maintained separate sleeping quarters. Ringling's failed hoking-up of a living ape contrasts with the fate of cinema's greatest ape: King Kong. Who can forget actor Robert Armstrong's epitaph for Kong: "It wasn't the airplanes. It was beauty killed the beast."[7] Thus we have the perfect equation for a sentimental melodrama. The most recent revival of the convention is the *Planet of the Apes* franchise. Interestingly enough, another French novel—*La Planète des singes* by Pierre Boulle (1963)—is the source. So far, there have been seven films, multiple comic books, a television series, and an animated series. In gaping at these uncaged, sentimentalized simians, audiences continue to give more tenderness to these theatricalized apes than God does.[8]

Returning to O'Neill's creation, *The Hairy Ape* demonstrates greater theatrical sophistication because O'Neill does not stoop to make Yank likeable. Yank never fully loses his brutishness (as noted, his fearsomeness completely diminishes by play's end, but he remains a brute). Even as he enters the gorilla's cage at the finale, he is assertive, if somehow pathetic. The aspects of animal behavior on stage are more important when considered from the perspective of the apeman in performance rather than as some sort of "Freudian" regression drama. It is the natural impulse of almost any audience member to have sympathy for a dumb creature. Significantly though, Yank talks just enough to lose that sympathy, yet in his attempt to communicate with his "lodge brother," the gorilla almost re-creates the drama and makes it into a different play, culminating when O'Neill's stage directions—a perfect example of Roman Ingarden's "secondary language"—imply that Yank "belongs."[9] In the previous scene, though, at the Industrial Workers of the World hall, Yank has indicted himself for the crime of being born, and mocks the policeman who does not even take Yank seriously enough to arrest him. Though the policeman does casually damn him by telling Yank to "go to hell" when the policeman responds "with a grin, indifferently" to Yank's plea of "Where do I go from here?"[10] Recall, though, that no one ever takes Yank's words seriously unless they carry the threat of violence.

In contrast to considering the play's absolute theatricality, traditional criticism sees the play primarily as a social text. Travis Bogard summarizes this view of the play's "thesis": "As the theatrical myth has it, materialistic America distorts and deforms the individual's spirit, destroying man's creative potential by divorcing him from those qualities of humanity which give him dignity and the sense of manhood. The materialistic system is his enemy and the core conflict of the fable is his battle with the exponents of that system."[11]

This thesis ignores the scene in which Yank is thrown out of the IWW hall and cavalierly dismissed by a passing policeman as a drunk not worth dragging to the station. Recall Bab's insight that the play's proletarian tragedy lies with its placement "before politics enters in."[12] It is important to note that Bab is not a Marxist, and *The Hairy Ape*'s unspecified radicalism was the sort of "bourgeois" attitudinizing that American Marxists particularly despised.[13] The play's politics are not even anarchist, since the IWW refuses to take Yank seriously and rejects his offer to take violent action.

In his explicitly political plays, O'Neill consistently calls for freedom from the industrialized model of enlightenment.[14] O'Neill is almost a pastoral radical, decidedly non-Marxist, and indeed antidoctrinaire (if he must be categorized, "pacifist anarchist" comes closest) in his depiction of the class struggle. To link, as Bogard's argument does, O'Neill with Elmer Rice and Arthur Miller is to elide the theatricality of O'Neill's play. To do so is to reduce it to another sort of a dramatic equation (Yank equals oppressed worker and nothing more). Bogard's critique is even reluctant to grant the play its expressionism, arguing that "the only genuinely non-naturalistic element in the early scenes is the pose which Yank assumes . . . when he sits in the attitude of Rodin's 'The Thinker.'"[15] Bogard, like almost all of O'Neill's critics, is holding a brief for the final autobiographical plays. Of the play's first four scenes, he avers, "Although scenic distortion in the expressionistic manner is possible, it is never essential."[16] Such commentary sees O'Neill's body of work as a dramaturgical Road to Damascus. O'Neill's true dramatic mission is to be a realistic writer of conversation plays steeped in bourgeois psychology, rendered unique via O'Neill's aesthetic of autobiography. All past plays are prologue to *Long Day's Journey into Night*. Without denying any of that play's greatness, nevertheless—save for the final, putatively autobiographical plays—O'Neill has scant interest in conversation plays. *The Hairy Ape*, in particular, given its precise subtitle (rare for O'Neill), coupled with Yank's confession that his capital crime was that he was "born," and combined with O'Neill's upending the conventional sentimentality of the ape-on-stage, absolutely removes the play from the sociological realm. Erika Rundle has exhaustively reviewed the simian ramifications of the play and states that *The Hairy Ape* is a "new genre." She discusses the serious ape on stage primarily in a Darwinian and "imperialist" context.[17] However, it can be argued that it is not the first play on the American stage with an ape-man to be taken seriously. The previously mentioned *Jocko*, in its English translation, was as great a hit in the United States as it was in Europe. What is more, Mazurier's American counterpart, the great Gabriel Ravel, caused such a sensation that Jocko became fodder for other popular entertainments.[18] Such a transmutation reveals how strongly audiences reacted to Jocko. Satire of contemporary melodramas was a staple of minstrel performance, for instance—Dumas *fils' La dame aux Camelias* being a perennial target. Of course, the extant images of performances of Jocko, whether ostensibly documentary in intent or as idealized illustrations,[19] cannot completely communicate to us the contemporary impact of the characterization of Jocko. We can, however, extrapolate that any mockery of the ape-man existed in proportion to how seriously the satirical object was taken by its audiences in its original form.

Postcolonial commentary has casually placed Jocko with later performers such as Krao the Laotian girl, who was billed as a member of the "Krao-Moneik tribe of monkey-men" as a means for explicating the relationship between the primates.[20] "Jocko" in the original play is a species of noble savage. Later versions reduce the Jocko figure to grinning and gibbering, thus degrading the ape-man and making empathy impossible.[21] Nevertheless, adaptations of "Jocko" persisted and were performed throughout the century, most often, though, in a pantomime version that was clearly in the spectacular more than the pathetic melodramatic mode. The nod that postcolonial commentary has given to on-stage ape-men makes it slightly interesting that the British stoker, Long, becomes the American Yank's mentor in radical agitation. Such discourse grows more complex when detailing the iterations of ape-in-the-wild versus ape-in-the-city.[22] Wildness is important in O'Neill's play as well; so long as Yank may threaten to "go ape," he dominates, but the moment he loses that savagery, the proud predator becomes confused prey. Witness the way that O'Neill dramatizes Yank's "descent," which unfolds so rapidly after his encounter with Mildred.

What is Yank trying to "t'ink" about after Mildred humiliates him? O'Neill makes no attempt to articulate Yank's intellectual aspirations, but in something that may be effectively reconsidered from a postcolonial perspective, O'Neill establishes a Museum of Natural History performance gallery in his stage directions.[23] Yank's stokehole comrades reduce him to a gazed-upon object, spoken about as though he were on exhibition. Keeping this in mind, one would again do well to question those who doubt the play's expressionism. Commentary such as this, which challenges O'Neill's right to categorize his own play, is surprising, since it comes from traditional O'Neill scholars who are usually willing to accept the playwright's authority as absolute and lack interest in any discourse prefixed by "post" or "meta." One wonders why there is such discontent with O'Neill's expressionism.

In *The Hairy Ape*, the question of belonging is a crucial one; indeed, it is the central question of the play. Since even this "theme" is presented in an expansively theatrical way, why would one resist the notion that the play is overtly symbolic and expressionistic, relying on imposing and obvious effects of language and stage devices to underscore its points? Contrasting with this unease is such critics' readiness to discuss Yank's "alienation," a crucial psychological aspect of expressionism. The play's theatricality is at once as local as its Manhattan milieu and as universal as the "thinker's" pose that Yank assumes. This brings us to the question of Yank himself: what is the significance of his name or, for that matter, of the play's name? Why are things in this drama at once specific and generalized? These questions augment the notion that *The Hairy Ape* relies not only on a sentimental convention to enable certain audience members to view Yank as a figure standing for all humanity. O'Neill accomplishes this through his variation of the theatrical convention of the sympathetic ape-man. O'Neill is stern enough to insist on Yank's death, even if the stage directions give him the possibility of transcendence. We want to feel sorry for Yank, as we do for all caged animals, and his inarticulate longings are generalized enough so that almost anyone can feel vicarious imprisonment. Yank is "evolved" just enough. The play does not draw primarily on psychology or philosophy, and I would argue this is why it has held the stage and has not dated in the way that *Strange Interlude* or *The Great God Brown* have. It is more important that Yank is a twentieth-century species of the theatricalized ape-man. The subtitle of the play, *A Comedy of Ancient and Modern Life*, is fascinating. As Bogard emphasizes, O'Neill was fond of Keats's line "Now more than ever does it seem rich to die," and he also favors Heinrich Heine's "Best of all, never to have been born."[24] Thus it is not surprising that given the author's "rich" morbidity, the concluding scene in which Yank is crushed is to be taken not as sad or even pathetic but as the inevitable, even natural, conclusion to the life of someone who has displaced himself.

To counter Bogard's sociopolitical "fable," one would do better to consider the play as a reversal and negation of the Pygmalion myth.

Nevertheless, it is neither beauty nor love that inspires here, nor anything aesthetic, but rather ugliness, labor, and social consciousness, all of which are ultimately transcended for something "perhaps" cosmic.[25] Thus we have a variation on O'Neill's later "hopeless hope" because "perhaps the hairy ape at last belongs."[26] And rather than Bogard's argument that the play is a brief for Willy Loman, it is Stanley Kowalski who resonates—a point briefly noted by Bert Cardullo in 2007, but one that he does not follow up on.[27] For a moment, before Yank enters the gorilla's cage, O'Neill would seem to have the brutes advance; Yank indeed prefigures Stanley. One hesitates to identify Mildred with Blanche, though both a film scenario O'Neill wrote and the screenplay for the 1944 film offer a predatorily libidinous Mildred. In O'Neill's play, Mildred is the enactment of attenuation, yet even her affected lassitude has tangible results: Yank is driven from the stokehole and his identity destroyed. Mildred is already damned when she visits the stokers' hell. An embodiment of *nostalgie de la boue*, Mildred's complicity with primitivism is something that conventional analysts of the play are most comfortable with. It is ironic, though, that Yank's alleged inarticulateness creates an idiom that encapsulates the human quest for relevance in the universe and is motivated by almost pure metaphor. Conversely, Mildred, whom we assume to be educated and who is laboriously articulate, is, in fact, merely carnal. Indeed, the on-screen Mildred neither shrinks from Yank's advances nor seducing her best friend's beau. Robert D. Andrews and Decla Dunning were solid professional screenwriters, and one wonders what they thought as they added plot and character details to the original, but one must also recall that Mildred's libido was part of O'Neill's screen treatment. O'Neill's scenario may have enabled their license.

The gorilla that kills Yank is an analogue for Yank in the stokehole. One might go so far as to argue that Yank takes on Mildred's role as the intruder or, for that matter, that the escaped gorilla conjures Yeats's "rough beast slouching toward Bethlehem."[28] One might also recall the denatured inhabitants of T. S. Eliot's *The Waste Land*. The gorilla has spent too much time caged to recognize Yank's attempted kinship; Yank lacks any rootedness as he previously saw himself as steel, part of the ship's machinery. "Robert Smith" is "Yank's" full name— its blandness almost an all-American mockery of the ethnic/national types who populate the stokehole. (Even "ethnic" alcoholic beverages play into this parody of patriotism.) Perhaps this is the first seriously comic routine of the play: nationalism is the opium of the people. In his argument, Cardullo stretches Smith's nickname to the point where the essay posits Yank as an ideal futurist hero because he is probably a World War I veteran—rather a wishful reading. If one must adhere to the typical approach to American drama and glean each scene of a play for biographical data, then Yank gives us plenty of autobiography in the play. Surely he would have mentioned military service, but ultimately, this sort of discussion smacks of drama criticism à la Lee Strasberg: figuring out the character's "life story" rather than looking at what he or she does on stage.[29] Moreover, to do so imposes the sort of naturalistic frame on the play that O'Neill rejects. To regard the play as the final chapter of Robert Smith's biography slathers a layer of sentimentality upon the play. After all, reading plays as biographies or, worse, extrapolating dramatic characters' "biographies" sentimentalizes because it anthropomorphizes what are theatrical figures.[30] It is not unlike prettifying the ugliness of the caged reality of two formerly free gorillas by naming them "Mr. and Mrs. Gargantua." Finally, if The Hairy Ape is recast as "the life and hard times of Robert Smith, "it takes away from the action of the play and makes it impossible to consider it as a comedy. The final words of the play are the key to its comedy: Yank at last belongs. He leaves mundane alienation behind and may just be on his way to oneness with the universe. This is what comedy does—it shows how the individual functions in a community. O'Neill is not limiting Yank to an earthly community. While Margaret Ranald asserts that O'Neill's non-autobiographical naturalistic works deserve more attention, she also argues that The Hairy Ape is essentially realistic. She argues that the characters are "symbolic rather than realistic." Thus discussions such as Bogard's, Cardullo's, and even Ranald's[31] cannot get beyond the play as sociology; such arguments fail to consider that O'Neill does not care about life as it is lived—that is not what he dramatizes here or in most of his other plays. To the contrary, he stridently and relentlessly wrote against any aspect of that sort of dramaturgy.

Thus O'Neill has Yank transcend death by a gorilla's crushing embrace. The irony is that when Yank asks the gorilla to shake and respond with the *secret grip of our order*, he condemns himself to death but not to oblivion. O'Neill's stage directions imply otherwise, yet what does it mean that he "belongs"? To what or to whom does he belong? It is a question as unanswerable as what Yank was trying to "t'ink" about earlier in the play. As to ancient and modern life, again there is almost no commentary on the "ancient" part of the subtitle. Witness Cardullo's explication of the play's relationship to futurism and Bogard's enumerating its precise expressionistic elements.

Another daunting issue is the anomaly of the play's title given the comparative hairlessness of the actors who have played Yank. Diana

Snigurowicz goes over the performance and social aspects, not to mention the scientific aspects, of Darwinism as a means of identifying humanity.[32] The outstanding characteristic of "the monkey" is hairiness. She discusses the "Jocko" phenomenon and also offers a detailed discussion of "Krao," the girl from the "monkey tribe." The microcephalic, hirsute Julia Pastrana and Mme. Delait, an early *femme à barbe*, are nineteenth-century cultural artifacts of the delineation of race and species identification via performance. The fascination such performers inspired perhaps solidified the theatrical craze that Mazurier had started. Conversely, the "anthropological" curiosity Krao, Pastrana, Delait, and later JoJo, the Dog-Faced Boy, stimulated lacked the intensity that "Jocko," an ape portrayed by a man, caused. So what we ought to consider is that Yank is part of a theatrical tradition that is at once sentimental but also a useful signifier in itself, for as many have allowed, the observance of the ape is the mirror of the soul. We judge ourselves by the way that the apes disport themselves. In the 1820s, Mazurier's performance was extraordinary because of the way he leapt from the stage into the audience. The French dancer's agitated and affecting performance was remarked on by William Darwin Fox[33] to none other than his cousin, Charles Darwin, who was himself aware of Jocko's impact. Recently it has even been argued that the vogue for performances with "monkey-men" set the stage for the public reaction to Darwin's theory.[34] Yank is disturbing because he threatens to leave the stokehole and bring his proletarian fury to Fifth Avenue. This is what gets him arrested. But I must insist that it is not the crude antibourgeois reification that matters here. What we are seeing is a twentieth-century nightmare vision of the lovable and ultimately catastrophic *Jocko le singe* who was kind and helpful, saving the life of a child only to be shot by an ignorant onlooker who mistook the ape's lifesaving for an attack. Yank, because he is only able to wrestle with his own demons and not able to excise anything beyond them is crushed by the real force of brute nature. In a real sense, Yank is only a pseudoape, easily controlled and destroyed. Another aspect that has been neglected is that Yank stops his pursuit of Mildred as soon as he learns that her father is the president of the steel trust. In jail, he resolves to destroy him and thereby completely stop the manufacture of steel. His aim is to destroy steel itself, which would, in his view, destroy everything. This is a cogent metaphor for loosing anarchy, but rather than bringing down capitalism, he only releases a "real" gorilla.

The play has been identified with Dante's *Inferno*, yet it is better to consider that there is more of Marlowe's *Doctor Faustus* here. From the first sight of Yank, he is in hell (from the audience's perspective), and from the moment he encounters Mildred, Yank is certainly in hell, and one might even link his questing Manhattan scenes with a Faustian journey of infernal fulfillment. It is not unusual to assume that Yank belongs to something primordial at play's end. But instead of an affirmation, it is O'Neill's final, bitter joke. The idea that the "secret order" has a "handshake" and is somehow a high sign of eternity is a joke that is purposefully not funny. This also allows us to consider the rhetorical for a moment, if we look not only at the Darwinian trope of the ape—the melodramatic image of *Jocko le singe*—but at the revered Ernst Robert Curtius, who may remind us of "the ape as metaphor," which goes back to the foundations of Western discourse and the *mos sidonianus* as a means of mimesis. This is another "ancient" aspect of the play. Curtius discusses the simian trope as one of the earliest indices of literary form.[35] As far as mimesis goes, there is much more than "monkey see, monkey do" afoot here, of course. The use of the metaphor allows O'Neill to create a character who is *more* human. Yank the "hairy ape" calls attention to the humanity of Bob Smith the stoker. Paulo Medeiros discusses the earliest scientific "look at apes" as a means of getting to our origins.[36] Of course, we now blink at the positivism of nineteenth-century interspecies genealogy and its relation to cultural Darwinism. Yank, though, has little interest in where he came from; he is, for most of the play, pragmatic, only interested in where he *is*. It is only at the conclusion, and even then only because he must, that he considers something more. But again, we must not forget that Yank is not a man; he is a function of O'Neill's play, and the author gives the possibility of a profound conclusion for Yank. In an essay comparing Yank to Caliban, Bernard Baum argues that Yank "displays the attributes of poet, philosopher and prophet" and is a "trenchant social critic" who baffles a policeman.[37] As mentioned, at the finale, Yank "must" consider something more, and we may see O'Neill's depiction of Yank as Rodin's *Thinker* as foreshadowing (irrespective of the scholarly commentary that explains Rodin's original intention placing the figure the gates of hell). It has become a given that Yank is inarticulate and strange, fearsome and brutal, and that the play is "experimental." As we have seen, almost all conventional criticism takes the play as some sort of Darwinian parable with at best a soupçon of O'Neillian despair tossed in at the finale. The rich theatrical and rhetorical resonances, which predate the "d/evolutionary" overlay critics have relished since the play's first performance, have barely been attended to. Returning to Bab's comment that the play is tragic because it is about a proletarian who is not political enables us to get through these layers of conventional commentary. Of course, Bab is drawing on a dramatic tradition that can summon Friedrich Hebbel's *Maria Magdalena*, usually considered the first working-class tragedy. Thus he is readily conversant in the theatrical discourse O'Neill presents. The American dramatic equivalent would be something like *Bertha, the Sewing Machine Girl*. I do not make the comparison frivolously. Almost all serious American plays are only interested in rendering sociopolitical issues in their attempts at gravitas. Playwrights such as Thornton Wilder or William Saroyan are the exception. Even Edward Albee, whom most commentators would consider otherwise, has insisted that he is primarily a political playwright.[38]

It is more valuable to look at Yank as a rhetorical/theatrical creation than as a fully fleshed-out human being because when one analyzes Yank in psychological-biographical terms, the gaps in our knowledge of Yank's life force us to venture offstage and speculate based on preconceived notions—what I earlier called "wishful" criticism. If, on the contrary, one considers only what Yank says and does in the play, we find a denser, much richer play than the sort of sociopolitical would-be expressionist play that it has been traditionally taken to be. This does not mean that one ought to consider Yank as a bloodless creation in a bell jar of performed rhetoric. No, he bangs on that glass until it breaks, hence the frequency of productions. Another reason to discount the quibbling over what "style" the play was written in is that it has not significantly dated, and directors through the twentieth and twenty-first centuries continue to challenge audiences with it. Indeed, it is all the more interesting that this example of high modernist drama lends itself to postmodernist analysis. One might even pick up on the Hegelian truth discovered through error that prepares a path to Jacques Lacan and Slavoj Žižek in this way. As Žižek has it, through Lacan, truth arises from misrecognition. Moreover, the fundamental human aspirations that Yank enacts perhaps come from what we see as a Lacanian construct, the unconscious being structured as language. Yank's desire to belong is something that anyone can identify with, but this is too essentialist for the twenty-first century. Yank is usually considered as a species of "dumb beast." On the other hand, consider that Yank is the thing itself; as we watch, his struggle is fascinating because he only *seems* to be a dumb creature, as has been noted by some commentators.[39] Žižek meditates on Leninism, brutality, and speciesism in "Of Apes and Men." Žižek's reading of the dictatorship of the proletariat and Peter Singer's valuation of ape versus human enables further rumination on the structure of language.

This allows Yank's inarticulation to be taken seriously. We must accept everything he does; we must watch the actor perform the role of Yank, not merely "listen" to his barbaric yawps. When we consider the totality of performance, we may use Žižek as a means of accepting that Yank makes himself his own object. (What is more, the concern that Žižek invites by directing us to what is "offstage" allows a nod to the on-screen libido of Susan Heyward's Mildred.) In this case, considering the truth revealed through error, Yank is not a sentimental thing itself but the brutal emergence of consciousness. By this I do not intend to make a special plea for Yank's theatrical/rhetorical presence; he is killed and his death serves comic rather than tragic ends. More important, this is not to be taken as inscribing any sort of ascendancy to Yank or Mildred. There is nothing of the Garden, Adam, or Eve in this play. To impute a tragically postlapsarian elevation of consciousness to the primitivism present in the play is sentimentality with a divine face (not to mention a rejection of O'Neill's subtitle).[40]

To consider the theatrical and rhetorical construction of Yank is to deepen our understanding of the play and provide insight into why it is one of the most frequently staged of O'Neill's earlier plays. Locating Yank in the ape-man performance tradition is only problematic if one wishes to sentimentalize Yank, which I fear is what happens when he is considered a pathetic brute. If we feel sorry for Yank rather than thinking about him—if indeed we fail to allow for the *Verfremdungseffekt* that was clearly at play in Peter Stein's acclaimed 1987 production and what I would argue Stein found in the text. It is useful to recall that prior to Brecht's "V-effekt" is Viktor Shklovsky's formalist notion from 1917 (before he embraced Marxism) of *ostranenie*. O'Neill was, of course, no Marxist, but it is important to distance the play from Marxism, so a "formalist" nod here allows us to situate the play as a modernist work, but by insisting on its theatricality rather than literary/socio/political "meanings," it can also comfortably be postmodern—hence the play's density.

It is *as though* Yank were in a monkey suit. He is compared to a hairy ape—though Mildred never calls him that—and the play is titled the same, but in none of the famous original production photographs does Louis Wolheim look at all hirsute. And he was one of the trio of performers that O'Neill felt had come closest to embodying his own vision. The actor was a cultivated man, a Cornell graduate (in the class of 1906, two years behind George Jean Nathan) who spoke several languages and was a mathematics professor at Cornell before becoming an actor at the urging of his friends the Barrymore brothers. So his acclaimed performance is all the more interesting and in keeping with the argument that Yank should be regarded as an intellectual rather than emotional or sensibilitized creature. If he is not considered this way, he may be reduced to a sentimental hero in a failed tragedy of all-too-human aspiration.

Finally, the recognition that Yank is performing the role of the "ape-man" enables us to remark on what the total performance of the role of Bob Smith achieves: transcendence from categorical or otherwise limiting planes of existence that reduce "Yank" to a failed worker, revolutionary, or human being. Instead he leaves the fleeting contemporary elements of the play, its mise-en-scène, and spirits away into something beyond exhibition, performance, or ancient or modern life.

NOTES

1. Julius Bab, "America's Foremost Playwright," in *O'Neill and His Plays: Four Decades of Criticism*, ed. Oscar Cargill, N. Bryllion Fagin, and William J. Fisher (New York: New York University Press, 1961), 350.

2. Thomas F. Connolly, *Genus Envy: Nationalities, Identities and the Performing Body of Work* (Amherst, NY: Cambria, 2010), 19–39.

3. Erika Rundle, "The Hairy Ape's Humanist Hell: Theatricality and Evolution in O'Neill's 'Comedy of Ancient and Modern Life,'" *Eugene O'Neill Review* 30 (2008): 48–144. This article thoroughly discusses Tarzan's permutations, as well as many other intellectual and aesthetic issues.

4. Gabriel Rochefort, *Jocko; ou, Le singe du Brésil.* (Paris: Chez Quoy Libraire, 1825), 22 August 2011 http://books.google.com/books?id=NAFBAAAAYAAJ&pg=PA14&dq=jocko+le+singe+de+bresil&hl=en&ei=LV3lTpeYCdCy0AHPvrWVCQ&sa=X&oi=book_result&ct=result&resnum=1&ved=0CC8Q6AEwADgK#v=onepage&q=jocko%20le%20singe%20de%20bresil&f=false.

5. Bernard Baum, "*Tempest* and *Hairy Ape*: The Literary Incarnation of Mythos," *Modern Language Quarterly* 14 (1953): 258–73.

6. George Brinton Beal Papers, circus collection. Harvard Theatre Collection.

7. Fran Walsh, Philippa Boyens, and Peter Jackson, *King Kong*, Internet Movie Script Database, 27 August 2011, http://www.imsdb.com/scripts/King-Kong.html.

8. R. H. Blyth: "We are being sentimental when we give to a thing more tenderness than God gives to it." ." J. D. Salinger quotes this in Raise High the Roof Beam, Carpenters and Seymour: An Introduction. Little, Brown, 1991. 78.

9. Eugene O'Neill, *The Hairy Ape*, in *Complete Plays 1920–1931*, ed. Travis Bogard (New York: Library of America, 1988), 163.

10. O'Neill, *Hairy Ape*, 160.

11. Travis Bogard, *Contour in Time: The Plays of Eugene O'Neill*, rev. ed. New York: Oxford University Press, 1988), 269.

12. Bab, "America's Foremost Playwright," 350.

13. John Howard Lawson, "The Tragedy of Eugene O'Neill," *Masses and Mainstream*, 7.3 (March 1954): 7–18.

14. John P. Diggins, *Eugene O'Neill's America: Desire under Democracy* (Evanston, IL: University of Chicago, 1997). Diggins elaborates on this idea throughout his book.

15. Bogard, *Contour in Time*, 246.

16. Bogard, *Contour in Time*, 247.

17. Rundle, "Hairy Ape's Humanist Hell," 54.

18. Mark Cosdon, *The Hanlon Brothers: from Daredevil Acrobatics to Spectacle Pantomime, 1833–1931* (Carbondale. IL: Southern Illinois University Press, 2010), 78–79.

19. The Harvard Theatre Collection has a selection of such images.

20. Paulo Medeiros, "Simian Narratives at the Intersection of Science and Literature," *Modern Language Studies* 23, no. 2 (Spring 1993), 59–73. Medeiros's argument is based on literary and scientific narratives. An older study places Yank with Caliban: Baum, "*Tempest* and *Hairy Ape*," 258–73. The argument about apes and men even expands to species-ism, see Slavoj Žížek, "Of Apes and Men," Lacan.com, 29 July 2011 http://www.lacan.com/thesymptom/?page_id=952.

21. Winthrop D. Jordan, *The White Man's Burden: Historical Origins of Racism in the United States* (New York: Oxford University Press, 1974), 13–18, 103–6. Jordan's text remains a classic history of the use of animality in the racist creation of identity in the United States.

22. Diana Snigurowicz, "Sex, Simians, and Spectacle in Nineteenth-Century France; Or, How to Tell a 'Man' from a Monkey," *Canadian Journal of History* 34, no. 1 (1999): 51–81.

23. Rosemarie K. Bank, "Representing History: Performing the Columbian Exposition," *Theatre Journal* 54, no. 4 (2002): 589–606. Bank offers insightful commentary on the ideology and practice of colonialist exhibition strategies.

24. Lines from John Keats's "Ode to a Nightingale" and Heinrich Heine's "Morphine." The latter echoes Matthew 26:24 and Mark 14:21.

25. O'Neill, *Hairy Ape*, 163.

26. Ibid.

27. Bert Cardullo, "Global Futurism, Divine Comedy, Greek Tragedy, and . . . *The Hairy Ape*," *Eugene O'Neill Review* 29 (2007): 7–20. Cardullo discusses comedy. Erika Rundle does as well; see "Hairy Ape's Humanist Hell." 130.

28. Yeats, 187.

29. Connolly, *Genus Envy*, 28.

30. Playwright David Mamet frequently takes issue with this approach. See *True and False: Heresy and Common Sense for the Actor* (New York: Vintage Books, 1999) or *Theatre* (New York: MacMillan, 2010).

31. Margaret Loftus Ranald, *The Eugene O'Neill Companion* (Westport, CT: Greenwood, 1984), 280–81. Ranald asserts that O'Neill's non-autobiographical naturalistic works deserve more attention, but that *The Hairy Ape* is essentially realistic. She argues that the characters are "symbolic rather than realistic."

32. Snigurowicz, "Sex, Simians, and Spectacle," 51–81.

33. Anthony W. D. Larkum, *A Natural Calling: Life, Letters and Diaries of Charles Darwin and William Darwin Fox* (Singapore: Springer Science, 2009): 18, 469.

34. Jane Goodall, *Performance and Evolution in the Age of Darwin* (London: Routledge, 2002), 52.

35. Ernst Robert Curtius, *European Literature and the Latin Middle Ages* (Princeton University Press, 1953), 539.

36. Medeiros, "Simian Narratives," 59

37. Baum, "*Tempest* and *Hairy Ape*," 271–72

38. Edward Albee (lecture at Suffolk University, Spring 1995).

39. Both an outstanding O'Neill scholar and a theatre director have made this argument. Michael E. Rutenberg, "Bob Smith Ain't So Dumb: Directing *The Hairy Ape*," *The Eugene O'Neill Newsletter* 3, no. 3 (January 1980), 1 September 2011, http://www.eoneill.com/library/newsletter/iii_3/iii-3f.htm; Doris M. Alexander, "Eugene O'Neill as Social Critic," *American Quarterly* 6, no. 4 (Winter 1954): 349–63.

40. James A. Robinson, "The Masculine Primitive and *The Hairy Ape*." *Eugene O'Neill Review* 19, no. 1–2 (1995): 94–109. This essay makes primitivist claims for Yank as an Adamic tragic hero with Mildred as Eve.

Works Cited

Alexander, Doris M. "Eugene O'Neill as Social Critic." *American Quarterly* 6.4 (Winter 1954): 349–63. Print.

Bab, Julius. "America's Foremost Playwright." *O'Neill and His Plays: Four Decades of Criticism*. Ed. Oscar Cargill, N. Bryllion Fagin, and William J. Fisher. New York: New York UP, 1961. 350. Print.

Bank, Rosemarie K. "Representing History: Performing the Columbian Exposition." *Theatre Journal* 54.4 (2002): 589–606. Print.

Beal, George Brinton Beal Papers, circus collection. Harvard Theatre Collection.

Baum, Bernard. "*Tempest* and *Hairy Ape*: The Literary Incarnation of Mythos." *Modern Language Quarterly* 14 (1953): 258–73. George Brinton Beal Papers, circus collection. Harvard Theatre Collection. Print.

Bogard, Travis. *Contour in Time: The Plays of Eugene O'Neill*. Rev. ed. New York: Oxford UP, 1988. Print.

Cardullo, Bert. "Global Futurism, Divine Comedy, Greek Tragedy, and . . . *The Hairy Ape*." *Eugene O'Neill Review* 29 (2007): 7–20. Print.

Connolly, Thomas F. *Genus Envy: Nationalities, Identities, and the Performing Body of Work*. Amherst: Cambria, 2010. Print.

Cosdon, Mark. *The Hanlon Brothers: From Daredevil Acrobatics to Spectacle Pantomime, 1833–1931*. Carbondale, IL: Southern Illinois UP, 2010. Print.

Curtius, Ernst Robert. *European Literature and the Latin Middle Ages*. Princeton: Princeton UP, 1953. Print.

Diggins, John Patrick. *Eugene O'Neill's America: Desire under Democracy*. Chicago: U of Chicago P, 1997. Print.

Goodall, Jane. *Performance and Evolution in the Age of Darwin: Out of the Natural Order*. London: Routledge, 2002. Print.

Ingarden, Roman. *The Literary Work of Art: An Investigation of the Borderlines of Ontology, Logic, and Theory of Language*. Trans. George C. Grabowicz. Evanston, IL: Northwestern UP, 1979. Print.

Jordan, Winthrop D. *The White Man's Burden: Historical Origins of Racism in the United States*. New York, NY: Oxford UP, 1974. Print.

Larkum, Anthony W. D. *A Natural Calling: Life, Letters, and Diaries of Charles Darwin and William Darwin Fox*. Medford, MA: Springer Science, 2009. Print.

Lawson, John Howard. "The Tragedy of Eugene O'Neill." *Masses and Mainstream*.Vol. 7 no. 3 (March 1954): 7–18. Print.

Mamet, David. *Theatre*. New York: MacMillan, 2010. Print.

———. *True and False: Heresy and Common Sense for the Actor*. New York: Vintage, 1999. Print.

Medeiros, Paulo. "Simian Narratives at the Intersection of Science and Literature." *Modern Language Studies* 23.2 (Spring 1993): 59–73. Print.

O'Neill, Eugene. *The Hairy Ape. Complete Plays 1920–1931*. Ed. Travis Bogard. 119–164. New York: Library of America, 1988. Print.

Ranald, Margaret Loftus. *The Eugene O'Neill Companion*. Westport: Greenwood, 1984. Print.

Robinson, James A. "The Masculine Primitive and *The Hairy Ape*." *Eugene O'Neill Review* 19.1–2 (1995): 94–109. Print.

Rochefort, Gabriel. *Jocko; ou, Le singe du Brésil*. Paris: Chez Quoy Libraire, 1825. *Google Books*. Google, 18 Mar. 2009. Web. 19 August 2011. http://books.google.com/books?id=NAFBAAAAYAAJ&pg=PA14&dq =jocko+le+singe+de+bresil&hl=en&ei=LV3lTpeYCdCy0AHPvrWVCQ &sa=X&oi=book_result&ct=result&resnum=1&ved=0CC8Q6AEwADgK #v=onepage&q=jocko%20le%20singe%20de%20bresil&f=false.

Rundle, Erika. "The Hairy Ape's Humanist Hell: Theatricality and Evolution in O'Neill's 'Comedy of Ancient and Modern Life.'" *Eugene O'Neill Review* 30 (2008): 48–144. Print.

Rutenberg, Michael E. "Bob Smith Ain't So Dumb: Directing *The Hairy Ape*." *Eugene O'Neill Newsletter* 3.3 (January 1980). *eOneill.com*. n.d. Web. 8 September 2011. http://www.eoneill.com/library/newsletter/iii_3/iii-3f.htm.

Snigurowicz, Diana. "Sex, Simians, and Spectacle in Nineteenth-Century France; or, How to Tell a 'Man' from a Monkey." *Canadian Journal of History* 34 (1999): 51–81. Print.

Walsh, Fran, Philippa Boyens, and Peter Jackson. *King Kong*. Script. *Imsb.com*. Internet Movie Script Database, n.d. Web. 8 September 2011. http://www.imsdb.com/scripts/King-Kong.html.

Yeats, William Butler. *The Collected Poems of W. B. Yeats. Richard Finneran, ed*. New York, NY: Scribner's, 1996.

Žižek, Slavoj. "Of Apes and Men." *Lacan.com*. n.d. Web. 23 July 2011. http://www.lacan.com/thesymptom/?page_id=952.

CHAPTER 10

WAITING FOR O'NEILL

THE MAKINGS OF AN EXISTENTIALIST

Steven F. Bloom

It was around 1941 when the 53-year-old Eugene O'Neill wrote the now well-known words that the 23-year-old Edmund Tyrone speaks toward the end of *Long Day's Journey into Night*: "It was a great mistake, my being born a man. I would have been much more successful as a sea gull or a fish. As it is, I will always be a stranger who never feels at home, who does not really want and is not really wanted, who can never belong, who must always be a little in love with death!"[1] Spoken in one of O'Neill's last plays, these words have come to be associated with the aging O'Neill and capture his mature vision of the human condition, a vision that aligns well with the existentialist beliefs that were becoming current by 1941: in the face of an apparently meaningless existence, all human beings are alone and responsible for their individual identities and actions. In fact, however, the sentiments conveyed by Edmund's words were very much akin to those with which the playwright himself wrestled as a young man and budding artist back in 1912, and they would manifest themselves in some of his earliest dramatic works, in particular the one-act sea plays written between 1914 and 1918.

It is common to think of the early sea plays as naturalistic dramas, and their expressionistic elements have been duly noted by many commentators. Less has been made, though, of their existentialist and absurdist elements. Although Michael Y. Bennett, in his 2011 book *Reassessing the Theatre of the Absurd*, builds a compelling argument based on recent scholarship that questions Martin Esslin's use of the term "absurd," O'Neill's sea plays do exhibit a number of qualities that are consistent with the plays Esslin included in his 1961 study *The Theatre of the Absurd*, and ultimately they can be seen as early precursors of existential drama.

Other scholars have already made some connections between O'Neill and so-called absurdist drama, most notably Normand Berlin in his 1988 essay "The Beckettian O'Neill" and Linda Ben-Zvi in her 1993 essay "O'Neill and Absurdity." Berlin focuses almost exclusively on *The Iceman Cometh* and *Long Day's Journey into Night*, making a strong and compelling connection between O'Neill's late plays and Samuel Beckett's early works, productions of which appeared in New York within months of each other in 1956 and 1957: "They are both children of their century, which means that each in his own way had to confront the terrifying prospect that there are no firm values, no scientific absolutes, no ultimate meanings, that there is no God, that man's struggle against necessity is self-destructive. And O'Neill's last plays and Beckett's first plays belong to a post-World-War-II atmosphere of suffering and despair, of irrational demonic forces at work, in man, of the possibility of catastrophic destruction."[2] Acknowledging the apparent paradox of comparing one of literature's most minimalist writers to one of literature's most expansive, Berlin mines the rich common thematic ground between them to identify what is modern about modern drama and how it revealed itself in two very different voices on stage within a span of a few months.

Ben-Zvi broadens the comparison, not only to some of O'Neill's other late plays but to his earlier works, where she finds central images and themes in the young dramatist's work that are consistent with the images and themes identified by Esslin as absurdist.[3] Her goal is to place O'Neill's complete works in the context of the theatre of the absurd and to demonstrate convincingly why Esslin should have included O'Neill "in that list of forerunners of absurdist theater, acknowledging O'Neill's kindred worldview and some of his dramatic experimentation that helped pave the way for later writers."[4]

Of the sea plays, *Bound East for Cardiff* receives the most attention from Ben-Zvi. She argues that several of its qualities qualify as elements of the theatre of the absurd, as defined by Esslin: its cramped, dark setting; its use of the repeated sound of the steamer's whistle blasts; the ineffectual, God-like Captain; and the desire for, and inevitability of, death in the face of the terror of which men seek the company of others to pass the time.[5] She similarly, and even more briefly, cites the setting, lack of a traditional plot, and nihilistic philosophy of *The Moon of the Caribbees* as absurdist elements.[6] Except for one other mention of the *Glencairn* sailors as "specters of modern alienation," in support of her argument that O'Neill created characters who are "generalized representatives of the modern period,"[7] which is consistent with the typical character delineation of Esslin's theatre of the absurd, that is the extent of Ben-Zvi's "revisionist readings" of the sea plays. As she herself suggests, though, there is more.

In *The Long Voyage Home*, Olson, who describes himself as a "poor devil sailor man,"[8] explains to Freda that, while he has been working at sea for over ten years, it has been his intention to return home to his mother and his brother on their farm in Sweden; yet whenever he is in port, he drinks too much and spends all his money so that he has to ship out on another voyage in order to make enough money to return home. Thus he seems to be doomed to repeating the same cycle eternally, not unlike Sisyphus, the mythical character doomed to pushing a boulder up a hill only to have it roll back down to the bottom every time he gets it to the top. In 1917, in *The Long Voyage Home*, O'Neill was mining the same metaphysical terrain as Camus did in 1942 in his *The Myth of Sisyphus*, although the works are very different in genre and details. While Bennett cogently argues against aligning Camus's *Myth* with Sartrean existentialism, it is what Bennett calls Sisyphus's "absurd punishment" as depicted in Camus's *Myth*—"his desire to roll the rock up to the top is always contradicted by the reality of the situation"[9]—that resonates with O'Neill's depiction of Olson in *The Long Voyage Home*.

Many of O'Neill's other sea plays are characterized by elements that are strikingly akin to specific elements of Beckett's *Waiting for Godot*. First and foremost, there is the waiting. In *Godot*, Beckett would many years later capture the essence of the modern human experience within the metaphor of waiting. In the famous story of the San Quentin prison production lie the powerful implications of this metaphor for modern times: prisoners in lifelong detention, waiting to die, could best relate to the situation of Vladimir and Estragon. In 1914, however, O'Neill captured it in the plight of men at sea, waiting—waiting for their next shift, waiting for the fog to lift, waiting to get to the next port, waiting to get home again, and as personified by Yank in *Bound East*, waiting for death.

In *Bound East*, all the men wait for the sound of the ship's bells signaling eight o'clock and a shift in the watch; throughout the first part of the play, some of the men leave to take their shift on deck, while others return below to sleep. They are all waiting for the weather to improve and the fog to lift, so that they can arrive in port at Cardiff, where Cocky falsely assures Yank that he will be "'avin your pint of beer . . . this day week."[10] Yank remains in his bunk, gravely ill and unable to move, unable to respond to the sound of the bell, waiting for the end of his life: "I'm goin' to die, that's what, and the sooner the better!"[11] he insists to Driscoll.

In *Ile*, the men aboard the *Atlantic Queen* have grown tired of waiting for the ice to break so they can continue northward on their quest for whale oil; they have been aboard ship for two years with no sign of progress north, and because of Captain Keeney's stubborn determination to return only with a ship full of oil, they have little hope for returning home. Early on, the Steward wails "*bitterly*," "Home! I begin to doubt if ever I'll set foot on land again."[12] The theme of waiting is articulated most eloquently and pathetically by Keeney's wife. Mrs. Keeney's plight is ironic. At first, she complained of being left at home while her husband went to sea: "I didn't want to wait back there in the house all alone as I've been doing these last six years since we were married—waiting, and watching, and fearing—with nothing to keep my mind occupied."[13] Now that she has accompanied him on his voyage, when Keeney promises that they will turn for home within one to three months once they have the oil, she cries, "But we can't wait for that—I can't wait . . . And the men won't wait."[14] No matter on land or at sea, life for Mrs. Keeney is always a matter of waiting. At one point, she even refers to her accommodations aboard the ship as a "prison cell of a room, and the ice all around, and the silence."[15] One can only guess that a production of *Waiting for Godot* aboard the SS *Glencairn* or the *Atlantic Queen* would have been as well received as it was at San Quentin.

In *Godot*, Beckett frequently calls attention to the passing *of* time as well as to Didi and Gogo's awareness of the need to pass the time, most memorably playing on the double meaning of the words "passing time" immediately after Pozzo and Lucky depart in Act One:

> **Vladimir**: That passed the time.
> **Estragon**: It would have passed in any case.
> **Vladimir**: Yes, but not so rapidly.[16]

Didi and Gogo pass the time while waiting for Godot. Godot's identity is never revealed, and it is never clear just what they are waiting for, but that is part of the profound mystery of this play. In O'Neill's sea plays, the characters also pass the time while waiting for something to happen, but in these cases, they are waiting for something more concrete: they are waiting for the fog to lift or the ice to melt, or, in

Yank and Driscoll's case in *Bound East for Cardiff*, they are waiting for death to come. After the Captain says there is nothing he can do for Yank, he leaves Driscoll with him to keep him company until he dies, and the two men pass the time complaining about life at sea, dreaming of a better life on land, reminiscing about their time together, and trying to figure out what it all means. This exchange passes the time while they wait for Yank to die, with no more practical impact on their lives than Didi and Gogo's "movements . . . elevations . . . relaxations . . . [and] elongations," which are the activities they do to pass the time "while waiting . . . to warm [them] up . . . to calm [them] down." This particular exchange between Didi and Gogo ends with Gogo asking, "Do you think God sees me?," which is not that different from Yank's uncertainty, when he asks Driscoll in his final moments, "You don't think He'll hold it up agin me—God, I mean."[17]

And then there is the camaraderie. In *Bound East for Cardiff*, as in the other sea plays, these men live in cramped, uncomfortable conditions for long periods of time, and they depend on each other to help pass the time. There is a great communal camaraderie among all the men, characterized by familiar teasing and mocking, carousing, and complaining about the pay, grub, and management. It is only the presence of their dying mate, Yank, and the reminders from his concerned friend Driscoll that interrupt the complaining; as each man awaits his shift on watch, he either sleeps or engages in these kinds of exchanges with his comrades. The friendship between Driscoll and Yank runs the deepest and is truly sustaining for both of them, as they declare to each other for the first time their common dream of saving their money to buy a farm where they can live together. In *Godot*, Estragon asks Vladimir, "How long have we been together all the time now?," to which Vladimir replies with some uncertainty, "I don't know. Fifty years maybe."[18] In *Bound East*, when the Captain asks Driscoll if he and Yank have been shipmates for a long time, Driscoll replies, "Five years and more, sorr," to which the Captain replies, "I see."[19] As with Didi and Gogo, it does not matter exactly how long they have been together; it has been an eternity, and one's company is all that matters for the other.

In *Ile*, the men have tired of waiting; they have been at sea for two years, and they have grown weary from passing the time. They want to go home. More important, Mrs. Keeney *needs* to go home. By inserting a woman into the man's world at sea, O'Neill dramatizes the consequences of not being able to pass the time in the company of others. Ben tells the Steward that Mrs. Keeney "does nothin' all day long now but sit and sew—and then she cries to herself without makin' no noise."[20] She tries to pass the time by sewing, but talks to no one any longer, and seems out of place and alone. Keeney says, "'Tis no fit place for a woman, that's sure. I was a fool to bring ye."[21] Without the camaraderie of others or the routine of work aboard ship, there is nothing for Mrs. Keeney to do to occupy her mind and to keep her from contemplating the emptiness of her existence. In *Waiting for Godot*, Vladimir sums up the human predicament: "All I know is that the hours are long, under these conditions, and constrain us to beguile them with proceedings which—how shall I say—which may at first sight seem reasonable, until they become a habit. You may say it is to prevent our reason from foundering. No doubt. But has it not long been straying in the night without end of the abyssal depths?"[22] The organ that Keeney has bought for his wife symbolizes the need for distracting activity. He explains, "I even sent to the city for that organ for ye, thinkin' it might be soothin' to ye to be playin' it times when they was calms and things was dull like."[23] It does not work for her though, and she says, "I feel as if the cold and the silence were crushing down on my brain."[24] Without the ability to pass the time, a human being may go mad, as Mrs. Kenney does: "It's killing me, this life—the brutality and cold and horror of it. I'm going mad. I can feel the threat in the air. I can hear the silence threatening me—day after gray day and every day the same. I can't bear it."[25] She is referring to the very specific plight of a woman trapped alone in a man's world aboard a ship stuck at sea, but she could also be describing the metaphysical plight of human beings: the reason why we find ways to pass the time, to avoid staring into the abyss, and to drown out the silence; the reason why a group of derelicts and bums in a later play by O'Neill will invest so much in pipe dreams.

What all these characters are simultaneously waiting for and distracting themselves from is death. In one way or another, death hovers over all of O'Neill's sea plays, just as death hovers over *Waiting for Godot*. Several times during the play, Vladimir and Estragon consider hastening the process by hanging themselves, but always find a reason not to do so; either they do not have a rope, or the belt is too short, or the cord is too weak. In act one, Estragon constructs a logical reason not to kill themselves: "This is how it is. (*He reflects.*) The bough . . . Gogo light—bough not break—Gogo dead. Didi heavy—bough break—Didi alone."[26] The fear of being alive and alone, not the fear of death, is what motivates them to stay alive, together. It is not a selfish motivation, either, for Vladimir asks, "But am I heavier than you?," to which Estragon replies, "So you tell me. I don't know. There's an even chance. Or nearly . . . Don't let's do anything. It's safer."[27] As tormenting as it can be to go on living on "this bitch of an earth,"[28] the prospect of being alive without the other's companionship is even less tolerable. Toward the end of act two, Estragon complains, "I can't go on like this," to which Vladimir retorts, "That's what you think,"[29] and, of course, he does go on.

Death hovers over O'Neill's sea plays even more palpably, simply because men at sea are always at risk of dying, and they often do. Death remains in the background of both *Ile* and *The Long Voyage Home*, but it is front and center in *Bound East for Cardiff*. Yank is dying; he knows that he is dying, and he is not afraid of it: "The sailor life ain't much to cry about leavin'—just one ship after another, hard work, small pay, and bum grub; and when we git into port, just a drunk endin' up in a fight, and all your money gone, and then ship away again."[30] This is the same Sisyphean life that Olson describes in *A Long Voyage Home*. In *Bound East*, Yank is aware of his misery and, faced with the end of it, he welcomes death: "I was just thinkin' it ain't as bad as people think—dyin'. I ain't never took much stock in the truck them sky-pilots preach. I ain't never had religion; but I know whatever it is what comes after it can't be no worser'n this."[31] Yank welcomes death, and unlike Sisyphus, in O'Neill's version, Yank is allowed to die.

He does have one regret, though: "I don't like to leave you, Drisc, but—that's all."[32] Based on the bond that is established between them in this scene, it is not unreasonable to suggest that his regret, like the anticipatory regret of Didi and Gogo when they contemplate suicide, is more about leaving Driscoll to endure this life alone, without Yank's companionship, than about his own death. Indeed, the sadness in the final tableau is the image of Driscoll, "*a brawny Irishman with the battered features of a prizefighter*,"[33] alone at the side of his dead friend, "[sinking] *down on his knees beside the bunk, his head on his hands. His lips move in some half-remembered prayer*."[34] When Cocky enters to announce, ironically, that the fog has lifted, he can only respond with awe, quietly and respectfully exclaiming, "Gawd blimey!"[35]

In her essay on O'Neill and absurdity, Ben-Zvi insists that she is "not trying to reinvent O'Neill as an absurdist,"[36] and that is not the purpose here either. It is, in fact, the endings of O'Neill's sea plays that pointedly differentiate them from *Waiting for Godot*, and relegate them to the lobby of the theater of the absurd. First and foremost, these early plays, still under the strong narrative influence of nineteenth-century melodrama, *had* endings; that is, something happens in the final moments of almost every play that gives it closure of some kind. As much as he was rebelling against his father's theatre,

O'Neill knew a good ending when he saw one; his loss of faith as a young man and a healthy dose of twentieth-century skepticism led him to make those endings ironic, but they still provided narrative resolution.

In *Bound East for Cardiff*, Yank dies, and right after that, the fog lifts. Unlike Didi and Gogo in *Godot*, Yank escapes life on "this bitch of an earth," and the irony is that had he survived a little while longer, he could have received medical attention and been saved once they arrived in port. There is nothing ironic about *Waiting for Godot*; Godot does not arrive—Didi and Gogo must keep waiting. Had Beckett written *Bound East for Cardiff*, the fog would have lifted in time for Yank to be saved, and he and Driscoll would have continued to pass the time interminably while waiting for their next watch at sea and for their next arrival in port.

The irony at the end of *Ile* is downright painful. Just after Keeney reluctantly acquiesces to his wife's desperate pleas to turn for home and is about to issue a command to his crew to do so, he receives word that the ice has broken up and that they now have clear passage to where the whales and the oil are. He continues on course for the oil at the expense of his wife's sanity and presumably his marriage. Had Beckett written *Ile*, the ice would never melt; every day, the crew and Mrs. Keeney would be convinced to wait one more day and they would continue to find ways to entertain and amuse themselves and each other, be it by playing the organ, by following the routines of life at sea, including threatening mutiny or by arguing and fighting.

In some ways, the ending of *A Long Voyage Home* comes closest to a Beckettian ending. Olson talks about making a change, to end the repetitive cycle of his life at sea, and he comes very close to accomplishing it, but he does not. This time, it is not the capricious force of destiny, but rather the malevolent force of greedy human beings, that interferes with his plans and dooms him to his Sisyphean fate. Even in this case, though, O'Neill hints at a more definitive conclusion. When Olson hears that the *Amindra* is in port, he says, "I pity poor fallers make dat trip round Cape Stiff dis time year. I bet you some of dem never see port once again."[37] Since the *Amindra* is exactly where the "Roughs" are contracted to deposit his unconscious body, the implication is that not only will Olson never get home, but it is highly likely that he will die and never see port again. Had Beckett written *A Long Voyage Home*, of course, Olson would have somehow been enticed into drinking his money away, thus forcing him back aboard ship for another day that would be just the same as all the days that had come before.

In many of O'Neill's early plays, then, there is an ironic twist at the end, a manifestation of what O'Neill called "ironic fate," explained by Travis Bogard as follows: "The lives of the characters are controlled, in despite of their wills, by a power of destiny that is inexorable, malevolent insofar as it can be said to have purpose, but in essence meaningless."[38] The meaninglessness of this inexorable force of destiny is not inconsistent with Esslin's vision of the theatre of the absurd, but the imposition of this force upon O'Neill's plays in a linear, narrative fashion is what, according to Esslin, would disqualify O'Neill from admission to the theatre of the absurd. Had the young O'Neill written *Waiting for Godot*, Vladimir and Estragon would kill themselves or leave, and Godot would arrive on stage at the end to exclaim, "Gawd Blimey! Why didn't they wait?"

Esslin differentiates the dramatists of the absurd from another group of writers, including Jean-Paul Sartre and Albert Camus, whose themes and subject matter are alike: "They present their sense of the irrationality of the human condition in the form of highly lucid and logically constructed reasoning, while the Theatre of the Absurd strives to express its sense of the senselessness of the human condition and the inadequacy of the rational approach by the open abandonment of rational devices and discursive thought."[39] That the linear style of many of O'Neill's plays, including virtually all the sea plays (perhaps *The Moon of the Caribbees* being the one exception), excludes O'Neill from the theatre of the absurd is inarguable. As both Berlin and Ben-Zvi point out, later in his career, O'Neill would write a few plays that are more fully comparable—not only in philosophical sensibility but, to some degree, in dramaturgical conventions as well—to those of Beckett and perhaps other dramatists of the absurd (*The Iceman Cometh* and certainly *Hughie*, for instance, reward reconsideration in this light). That he belongs, however, with that other group of dramatists—call them the existentialist dramatists—is certainly more arguable, and there is evidence for it in many of the sea plays, as well as other early one-acts. One might say that in his earliest years as a dramatist, given his nascent dramaturgical sensibilities and the theatrical tenor of his times, O'Neill may not have been quite able, or even trying, to touch what Beckett and the others would attempt to accomplish on stage years later, but he certainly had the *makings* of an existentialist, at the very least.

NOTES

1. Eugene O'Neill, *Long Day's Journey into Night* (New Haven, CT: Yale University Press, 1956), 153–54.
2. Normand Berlin, "The Beckettian O'Neill," *Modern Drama* 31 (March 1988): 31.
3. Linda Ben-Zvi, "O'Neill and Absurdity," *Around the Absurd: Essays on Modern and Postmodern Drama*, ed. Enoch Brater and Ruby Cohn (Ann Arbor: University of Michigan Press, 1990), 38–39.
4. Ibid., 36.
5. Ibid., 39–40.
6. Ibid., 41.
7. Ibid., 44.
8. Eugene O'Neill, *Collected Shorter Plays* (New Haven, CT: Yale University Press, 2007), 99.
9. Michael Y. Bennett, *Reassessing the Theatre of the Absurd: Camus, Beckett, Ionesco, Genet, and Pinter* (New York: Palgrave Macmillan, 2011), 12–13.
10. O'Neill, *Collected Shorter Plays*, 10.
11. Ibid., 16.
12. Ibid., 117.
13. Ibid., 131.
14. Ibid., 132.
15. Ibid., 130.
16. Samuel Beckett, *Waiting for Godot* (New York: Grove, 1954), 31.
17. O'Neill, *Collected Shorter Plays*, 49.
18. Beckett, *Waiting for Godot*, 35.
19. O'Neill, *Collected Shorter Plays*, 16.
20. Ibid., 119.
21. Ibid., 134.
22. Beckett, *Waiting for Godot*, 51.
23. O'Neill, *Collected Shorter Plays*, 131.
24. Ibid., 132.
25. Ibid., 136.
26. Beckett, *Waiting for Godot*, 12.
27. Ibid.
28. Ibid., 25.
29. Ibid., 60.
30. O'Neill, *Collected Shorter Plays*, 17.
31. Ibid.
32. Ibid.
33. Ibid., 4.
34. Ibid., 22.
35. Ibid., 23.
36. Ben-Zvi, "O'Neill and Absurdity," 38.
37. O'Neill, *Collected Shorter Plays*, 109.

38. Travis Bogard, *Contour in Time: The Plays of Eugene O'Neill*, rev. ed. (New York: Oxford University Press, 1988), 17.
39. Martin Esslin, *The Theatre of the Absurd*, rev. ed. (Garden City, NY: Anchor Books, 1969), 6.

WORKS CITED

Beckett, Samuel. *Waiting for Godot*. New York: Grove, 1954. Print.

Bennett, Michael Y. *Reassessing the Theatre of the Absurd: Camus, Beckett, Ionesco, Genet, and Pinter*. New York: Palgrave, 2011. Print.

Ben-Zvi, Linda. "O'Neill and Absurdity." *Around the Absurd: Essays on Modern and Postmodern Drama*. Ed. Enoch Brater and Ruby Cohn. Ann Arbor: U of Michigan P, 1990. 33–55. Print.

Berlin, Normand. "The Beckettian O'Neill." *Modern Drama* 31 (March 1988): 28–34. Print.

Bogard, Travis. *Contour in Time: The Plays of Eugene O'Neill*. Rev. ed. New York: Oxford UP, 1988. Print.

Esslin, Martin. *The Theatre of the Absurd*. Rev. ed. Garden City: Anchor, 1969. Print.

O'Neill, Eugene. *Long Day's Journey into Night*. New Haven: Yale UP, 1956. Print.

———. *Collected Shorter Plays*. New Haven: Yale UP, 2007. Print.

CHAPTER 11

O'NEILL'S *HUGHIE*

THE SEA PLAYS REVISITED

Robert Combs

Although Eugene O'Neill is well known for the expansiveness of his dramatic innovations (*Strange Interlude* was so long it needed a dinner intermission, *Mourning Becomes Electra* required three nights to be performed, his most famous play is called *Long Day's Journey into Night*, and he planned an 11-play cycle treating the spiritual history of America from 1755 to 1932), a contrary, and significant, impulse in his dramatic practice is the one-act play. He began his career with *Bound East for Cardiff* and other sea plays. And at the end of his life, O'Neill was planning six one-acts to be called collectively *By Way of Obit*, of which only *Hughie* survives.

There are revealing parallels between *Hughie* and the sea plays, although on the surface they appear quite dissimilar. The sea plays present common sailors of various nationalities separated from their pasts and their families, facing not so much the dangers associated with adventurous sea stories as those of a more existential kind: confrontations with self, other, and nothingness. Their pasts have dropped away, their futures are uncertain, and they are in constant proximity to the great symbol of illimitable life and death, the sea. *Hughie*, on the other hand, takes place in a run-down hotel lobby in midtown Manhattan in 1928. Isolated not in the sea, but in the lonely night of a vast city, a guest and a night clerk attempt to have a conversation. The guest, Erie Smith, a small-time gambler described as a "a teller of tales" in the *dramatis personae*, attempts to engage the new night clerk, Charlie Hughes, with his self-aggrandizing monologues, while Hughes, who has just replaced the deceased former night clerk and Erie's longtime companion—coincidentally also named Hughes—pretends to listen. In the course of this short play, the extent of both men's despair is revealed, and the difficulty—perhaps the impossibility—of actual human contact is explored. Nevertheless, by the end Erie's association with the famous gambler Arnold Rothstein gets the night clerk's attention; a friendship begins to develop that may be a foundation for present and future conversations through the mediation of the roles of "wise guy" and "sucker," roles the two men gratefully embrace.

Hughie and the sea plays, read together, highlight a number of O'Neill's themes, as well as the dramatic means by which they are presented: human isolation expressed through dialogue—that is often really monologue—in a highly atmospheric, quasi surreal setting; a paradoxical discovery of hopefulness when people reach each other through irresolvable conflicts in impossible situations; and a pervasive sense of irony, which is often at the heart of modern one-act plays and short stories. A symbolist naturalism that resists resolution infuses the sea plays and *Hughie*; in several ways, it epitomizes the art of Eugene O'Neill. I will focus on four of the sea plays, originally published together as *SS Glencairn: Bound East for Cardiff, In the Zone, The Long Voyage Home*, and *The Moon of the Caribbees*, all written between 1913 and 1916. Taking his cue from Joseph Conrad, according to Travis Bogard,[1] O'Neill had found his great theme: man's destiny of belonging to an elemental life force that can never be understood.

Two of the *Glencairn* plays express this theme powerfully with almost no plot. In *Bound East for Cardiff*, Yank has injured himself falling from a ladder and is carried to his bunk below deck, where he dies, accompanied only by his friend Driscoll. That is all that happens. But every detail contributes to a paradoxical picture of chilling helplessness mixed with acceptance, and even affirmation. The ship is enveloped by night and fog, which make the characters feel lost and trapped. The crew, composed of Melvillean orphans and their pretentious captain, are reduced to spectators of a fate that could just as well be theirs. The dramatic interest of the scene lies in the companionship of Yank and Driscoll, specifically in the intense human contact that the extremity of Yank's situation makes possible. Yank describes life on the sea with great frankness: "This sailor life ain't much to cry about leavin'—just one ship after another, hard work, small pay, and bum grub; and when we git into port, just a drunk endin' up in a fight, and all your money gone, and then ship away again."[2] Yet the two sailors share memories of experiences that have been undeniably fulfilling, and they express love for each other in a shared fantasy of one day owning a farm together far from the sea. Rolf Scheibler makes the important point that "pipe dreams," such as this one, which are so fundamental to O'Neill's conception of how people endure life, do not refer simply to illusions as such, but to the necessity of relating to people through conventions, especially improvised conventions that have symbolic meaning for those who believe in them. As Scheibler says, "O'Neill is not concerned with preaching theories, he is concerned with establishing the paradoxes of life and making them transparent."[3] Only at the point of complete defeat can a pipe dream, a mutually agreed upon convention, be seen for what it is, a means of forming a connection with another person.[4]

In *The Moon of the Caribbees*, the sailors play an even smaller role, relative to the symbolist world of the drama, than they did in *Bound East for Cardiff*. As O'Neill said of this poetic play, "the spirit of the sea . . . is . . . the hero."[5] A motley group of sailors awaits the arrival of some island women bringing rum. O'Neill, as he does to an even greater extent in *Hughie*, conveys the meaning of the scene through stage directions: "*A melancholy Negro chant, faint and far off, drifts, crooning, over the water.*" It is, he says, "*the mood of the moonlight made audible.*"[6] As the women arrive, the men come to life, singing, dancing, loving, and fighting, until their disruption of naval order is discovered by the first mate and the women are thrown off the ship. The moonlight and the native chant remain to suggest that a larger world envelopes the men before and after their experiences aboard the ship. Smitty, the most individualized of the sailors, seems to intuit a connection between this larger world and an inner world of memory. He wishes the natives would stop their song because "it makes you think of—well—things you ought to forget."[7] In O'Neill's later plays, of course, memories have the power to engulf his characters in a trance-like, immaterial world they cannot escape. These early two plays contain O'Neill's first glimpse of the depths he would explore in later masterpieces.

In the Zone and *The Long Voyage Home* seem perhaps less original than the plays just discussed because they rely on plot and situation more than they do on symbolist dramatic techniques to make their points. But their plots move O'Neill's dramaturgy forward, placing his central characters between two different sets of forces: one, the spiritual and psychological world, which is rendered symbolically— the sea, moonlight, music, and death—and two, the sociopolitical world, which is rendered naturalistically. *In the Zone* is set aboard a ship in wartime, the "zone" representing a physical location where submarines may lurk, and also a less tangible location of vulnerability to betrayal or to the fear of being betrayed by a spy. Here Smitty is perceived by his shipmates as acting suspiciously by hiding a black box in his bunk and neglecting to close a porthole whose light might be visible to a sub nearby. As the play unfolds, we learn that the box actually contains love letters and a final rejection of Smitty by the woman he loves as a result of his drinking. The shipmates restrain Smitty as they read the letters out loud, cruelly exposing his private life.

The play continually juxtaposes private experiences with public accounts of them. The sailors gossip about Smitty behind his back. The light from the porthole is imagined from opposite directions, being from the "inside" a place of safety to be guarded by the sailors and from the "outside" a target that could attract enemy subs. Smitty's real name, Sidney Davidson, and the girl's, Edith, are known only when the letters are read aloud. Even the girlfriend's breakup with Smitty proceeds from secondhand information of a report of drunkenness from a third party. Private, personal realities are caught in a war zone of public ambiguity and are suspended in the isolation of life at sea.

The Long Voyage Home dramatizes the cruel cycle of a sailor's life described by Yank as he lies dying in *Bound East for Cardiff.* The play is set not at sea, but in a waterfront bar in London at that point in the cycle when a sailor believes he has a brief chance between voyages to escape the sea and return home. Olson has decided to stay sober, keep his money, and buy a ticket back to Sweden, where he hopes to be reunited with his aged mother on the family farm. He does stay sober, but only to fall into the hands of thugs who drug, rob, and shanghai him. Olson's story, told in this play with its title of ironic understatement, is O'Neill's version of "you can't go home again." Life experience, since it takes place in irreversible time, is a paradox of memory coexisting with loss. The more one remembers, the farther away the content of memory appears. Memory becomes a futile cycle of return to nowhere.

After the sea plays, O'Neill seems to require longer and larger dramatic forms for this subject of existential abandonment, as if the stage itself had to stretch to accommodate the complex historical and personal worlds in which his individual souls were lost. Kurt Eisen has shown how O'Neill appropriates the novel to dramatic purposes not only because of a need for its epic scope but also because only its "inner" narrative practices can do justice to the warring opposites within and among his characters. As Eisen says, "O'Neill's primary interest as a playwright was not in suppressing the inner contradictions of character as the melodramatist must do but in revealing 'the inner strength of opposites in the individual which is fate' by 'constantly overreaching the (dramatic) medium.'"[8] In *Strange Interlude*, for example, O'Neill uses asides that generate "simultaneously inner and outer dramatic exposition," a theatrical experiment Eisen compares to Henry James's experiments with point of view. O'Neill wrote his plays with an eye to their publication as well as their production. And when experiencing an O'Neill drama an audience sometimes feels as if they are reading a novel and seeing a play at the same time.

The sea plays, at the beginning of O'Neill's career, and *Hughie*, at the end, illustrate another debt to prose narrative, that of the short story. The one-act play and the short story bear a family resemblance, and critics have been struck, particularly, by *Hughie*'s resemblance to this form. John Henry Raleigh says that the play is "really a short story"; he doubts that it could be effectively performed because of the extensive thought asides given to Charlie, the night clerk. Timo Tiusanen agrees, suggesting that the play might work better on the radio. Rolf Scheibler calls *Hughie* "a one-act play for the imaginary theatre," essentially consigning it to the domain of closet drama.[9] And O'Neill himself shrugged off responsibility for the production challenges. According to Arthur and Barbara Gelb, O'Neill said, "It would require tremendous imagination. Let whoever does it figure it out. I wouldn't want to be around to see it."[10] It is not only the thought asides that render the play literary as well as theatrical. Frank O'Connor, Nadine Gordimer, and Péter Egri, all discuss the short story in terms that apply to O'Neill's one-acts. And critic Robert Langbaum's discussion of the dramatic monologue—a "poetry of experience," which arguably led to the Romantic short story as practiced by Poe and others—sheds light on O'Neill's handling of dramatic characters throughout his career.

Influenced by Edgar Allan Poe, who considered "unity of impression" the *sine qua non* of the short story form, modern critics have resisted defining the short story according to length. A short story is not simply a story that is short, but a very special breed of literature. Frank O'Connor places great stress on the kinds of characters who inhabit the short story. He asserts that the short story "has never had a hero." Its characters constitute a "submerged population group," by which O'Connor means people who are defeated "in a society that has no sign posts, a society that offers no goals and no answers." These outlaw figures sometimes echo or caricature symbolic figures such as Christ or Socrates, but they remain remote from any sense of normal community; they are "romantic, individualistic, intransigent."[11] Yank, Driscoll, Smitty, and Olson all illustrate O'Connor's view though they live in O'Neill's one-act sea plays rather than short stories. Erie Smith and Charlie Hughes also inhabit the social margins O'Connor is describing. Originally from Erie, Pennsylvania, and Saginaw, Michigan, respectively, Erie and Charlie, in their different ways, inhabit a New York that is a kind of limbo for them. And in this situation they are not unique. Erie claims that most of the people he knows in New York originally came from "the sticks." In other words, New York, the Mecca of American dreams, becomes for many not a destination, but a condition of marching in place, a state characterized simply by endurance.

According to O'Connor, the short story provides an "intense awareness of human loneliness." The opposite of companionship, a story can nevertheless be existentially reassuring, representing a dramatic experience of self not ordinarily available for public observation, perhaps even epitomizing a character's whole life. As O'Connor says, "Since a whole lifetime must be crowded into a few minutes, those minutes must be carefully chosen indeed and lit by an unearthly glow, one that enables us to distinguish present, past, and future as though they were all contemporaneous."[12] As if picking up on O'Connor's phrase "unearthly glow," author Nadine Gordimer likens the vision provided by short stories to the "flash of fireflies, in and out, now here, now there, in darkness." Modern consciousness, says Gordimer, consists of "flashes of fearful insight alternating with near-hypnotic states of indifference," which short story writers have learned how to imitate in their "fragmented and restless form." Gordimer puts it very plainly: "The increasing loneliness and isolation of the individual in a competitive society"[13] is the modern condition. Péter Egri sees a profound connection between this socioeconomic condition, the ethos of the short story, and the great late plays of O'Neill: "The opposition between the real world of alienation and the capillaric activity of human resistance has brought about an organic merger of the short story model and the dramatic mould in the O'Neill canon. O'Neill's late plays 'crystallize a veritable synthesis of the short story and drama with dramatic antithesis, epic interest and lyric yearning.'"[14]

The dramatic antitheses of virtually all of O'Neill's plays are epitomized in his sea plays and *Hughie*. It would take several novels to elaborate all that is of epic interest in the sea plays: naval history, labor and capital, women, men, prostitution, smuggling, submarine warfare, spies, crimping, alcohol, drugs, the various nationalities represented; all these are the stuff of melodramatic and naturalistic novels. Similarly, *Hughie* touches on hotels; their employees and guests; the history and geography of New York; the growth of cities after the industrial revolution; services such as garbage collection and fire departments; police and crime, organized and otherwise; gambling, including horse racing; prohibition; alcohol; middle-class marriage; prostitution; the sociopolitical conditions of women and men; hospitals; funerals;, and so on. Egri argues that O'Neill abandoned his plans for an 11-play cycle because of the sheer weight of such a novelistic dramatic endeavor. He did not have the time to become America's dramatic Balzac or Zola. When he turned his attention to his autobiographical dramas, starting with *Iceman*, he moved, according to Egri, in a Chekhovian direction, a direction others—Tennessee Williams, Thornton Wilder, Arthur Miller, and Edward Albee—would also follow. Describing this development in terms of political and psychological typology, not influence, Egri writes, "The presentation of the world of alienation moves drama towards fiction; the expression of the counter-world of alienation takes drama in the direction of the lyric."[15] In Chekhov's short stories and O'Neill's late plays, Egri finds a mosaic art of isolated, lonely voices, held together by "a promise of a distant and rather indistinct future."[16] In his late plays, we could even say, O'Neill goes *back* to the future, reincarnating the lyrical, lonely angst of the sea plays in his own version of relatively plotless, Chekhovian tragicomedy.

Robert Langbaum sees in the dramatic monologue the point when a poetry of experience emerged from the Romantic tradition, but he could just as well be describing the short story when he speaks of "a poetry constructed upon the deliberate disequilibrium between experience and idea, a poetry which makes its statement not as an idea but as an experience from which one or more ideas can be abstracted as problematical rationalizations."[17] Like Robert Browning's "My Last Duchess" and Alfred Tennyson's "Ulysses," short stories such as Poe's "The Tell-Tale Heart" and Herman Melville's "Bartleby, the Scrivener," with their unreliable narrators, focus the reader's attention on a middle ground between the narrator's persona (mask) and the events the speaker is describing. The reader witnesses sympathetically the narrator's efforts to make sense of troubling events in his life, yet scrutinizes his words, as a private investigator or a psychoanalyst might, for clues to describe the processes almost being disclosed.

The dramatic monologue is not a soliloquy, which is self-directed. It is an incidental self-revelation that occurs as one half of a dialogue is being overheard.[18] It presents "not an Aristotelian complete action, but habitual action"[19] in which the speaker encounters the mysteries embedded in his own life. A stranger to himself—as he is to his listener—the narrator of a dramatic monologue is publically suffering what modern people privately fear: that one's life may not have an "objectively verifiable meaning" at all but only such self-justifying meaning as life has itself.[20]

O'Neill's *Hughie* is a double dramatic monologue. Erie Smith attempts to engage the night clerk in conversation, but the night clerk's own interior monologues about the sounds of the city night keep him from paying attention. And Erie is not really interested in the night clerk anyway, as he is only a means for delaying his own encounter with absolute loneliness in room 492. Because of the thought asides and stage directions, the audience sees the play from Erie's point of view and also from Hughie's. O'Neill must have thought the structure of this play of considerable interest because he planned to write six plays in his *By Way of Obit* cycle, which he describes in this way: "In each the main character talks about a person who has died to a person who does little but listen. Via this monologue you get a complete picture of the person who has died—his or her whole life story—but just as complete a picture of the life and character of the narrator. And you also get, by another means—use of stage directions, mostly—an insight into the whole life of the person who does little but listen. These plays are written more to be read than staged, although they could be played."[21] What is remarkable about this triangular dramatic structure is how balanced it is. The three component characters seem to be parts of a whole, as if they belonged together. When the lives of the three characters are completely unpacked, they appear similar in that their existence depends on knowing and being known within this structure.

The two living characters are mostly elsewhere, yet each is frighteningly present in a struggle to go on living when there seems to be no reason to do so. In the *dramatis personae*, Erie is called a "teller of tales," implying someone requiring an audience, perhaps also someone living by his wits with the help of lies. The night clerk is "a dummy," "a drooping waxwork." He is described with graveyard humor as speaking with "the vague tone of a corpse which admits it once overheard a favorable rumor about life"—a line Flannery O'Connor might have admired. Critics have read the play as a parable about the life-sustaining power of performance. In "O'Neill's Endgame," C. W. E. Bigsby describes *Hughie* as a play that "holds death at arm's length by language."[22] Keeping Hughie alive in memory until he can be replaced by his namesake, Erie is able to continue performing himself, lending life to his new audience in the process. Sally Harvey draws parallels between *Hughie* and Edward Albee's *The Zoo Story*, a play she sees as celebrating storytelling as a vehicle for human contact.[23] A number of American two-character plays and films could be mentioned that explore the intersections of life, death, and storytelling: LeRoi Jones/Amiri Baraka's *Dutchman*, Wallace Shawn/André Gregory's *My Dinner with André*, Marsha Norman's *'night, Mother*, A. R. Gurney's *Love Letters*, and David Mamet's *Oleanna*, to name a few. In these plays, stories make human contact possible, to be sure, but they also have the power to kill. Perhaps only Samuel Beckett's *Waiting for Godot* could be said to celebrate the life-sustaining power of performance as unequivocally as *Hughie*.[24]

In his psychoanalytic biography of O'Neill, Stephen Black sees *Hughie* as "O'Neill's paradigm of mourning."[25] After completing *Long Day's Journey into Night*, O'Neill was able to express in this one-act play, Black argues, the process by which someone lets go of the past and simultaneously reincarnates it in new forms of the present. The play represents an almost comic equivalent of Mary Tyrone's reply to James in *Long Day's Journey* when he urges her to forget the past: "Why? How can I? The past in the present, isn't it? It's the future, too. We all try to lie out of that but life won't let us."[26] It is as if the process of living in a world where all one's friends and family are destined to die at different times requires a sort of psychological recycling carried out by endless talking; the difficulty lies in finding someone who will listen.

The rigidity of a social role—whether that of a hard-boiled gambler or a night clerk—makes compassionate understanding unlikely, so some dramatic means must be found to broaden and deepen the audience's grasp of character. O'Neill uses the omniscient voice of the stage directions, narrative digressions into back story, and the presence of death to create what Langbaum calls "a disequilibrium between experience and idea." The stage directions comment on Erie, "yet, there is something phoney about his characterization of himself, some sentimental softness behind it which doesn't belong in the hard-boiled picture."[27] Rolf Scheibler convincingly elaborates this picture of Erie, who "prefers the world of the failed, the gamblers, and the criminals to that of the civilized society for the simple reason that, there, the desire for power and wealth is given uninhibited expression and is not hidden under the veil of hypocrisy and lies."[28] Now we have a character capable of understanding the failed dreams of a night clerk who, becoming bored with his job as night clerk in Saginaw, Michigan, came to New York, where the only job he could get was that of night clerk, and who has been at it ever since.

Erie's descriptions of his failed efforts to enter Hughie's home life as a visitor give us glimpses into how social roles make real human connections maintained by hard work possible but also how they can be quite disappointing. Hughie's wife, Irma, is resistant to the alien influence of Erie trying to come into their lives. And Erie, demonstrating remarkable insight, refuses to allow Hughie to jeopardize his domestic relationships by gambling with his wife's money. And most poignantly, he accepts his role as an outsider when he is forbidden to visit Hughie on his deathbed. Erie is profoundly conscious of the importance people place on their conventionally moral life styles, although he lives the life of a small-time gambler and crook himself. And he is profoundly conscious of everyone's need for fantasies. Something of an amateur psychologist, he explains, "I guess he saw me like a sort of dream guy, the sort of guy he'd like to be if he could take a chance. I guess he lived a sort of double-life listening to me gabbin' about hittin' the high spots."[29] Yet nowhere in the play does Erie sound more like the speaker in a dramatic monologue, an unreliable narrator, than in this passage. The audience immediately wonders if it is not Erie who lives a double life by means of his listener. The picture forming is that of two men who enjoy fantasies of derring-do, whether in the role of talker or listener, while both privately live highly circumscribed existences.

The human condition that makes fantasies necessary for human contact to occur is presented by O'Neill as nearly unbearable. Erie and the night clerk both have clearly suicidal fantasies. Erie envies Hughie for being dead, for being out of the racket that is life. The night clerk's dramatic monologue is even more disturbing. He sits night after night simply waiting for time to pass, measured by sounds in the street. Fire trucks, ambulances, garbage pickups are all occasions for violent, apocalyptic fantasies; the night clerk even wishes for a fire big enough to burn down the whole city. And his fantasies are not kind to Erie, whom he imagines only as the annoying hotel guest to whom he must pretend to listen. Though a comic figure, the night clerk resembles the sinister, antisocial monologists of Browning and Poe. It is significant that the dramatic shift that makes an ending possible for this play comes not as a result of anything done or said by the characters, but seemingly by accident. Neither Erie nor the night clerk seems able to escape this despairing human condition by any act of will on their own. A low point has been reached when the night clerk picks up the word "truth" in Erie's monologue and absent-mindedly asks, "Truth? I'm afraid I didn't get—What's the truth?" Erie replies, in total defeat, "Nothing, Pal. Not a thing." This allusion to Pontius

Pilate's question to Christ (John 18:38) passes without significance, like any other sound in the night, though for some reason "the night vaguely reminds him of death and he is vaguely frightened."[30]

The felt presence of death frightens the night clerk into using Erie for his own purposes, to help him "live through the night." And when he hears the name Arnold Rothstein, he decides to engage Erie in conversation about this celebrity of the underworld. Now, as though miraculously, an avenue for communication has opened up between the two men. Instantly becoming the friend of Arnold Rothstein, Erie regales the night clerk with tales of the great gambler. The night clerk melds into Hughie. Hughie is alive again. And Erie feels "*his soul is purged of grief, his confidence restored.*"

Samuel Bernstein sees a vitalist message of universal human connection pulsing through the play on several levels. The name Hughes sounds like the plural slang of "you," "yous," suggesting a reminder of mankind's common mortality. Bernstein asserts that "in *Hughie*, *The Iceman Cometh* and *Long Day's Journey into Night*, camaraderie, particularly among men, and love suggest a mystical connection among suffering humanity and a source of goodness and salvation in the universe."[31] Surely, the play asks questions about the thin line separating life and death. The casual sounding title *By Way of Obit* raises the question of how anyone determines the value of a human life once it is over. The routine newspaper obituary calls attention to its own inadequacy for such a purpose. *Hughie* is perhaps an ironic and comic reflection on that question.

Two works need to be mentioned that shed light on O'Neill's *Hughie*: James Thurber's 1939 short story "The Secret Life of Walter Mitty," and Joseph Conrad's 1899/1900 novel *Lord Jim*. Though not a dramatic monologue, "Walter Mitty" is a burlesque treatment of one of O'Neill's great themes, the human need for illusion. And *Lord Jim*, which critics have discovered to be a source for Thurber's famous story, is helpful in bringing a discussion of O'Neill's late one-act masterpiece home to its origins in his early one-act plays of the sea, owing so much to Conrad.

Thurber's iconic story opens in the midst of one of Mitty's fantasies, but in his reality he is accompanying his wife on a shopping trip to Waterbury, where he will buy overshoes and puppy biscuits under her direction. The story vacillates back and forth between his escapist fantasies, in which he is a commander, a millionaire banker, a surgeon, a defendant on trial for murder, a captain, and a man about to be executed by firing squad, and his passive suffering of his wife's seemingly endless nagging and solicitude for his health. His fantasies, in style and substance, are taken from pulp fiction of his time, and as Carl Lindner points out, many of his fantasies contain inaccuracies, such as calling a medical condition "coreopsis," a botanical term for a genus of plants.[32] A descendant of Rip Van Winkle and Tom Sawyer, as well as Don Quixote, Walter Mitty has entered popular American culture as a pathetic, yet mysteriously endearing example of romantic heroism in an age of industrialism, specialization, and domestic servitude. Mitty's fantasies do not really achieve for him any escape, of course, but only intensify his sense of inadequacy, leading him to the verge of insanity. In his study of Thurber, Stephen Black (who also wrote *Eugene O'Neill: Beyond Mourning and Tragedy*) diagnoses Mitty in this way: men of Mitty's class and time "compete not only with other men, but also against the dominant forces in a society designed for the protection of women and children. No longer the numb paladins who casually brave romantic perils for the sake of a shadowy heroine, men are sensitive, frustrated creatures whose very sensitivity and intelligence render them vulnerable and ineffectual."[33] And while Ann Mann is undoubtedly right in raising the question of how it would feel to be married to Walter Mitty,[34] still the comic figure has never become a general object of contempt, but seems to be, in some way, an inevitable image of masculine middle-class life.

According to Robert Morsberger, Walter Mitty was particularly popular with American troops in World War II, when Thurber's story was reprinted in *The Reader's Digest*. During the Battle of the Bulge, General Hoge made Thurber's "The Day the Dam Broke" required reading for his staff. And there was a Mitty International group in Europe and a Mitty Society in the South Pacific, with the password "Pocketa-pocketa-pocketa."[35] Morsberger sees this Mitty phenomenon chiefly as a kind of patriotic comic catharsis. But there are surely several layers of meaning to this story. Mitty is experiencing fantasies that are flattering to the heroism of those actually risking their lives. His fantasies thus pay a certain tribute to their sacrifices. Of course, Mitty could perform neither the tasks he is imagining nor the tasks soldiers were performing in reality. So again, the story might make the real soldiers feel pride in their efforts. Obviously, the troops are at war, and Walter Mitty is at home. Why? Is he medically or psychologically unfit to serve? Then he is part of the home front the soldiers are fighting to preserve, along with the women and children. The soldiers are fighting a real war that he is incapable of even imagining correctly. He needs to be protected, and the troops are protecting him. Perhaps they have a certain fondness for him, as though he were a weak, younger brother.

On the other hand, Walter Mitty may be the image of a writer (he makes up stories and insists to his wife that he is *thinking*) who is experiencing a cultural shift in a particularly painful way. He is, as Black suggests, an intellectual, sensitive kind of man who does not really define himself as a fighter, but as part of a new order, whose only heroism is the endurance of essentially meaningless, mundane habitual activities defined by and carried out for someone else. His secure middle-class position in society has become his prison. His wife cannot imagine that he has any legitimate reasons to feel unhappy, and he is not convinced that he does either. But Mitty knows that he is ineffective, anxious, and unhappy. He is, obviously, anticipating the age of psychotherapy, which would be ushered into middle-class life, never to depart, due to widespread posttraumatic stress disorder following World War II. It is as if Mr. and Mrs. Mitty, not being able to imagine war-related experiences except on a fantasy level, would have to imagine the personal consequences of war simply as something a doctor should be able to take care of.

From this point of view, Mitty is experiencing the absurdity of his life in a way analogous to that of Erie Smith in *Hughie*. Both Walter Mitty and Erie Smith need others to act as human mirrors for them so they can stabilize their identities. Erie cannot really explain to anyone, least of all to the new night clerk, what Hughie meant to him. But their symbiotic coimagining of life was profoundly satisfying for Erie and the night clerk. Erie's efforts to explain it are little more than rationalizations. Yet when the night clerk, for his own selfish reasons—which he does not understand either—decides to take a chance on Erie (they are playing dice at the end), something seems to click, and life can now go on. The terrible arbitrariness of human suffering has been met and dealt with one more time.

If "The Secret Life of Walter Mitty" explores O'Neill territory from a bourgeois, comic angle, Conrad's *Lord Jim* finds the dark heart of man's need for conventional, self-serving beliefs in what Albert Guerard calls a "psycho-moral drama which has no easy solution."[36] Jim is first mate on a ship carrying eight hundred pilgrims to Mecca. He has chosen the life of the sea because of his innate hunger for heroic adventure, but when his ship founders and the captain and other officers abandon their charge, he follows suit, only to be tried and found guilty, losing his certification, for a crime that, ironically, had little effect on reality. The ship he abandoned did not sink, but was simply towed to safety. Jim's shame follows him everywhere he goes, until the narrator, Marlow, choosing to believe in Jim's essential integrity, helps get him a post in a remote village where Jim is the only white man and where he can live in peace with himself because of his continuous heroic efforts to help the villagers. He becomes Lord Jim. All goes well until, as fate would have it, Gentleman Brown, a pirate foil of Jim, invades the village, intuits Jim's secret past, and undermines him from within. Holding to his fragile moral dream of himself, Jim honorably allows Brown to leave, whereupon, Brown savagely kills the native chief's son out of sheer spite, and leaves Jim to his fate. Jim finds a kind of redemption in accepting his own death at the hands of the native chief, facing him in the extremity of his grief.

Conrad's epigraph from Novalis makes clear the connection between *Lord Jim*, "The Secret Life of Walter Mitty," and *Hughie*: "It is certain my Conviction gains infinitely, the moment another soul will believe in it." Conrad's novel is driven not by the moral self-doubts of Jim, but by Marlow's continuing search to understand Jim's thought processes and, even more, to understand why Jim has come to mean so much to him. In the spirit of a mature man seeing himself in his younger brother, Marlow vacillates between criticism and compassion, finally seeing Jim as a universal symbol for self-doubt about one's, anyone's, ability to do the right thing. He accepts Jim's rationalization that he is a good man even if he does a bad thing as mankind's necessary fiction. One is never "good enough,"[37] Marlow says. If events occur that force this truth upon a man, he lives a sort of posthumous existence until the end of his physical life. Jim, Walter Mitty, and both Erie and the night clerk, all enter that no-man's land of knowing they can never be good enough. Having eaten this forbidden fruit of knowledge, however, they choose to carry on, with the help of stories they tell themselves, hoping to enlist others as listeners and confidants, necessary partners in their desperate endeavors to keep on living.

Morseberger points out that the word "inscrutable" is used to describe Jim and Mitty at the end of their respective narratives. Jim "is gone, inscrutable at heart." Walter Mitty is "proud and disdainful . . . the undefeated, inscrutable to the last."[38] The phrase "to the last" is also significant, being associated with Jim's romantic attitude toward his dream of himself *usque ad finem*, "until the end."[39] Being a stranger to oneself and to others is a lonely way to live and die. Loneliness, the price paid for learning that one is not "good enough," is what makes one character inscrutable to another. As Conrad says, "It is as if loneliness were a hard and absolute condition of existence; the envelope of flesh and blood on which our eyes are fixed melts before the out-stretched hand, and there remains only the capricious, unconsolable, and elusive spirit that no eye can follow, no hand can grasp."[40]

From the very beginning of O'Neill's career, he took *loneliness until the end* as his subject matter. It was the necessary condition for his characters and themes to come alive on the stage, as we see first in his sea plays. With *Bound East for Cardiff*, he felt he had made his beginning as an artist. In that short play, two men share stories of their adventures, hopes, and fears, as one of them is dying. The death of Yank, witnessed by the helpless Driscoll, establishes the dramatic context of most relationships among O'Neill's characters. At any given moment, some know they are dying, or have already died in a sense, and some don't. But the wheel of time turns. And eventually nearly everyone, perhaps, will be able to say with Cocky the last words of the play, "Gawd blimey."

Hughie is O'Neill's return to the attractive, short-story-like form, the one-act play, so well suited to communicate his soulful stare into the darkness.

NOTES

1. Travis Bogard, *Contour in Time: The Plays of Eugene O'Neill*, rev. ed. (New York: Oxford University Press, 1988), 38–42.
2. Eugene O'Neill, *Bound East for Cardiff*, in *Eugene O'Neill: Complete Plays 1913–1920*, ed. Travis Bogard (New York: Library of America, 1988), 195.
3. Rolf Schreibler, "*Hughie*: A One-Act Play for the Imaginary Theatre," *English Studies* 54 (1973): 243.
4. Ibid., 242.
5. Bogard, *Contour in Time*, 85.
6. Eugene O'Neill, *The Moon of the Caribbees*, in *Eugene O'Neill: Complete Plays 1913–1920*, ed. Travis Bogard (New York: Library of America, 1988), 544.
7. Ibid., 530.
8. Kurt Eisen, *The Inner Strength of Opposites: O'Neill's Novelistic Drama and the Melodramatic Imagination* (Athens, GA: University of Georgia Press, 1994), 25–26.
9. Laura Shea, "An E(e)rie Sound: The Stage Directions in O'Neill's *Hughie*," *Eugene O'Neill Review* 23, no. 1–2 (Spring–Fall 1999): 135.
10. Arthur Gelb and Barbara Gelb, *O'Neill* (New York: Harper and Row, 1973), 844.
11. Frank O'Connor, "The Lonely Voice," in *Short Story Theories*, ed. Charles E. May (Athens, OH: University of Ohio Press, 1976), 86–88.
12. Ibid., 89.
13. Nadine Gordimer, "The Flash of Fireflies," in *Short Story Theories*, ed. Charles E. May (Athens, OH: University of Ohio Press, 1976), 178–81.

14. Péter Egri, *Chekhov and O'Neill: The Uses of the Short Story in Chekhov's and O'Neill's Plays* (Budapest: Akadémiai Kiadó, 1986), 155.

15. Ibid., 155.

16. Ibid., 167–68.

17. Robert Langbaum, *The Poetry of Experience: The Dramatic Monologue in Modern Literary Tradition* (New York: W. W. Norton, 1957), 35–36.

18. Ibid., 146.

19. Ibid., 157.

20. Ibid., 227.

21. Bogard, *Contour in Time*, 531.

22. C. W. E. Bigsby, "O'Neill's Endgame," in *Eugene O'Neill and the Emergence of American Drama*, ed. Marc Maufort (Amsterdam: Rodopi, 1989), 165.

23. Sally Harvey, "O'Neill's *Hughie* and Albee's *The Zoo Story*: Two Tributes to the Teller and His Tale," *The Journal of American Drama and Theatre* 3, no. 2 (1991): 14.

24. See Michael Y. Bennett, "The Parable of Estragon's Struggle with the Boot in Samuel Beckett's *Waiting for Godot*," in *Reassessing the Theatre of the Absurd: Camus, Beckett, Ionesco, Genet, and Pinter* (New York: Palgrave Macmillan, 2011), 27–51.

25. Stephen Black, *Eugene O'Neill: Beyond Mourning and Tragedy* (New Haven, CT: Yale University Press, 1999), 451.

26. Eugene O'Neill, *Long Day's Journey into Night*, in *O'Neill: Complete Plays 1932–1943*, ed. Travis Bogard (New York: Library of America, 1988), 765.

27. Eugene O'Neill, *Hughie*, in *O'Neill: Complete Plays 1932–1943*, ed. Travis Bogard (New York: Library of America 1988), 832.

28. Scheibler, "*Hughie*," 240.

29. O'Neill, *Hughie*, 844.

30. Ibid., 846.

31. Samuel J. Bernstein, "*Hughie*: Inner Dynamics and Canonical Relevance," *Eugene O'Neill Review* 22, no. 1–2 (Spring–Fall 1998): 102.

32. Carl M. Lindner, "Thurber's Walter Mitty—The Underground American Hero," *Georgia Review* 28 (1974): 285.

33. Stephen A. Black, *James Thurber: His Masquerades* (The Hague: Mouton, 1970), 17.

34. Ann Ferguson Mann, "Taking Care of Walter Mitty," *Studies in Short Fiction* 19, no. 4 (Fall 1982): 351–57.

35. Robert E. Morsberger, *James Thurber* (New York: Twayne, 1964), 46.

36. Albert J. Guerard, "*Lord Jim*," in *Joseph Conrad Lord Jim: Authoritative Text, Backgrounds, Sources, Criticism*, 2nd ed., ed. Thomas C. Moser (New York: W. W. Norton, 1996), 397.

37. Joseph Conrad, *Lord Jim: Authoritative Text, Backgrounds, Sources, Criticism*, 2nd ed., ed. Thomas C. Moser (New York: Norton, 1996), 189.
38. Morsberger, *James Thurber*, 45.
39. Conrad, *Lord Jim*, 130.
40. Conrad, *Lord Jim*, 109.

WORKS CITED

Bennett, Michael Y. "The Parable of Estragon's Struggle with the Boot in Samuel Beckett's *Waiting for Godot*." *Reassessing the Theatre of the Absurd: Camus, Beckett, Ionesco, Genet, and Pinter*. New York: Palgrave, 2011. 27–51. Print.

Bernstein, Samuel J. "*Hughie*: Inner Dynamics and Canonical Relevance." *Eugene O'Neill Review* 22.1–2 (Spring–Fall 1998): 77–104. Print.

Bigsby, C. W. E. "O'Neill's Endgame." *Eugene O'Neill and the Emergence of American Drama*. Ed. Marc Maufort. Amsterdam: Rodopi, 1989. 159–68. Print.

Black, Stephen A. *Eugene O'Neill: Beyond Mourning and Tragedy*. New Haven: Yale UP, 1999. Print.

———. *James Thurber: His Masquerades*. The Hague: Mouton, 1970. Print.

Bogard, Travis. *Contour in Time: The Plays of Eugene O'Neill*. Rev. ed. New York: Oxford UP, 1988. Print.

Conrad, Joseph. *Lord Jim: Authoritative Text, Backgrounds, Sources, Criticism*. 2nd ed. Ed. Thomas C. Moser. New York: Norton, 1996. Print.

Egri, Péter. *Chekhov and O'Neill: The Uses of the Short Story in Chekhov's and O'Neill's Plays*. Budapest: Akadémiai Kiadó, 1986. Print.

Eisen, Kurt. *The Inner Strength of Opposites: O'Neill's Novelistic Drama and the Melodramatic Imagination*. Athens: U of Georgia P, 1994. Print.

Gelb, Arthur, and Barbara Gelb. *O'Neill*. New York: Harper, 1973. Print.

Gordimer. Nadine. "The Flash of Fireflies." *Short Story Theories*. Ed. Charles E. May. Athens: U of Ohio P, 1976. 178–81. Print.

Guerard, Albert J. *Lord Jim. Joseph Conrad Lord Jim: Authoritative Text, Backgrounds, Sources, Criticism*. 2nd ed. Ed. Thomas C. Moser. New York: Norton, 1996. 397–423. Print.

Harvey, Sally. "O'Neill's *Hughie* and Albee's *The Zoo Story*: Two Tributes to the Teller and His Tale." *The Journal of American Drama and Theatre* 3.2 (1991): 14–26. Print.

Langbaum, Robert. *The Poetry of Experience: The Dramatic Monologue in Modern Literary Tradition*. New York: Norton, 1957. Print.

Lindner, Carl M. "Thurber's Walter Mitty—The Underground American Hero." *Georgia Review* 28 (1974): 283–89. Print.

Mann, Ann Ferguson. "Taking Care of Walter Mitty." *Studies in Short Fiction* 19.4 (Fall 1982): 351–57. Print.

Morsberger, Robert E. *James Thurber*. New York: Twayne, 1964. Print.

O'Connor, Frank. "The Lonely Voice." *Short Story Theories*. Ed. Charles E. May. Athens: U of Ohio P, 1976. 178–81. Print.

O'Neill, Eugene. *Bound East for Cardiff*. *Complete Plays 1913–1920*. Ed. Travis Bogard. New York: Library of America, 1988. 185–99. Print

———. *Hughie*. *Complete Plays 1932–1943*. Ed. Travis Bogard. New York: Library of America, 1988. 829–51. Print

———. *In the Zone*. *Complete Plays 1913–1920*. Ed. Travis Bogard. New York: Library of America, 1988. 469–88. Print.

———. *Long Day's Journey into Night*. *Complete Plays 1932–1943*. Ed. Travis Bogard. New York: Library of America, 1988. 713–828. Print.

———. *The Long Voyage Home*. *Complete Plays 1913–1920*. Ed. Travis Bogard. New York: Library of America, 1988. 507–23. Print.

———. *The Moon of the Caribbees*. *Complete Plays 1913–1920*. Ed. Travis Bogard. New York: Library of America, 1988. 525–44. Print.

Scheibler, Rolf. "*Hughie*: A One-Act Play for the Imaginary Theatre." *English Studies* 54 (1973): 231–48. Print.

Shea, Laura. "An E(e)rie Sound: The Stage Directions in O'Neill's *Hughie*." *Eugene O'Neill Review* 23.1–2 (Spring–Fall 1999): 134–40. Print.

CHAPTER 12

CONDENSED COMEDY

THE NEO-FUTURISTS PERFORM
O'NEILL'S STAGE DIRECTIONS

Zander Brietzke

The New York Neo-Futurists' original production, *The Complete and Condensed Stage Directions of Eugene O'Neill, Vol.1, Early Plays/ Lost Plays,* elicited a lot of laughter from the audience at the tiny Kraine Theater in the East Village during its run in the fall of 2011. O'Neill's heavy verbosity coupled with his lofty status as America's only Nobel Prize–winning playwright created a sizable target for parody that the troupe did not miss.[1] Ignoring the main lines, they dramatized the playwright's penchant for extensive, elaborate, detailed, literary, and often bizarre stage directions. Indeed, the italicized text served as the only text in this production. That the production took place in a venue quite similar to the Provincetown Playhouse—the theater in the West Village on Macdougal Street at which most of O'Neill's early plays were first produced—returned O'Neill to the downtown context of an experimental artist trying to forge a new kind of theater. The Neo-Futurists' experiment with O'Neill produced a comedy that exposed a gap between the playwright's overwrought, literary ambitions and the physical abilities of actors to execute those intentions faithfully in a theatrical performance. The fact that the selected works of O'Neill's early efforts number among his bleakest (and worst, really) added to the comic romp.

Omitting dialogue in favor only of the stage directions is not entirely new. Henry Alford penned a short spoof in *The New Yorker* in 1998 that used stage directions culled from the oeuvre of O'Neill to create a Strindbergian conflict between a man named John and a woman named Mary, whose "physical attraction," in a description lifted from *Desire Under the Elms*, "becomes a palpable force quivering in the hot air."[2] Unlike Alford's playlet, though, the Neo-Futurists did not present a collage or master text of stage directions, but performed several early and rather obscure plays by O'Neill in their entirety, including five one-acts (*A Wife for a Life, The Web, Thirst, Bound East for Cardiff*, and *Before Breakfast*) and two full-length plays (*Servitude* and *Now I Ask You*). The overall title of the piece alludes to another parody of a literary heavyweight, *The Complete Works of William Shakespeare (Abridged)*, created and performed by the Reduced Shakespeare Company, in which three performers race through the bard at breakneck speed, clocking in with *Hamlet*, for example, in as little as 43 seconds.

The Neo-Futurists' performance was condensed as well, but not completely with respect to O'Neill's early and "lost" plays.[3] They skipped plays such as *Recklessness, Warnings, Fog, Bread and Butter, Abortion, The Movie Man, The Sniper, The Personal Equation, Ile, The Rope* and the rest of the *Glencairn* sea plays (*In the Zone, The Long Voyage Home, The Moon of the Caribbees*) before a natural stop in front of O'Neill's first commercial success, the Pulitzer Prize–winning *Beyond the Horizon* (1918). Overall, the set of plays that comprise *The Complete and Condensed Stage Directions* is an odd lot. The two full-length plays parody Ibsen badly and were never produced. Among the one-act plays, *A Wife for a Life* is a vaudevillian trifle and *The Web* is a melodramatic mess. *Thirst* represents O'Neill's first published play (his father, James, paid for printing costs), while *Bound East for Cardiff* is O'Neill's first produced play, staged by the Provincetown Players at the Wharf Theatre in 1916, and excellent in its own right. According to theatrical lore and as fellow playwright Susan Glaspell elegantly recorded, after the first reading of O'Neill's play the members of the Provincetown Players "knew what [they] were for."[4] The last one act, *Before Breakfast*, another slight play, tests the audience's capacity to endure a monologue.

Perhaps the thematic link that held the disparate pieces together in their performance was nothing more than the time of day. The major set piece on stage was an upright flat upstage right that displayed seven clocks with workable hands and the name of one of the plays under each. A stage manager sat downstage left at a table with a microphone and read all the text for the performance, which consisted, of course, only of the stage directions. Each play started when an actor set the time of the play on the respective clock in response to a cue from the stage manager. Six actors played all the required roles, but instead of speaking O'Neill's dialogue, they responded to what the stage manager described. Much of the action relied on pantomime on a bare stage that sported only the modular chairs or table that an individual play minimally required. All was not silent, though. When the stage directions indicated that a character was to "*spit disgustedly*," as in *Bound East for Cardiff*,[5] the actor tried to do so as well. When "*a stifled groan of pain from the next room*"[6] sounds in *Before Breakfast*, an actor offstage tried to produce that effect as well. And when the heroine of *The Web* "*cries bitterly, mournfully, out of the depths of her desolation*,"[7] the woman playing the part attempted to carry out O'Neill's intent. The stage manager and performers sustained the comic call-and-response rhythm of the performance throughout the evening.

Director and adapter Christopher Loar explained the genesis of the production in the program notes. Initially, he had toyed with the idea of twisting *Long Day's Journey into Night* to fit within the bandwidth of the Neo-Futurists' signature work to date, *Too Much Light Makes the Baby Go Blind*, in which the actors performed thirty original works in sixty minutes and the repertoire of individual plays changed regularly according to the whims of performers and audience members alike. According to the company website, "The single unifying element of these plays is that they are performed from a perspective of absolute honesty. We always appear as ourselves on stage, speaking directly from our personal experiences."[8] The presentational, nonmimetic aesthetic of the company seemed ill-suited to tackle O'Neill's domestic, family drama of deep-rooted love and bitterness fostered by years and years of living together in close quarters. Long interested in O'Neill's heavy use of stage directions, Loar wondered if a performance could be crafted using only the stage directions as text. This route, he surmised, would allow the company to play themselves instead of characters and provide an audience with a glimpse of what is usually never seen in performance. After all, didn't actors routinely begin rehearsals by crossing out the printed stage directions; or, barring that, simply ignoring them? Here, Loar hoped to use the stage directions, which make up a sizable load of each play, as the centerpiece of the production and the exclusive text. The most important question, he thought, was simply this: could the plays be presented meaningfully without the words of the characters?

Given the amount of comic business onstage, understanding the plot ultimately seemed hardly the point of this production. Laughter during the performance seemed to belie the seriousness of purpose with which O'Neill must have written each play. In *A Wife for a Life*, for example, a younger man prepares to run off with his older friend's wife, though he doesn't know that his friend is her husband, making the events more painful for the older man. The diseased prostitute, Rose, loses her child to the law at the end of *The Web*. A trio of shipwreck survivors falls out of a lifeboat and into the jaws of hungry sharks in *Thirst*. In *Bound East for Cardiff*, a mortally wounded sailor recounts his lonely life before dying at sea. A woman berates and belittles her husband into committing suicide in *Before Breakfast*. This is not a cheery group of plays, but as performed by the Neo-Futurists, the sad plight of the characters did not get much attention; instead, the performers drew attention to themselves as they struggled to act out O'Neill's stage directions. Rather than depicting the grim realities of tenement housing, the plight of the poor and dispossessed, the daily lives of the working class, or the poetic aspirations of a struggling artist, the Neo-Futurists created a comedy by presenting how difficult it is for actors to carry out the stated intentions and directions of a great, if controlling, playwright.

When, for example, the old man in *A Wife for a Life* realizes the stakes of his young friend's future happiness, he "*seems to crumple up.*" O'Neill's stage directions expound on the moment: "*Nothing seems alive about him but his eyes, staring horribly, and his right hand which nervously fingers the gun in the belt around his waist.*"[9] Despite whatever dramatic tension that may exist in the text at that point, the actor turned the scene to comedy when he tried to "crumple up" and then to "stare horribly." The terribly sad ending of *The Web* ran against the comic physical display inspired by one of the final stage directions in that play: "*Rose seems in a trance. Her eyes are like the eyes of a blind woman. She seems to be aware of something in the room which none of the others can see—perhaps the personification of the ironic life force that has crushed her.*"[10] How does an "ironic life force" look? The opening moments of *Before Breakfast* require a similarly impossible expression. As she reads a letter from her husband's mistress, Mrs. Rowland undergoes a transformation: "*At first her expression is one of hatred and rage, but as she goes on to the end it changes to one of triumphant malignity.*"[11] How does one show "triumphant malignity" and, even if it were possible, could it be named as such? The actors' attempts to display these emotions result in demonstratively melodramatic gestures that have little to do with actual human responses and emotions and therefore appear wildly comic.

Some of the most humorous moments in the performance came about because the actors onstage could not materially produce what the playwright conceived in his imagination. *The Web* calls for a sick and crying baby to be onstage the entire length of the performance. And while it is all well and good for O'Neill to specify when the baby cries and when it coughs, a real baby has a will of its own and will do as it pleases at any time. Of course, a producer could devise some sort of fake baby with the help of the properties department, but wouldn't the artificiality of such a construction interfere with the bleak realism that the action purports? The Neo-Futurists solved the problem by substituting an alligator hand puppet for the human baby but treating it as if it were a child. It was a funny choice, yes, but the real humor lay in the recognition of this choice as the lesser of other evils and as a solution to a performance problem that was created by the playwright. Something similar happened in *Thirst* when three actors donned little hats with fins to represent sharks and then ran around a blue sheet that stood for an endless ocean upon which drifted a solitary raft. There is nothing remotely funny about O'Neill's play, but the human sharks created a constant sight gag and made it impossible, really, to listen to the play at all. The final lines of the play, stage directions, are absolutely beautiful, but no audience sitting in a theater could actually see what the playwright describes: "*The black stain on the water widens. The fins circle no longer. The raft floats in the midst of a vast silence. The sun glares down like a great angry eye of God. The eerie heat waves float upward in the still air like the souls of the drowned. On the raft a diamond necklace lies glittering in the blazing sunshine.*"[12] The literary narrative of this passage simply does not translate to a theatrical space.

O'Neill always preferred the play as written to the play as performed. The printed text was his alone, while a theatrical production required the work of the playwright, producer, director, designers, technicians, and actors (whom O'Neill liked least of all). From early in his career to the end, O'Neill voiced a virulent antitheatrical prejudice, spawned in his youth from watching the melodramas in which his father performed, by his own shaky performances as an actor (he played the original "hand" in *Before Breakfast*), and by rebellion against his own father, a famous actor, and his desire to make a mark as a playwright.[13] As early as 1924, when he was a young but established commercial playwright, O'Neill boasted in an interview, "I don't go to the theatre because I can always do a better production in my mind than the one on stage. I have a better time and I am not bothered by the audience.[14]" In a letter from France, where he was living at the time in 1929, O'Neill rationalized to Eleanor Fitzgerald, the beloved former secretary of the Provincetown Players, why he did not attend the theater regularly: "My interest in the productions steadily decreases as my interest in plays as written increases. They always—with the exceptions you know—fall so far below or beside my intent that I'm a bit weary and disillusioned with scenery and actors and the whole uninspired works of the Show Shop."[15]

Two other letters later on switch focus from the problems of theatrical production in general to the problems of actors in particular. To critic Barrett Clark he wrote, in 1937, arguing against producing any of his cycle plays until all were complete: "Outside of the financial aspect, productions are only nerve-racking interruptions to me—'show business'—and never have meant anything more. The play, as written, is the thing, and not the way actors garble it with their almost-always-alien personalities (even when the acting is fine work in itself)."[16] About *The Iceman Cometh*, O'Neill voiced a similar concern to friend and critic George Jean Nathan in 1940: "I'm not giving a thought to production. In fact, I hate to think of it being produced—of having to watch a lot of actors muscle in their personalities to make strange for me these characters of the play that interest me so much—now, as *I* have made them live!"[17] The play as written is perfect, according to O'Neill, because he can envision a performance in which all theatrical elements align with his imagination.

In his program notes for the Neo-Futurists' production, director Christopher Loar reasons that O'Neill's elaborately extensive stage directions "were an insurance policy of sorts against anyone screwing up his plays." But the Neo-Futurists proved with their performance that fidelity to what O'Neill wrote ensures a laughable production. By not interpreting the texts but only trying to do what was in the texts, the players ended up poking fun at O'Neill as if to get back at him for trying to do their creative jobs by himself. The comic response to the performance signified that the playwright could not play all the parts and needed the imaginative and interpretive skills of actors to bring truly his words to life on stage. The experimental and avantgarde production resolved the conflict between the page and stage, between word and action, between the rebellious son (Eugene) and the domineering father (James) by siding with the actor-father against the playwright-son. In a refreshing twist of the old comic trope in which youth triumphs against old age, the Neo-Futurists took the part of the old man only to defeat the father of American drama.

When folks see a production that they don't like of a play that they do admire, they might complain, "Why can't they just *do* the play?," as if there were a play to do apart from figuring out what O'Neill or any other playwright actually meant word by word and line by line. Distinguishing between what O'Neill said and what he may have meant by what he said requires patience, diligence, and even sometimes the spark of genius. Most productions fall short, naturally, and are terrible. That is another lesson brought home by the Neo-Futurists' production: theater is very hard to do. Theatrical production is not, after all, akin to an archaeological dig that excavates *the* original performance that perfectly mirrors the dramatic text. More often, an outstanding performance of a text reveals *an* original aspect about a play that had never been seen or even noticed previously. And it is highly likely that a memorable production of an O'Neill play might reveal more insights in the play than ever the playwright even dreamed existed. Actors, directors, and designers do conspire, at times, to ruin plays. At the same time, though, they can occasionally make old plays new and great plays great again in new and exciting ways. The odds for greatness may not be good, but they might just be worth the risk.

Indeed, theatrical productions resurrected O'Neill's career posthumously, beginning in 1956 with the landmark revival of *The Iceman Cometh* at the Circle in the Square Theatre in Sheridan Square and then the American premiere of *Long Day's Journey into Night* on Broadway later that same year, both of which made actor Jason Robards a star and the leading interpreter of O'Neill for a generation. Since that time over fifty years ago, there have been many thrilling and successful O'Neill productions on and off Broadway and in and out of New York that have inspired and challenged creative talents. The hope of finding new meanings in the works keeps begging for more productions, traditional and avant-garde, and continues to draw audiences back into the theater to experience what happens in that space. The humorous intent of *The Complete and Condensed Stage Directions of Eugene O'Neill, Vol. 1, Early Plays/Lost Plays* sounded immediately with its long-winded title: bookish, boring, and encyclopedic, as if it were a heavy tome gathering dust on some forgotten reference-library shelf. Inclusion of a volume number suggests companion editions to be found in an equally desolate spot. While such books would be bound and stitched in between cloth covers, the theatrical performance by the physically gifted Neo-Futurists demonstrated a need and a desire to transcend the literary text. Even though O'Neill's words constrained them, the actors relished the liberating freedom of theatrical performance.

NOTES

1. O'Neill's experimental and ambitious plays of the 1920s, including works such as *The Great God Brown* and *Strange Interlude*, received parodic treatment frequently. For an excellent catalogue of satiric responses to O'Neill's work during that decade, see Felicia Hardison Londre, "Twitting O'Neill: His Plays of the 1920s Subjected to *La Critique Créatrice*," *Eugene O'Neill Review* 26 (2004): 118–43.

2. Henry Alford, "Unspoken O'Neill," *New Yorker*, November 30, 1998, 68; Eugene O'Neill, *Desire Under the Elms*, in *Complete Plays 1920–1931*, ed. Travis Bogard (New York: Library of America, 1988), 341.

3. Gotham Press of Boston published *Thirst and Other One Act Plays* in 1914 in a volume that also included *The Web, Warnings, Fog*, and *Recklessness*. *Lost Plays of Eugene O'Neill* appeared in 1950 (New Fathoms) and included *A Wife for a Life, Servitude, Abortion, The Movie Man*, and *The Sniper*. Carlotta O'Neill authorized Random House to publish *Ten "Lost" Plays* in 1964 in a volume that consisted of all of the above plays.

4. Susan Glaspell, *The Road to the Temple*, ed. Linda Ben-Zvi (Jefferson, NC: McFarland, 2005), 204.

5. Eugene O'Neill, *Complete Plays 1913–1920*, ed. Travis Bogard (New York: Library of America, 1988), 190.

6. Ibid., 398.

7. Ibid., 28.

8. Christopher Loar, The Complete and Condensed Stage Directions of Eugene O'Neill, 22 Sept. 2011.

9. O'Neill, Complete Plays 1913– 1920, 7.

10. Ibid., 28.

11. Ibid., 392.

12. Ibid., 51.

13. I have borrowed the term "antitheatrical prejudice" from the title of the book by Jonas Barish (Berkeley: University of California Press, 1981). I am indebted to Professor Barish's work. About O'Neill, he says only this: "[O'Neill] registered repeated dismay at what he scathingly called the 'show-shop' of the theater, recording his sense of betrayal at what actors, including the most gifted and dedicated actors, made of the characters he had forged in the silence of his imagination" (133).

14. Oscar Cargill, N. Bryllion Fagin, William J. Fisher, eds., *O'Neill and his Plays: Four Decades of Criticism* (New York: New York University Press, 1961), 112.

15. Eugene O'Neill, *Selected Letters of Eugene O'Neill*, ed. Travis Bogard and Jackson R. Bryer (New York: Limelight, 1994), 338.

16. Ibid., 467.

17. Ibid., 501.

WORKS CITED

Alford, Henry. "Unspoken O'Neill." *The New Yorker* 30 Nov. 1998: 68. Print.

Jonas Barish. *The Antitheatrical Prejudice.* Berkeley: U of California P, 1981. Print.

Cargill, Oscar, N. Bryllion Fagin, and William J. Fisher, eds. *O'Neill and his Plays: Four Decades of Criticism.* New York: New York UP, 1961. Print.

Glaspell, Susan. *The Road to the Temple.* Ed. and Intro. Linda Ben-Zvi. 1926. Jefferson, North Carolina: McFarland, 2005. Print.

Loar, Christopher. Program note. *The Complete and Condensed Stage Directions of Eugene O'Neill.* Perf. New York Neo-Futurists. Kraine Theater, New York. 22 Sept. 2011.

Londre, Felicia Hardison. "Twitting O'Neill: His Plays of the 1920s Subjected to *La Critique Créatrice.*" *Eugene O'Neill Review* 26 (2004): 118–43.

New York Neo-Futurists. Home page. N.d. Web. 24 Oct. 2011. http://www.nynf.org.

O'Neill, Eugene. *Complete Plays 1913–1920.* Ed. Travis Bogard. New York: Library of America, 1988. Print.

———. *Desire Under the Elms. Complete Plays 1920–1931.* Ed. Travis Bogard. New York: Library of America, 1988. 317–78. Print.

———. *Selected Letters of Eugene O'Neill.* Ed. Travis Bogard and Jackson R. Bryer. 1988. New York: Limelight, 1994. Print.

Notes on the Authors

Phillip Barnhart wrote his undergraduate thesis on Marcel Proust at Bennington College (BA 1991). He has an MFA in writing and poetics from the Jack Kerouac School of Disembodied Poetics at Naropa University in Boulder, Colorado; an MLS in theatre and community from the Rackham School of Graduate Studies at the University of Michigan—Flint; and is currently in a PhD theatre director/scholar program at Wayne State University in Detroit. He is a lecturer in the Department of Theatre and Dance at the University of Michigan—Flint. Barnhart also manages a website on queer theatre historiography at http://www.lavenderstage.com.

Michael Y. Bennett is an assistant professor of English in Drama at the University of Wisconsin-Whitewater. He is the author of three books: *Reassessing the Theatre of the Absurd: Camus, Beckett, Ionesco, Genet, and Pinter* (Palgrave Macmillan, 2011); *Words, Space, and the Audience: The Theatrical Tension between Empiricism and Rationalism* (Palgrave Macmillan, 2012); and *Narrating the Past Through Theatre: Four Crucial Texts* (Palgrave Pivot, forthcoming Autumn 2012). He is also the editor of *Refiguring Oscar Wilde's* Salome (Rodopi, 2011).

Steven F. Bloom is the author of *Student Companion to Eugene O'Neill*, published by Greenwood Press in 2007, and the editor of *Critical Insights: Eugene O'Neill*, published by EBSCO/Salem Press in 2012. Bloom has served on the Eugene O'Neill Society's board of directors since 2000, and he has been president of the Society and chairman of the board. He was the book reviews editor of *The Eugene O'Neill Review* from 1988 until 2004. He has published numerous articles and reviews in *The Eugene O'Neill Review* and elsewhere and has spoken on O'Neill at many professional conferences and public forums. Bloom received his PhD in English and American literature from Brandeis University. He is currently the associate vice president for academic affairs at Lasell College in Newton, Massachusetts.

Zander Brietzke teaches modern and American drama at Columbia University. He earned a BA in theater from Missouri Southern, an MFA in directing from the University of Alabama, and a PhD in directing and dramatic criticism from Stanford University. He has taught at Lehigh University in Pennsylvania, the College of Wooster in Ohio, and Montclair State in New Jersey where he now makes his home. A former president of the Eugene O'Neill Society, he is the author of *The Aesthetics of Failure: Dynamic Structure in the Plays of Eugene O'Neill* (McFarland 2001), *American Drama in the Age of Film* (Alabama 2007), which was named by the Theatre Library Association as a finalist for the Richard Wall Memorial Award, and *Teaching with the Norton Anthology of Drama* (2009), an instructor's manual. Zander edited the annual *Eugene O'Neill Review* at Suffolk University in Boston from 2004 to 2010. Currently, he is writing a manuscript on modern drama masters Henrik Ibsen, Anton Chekhov, and August Strindberg.

Lesley Broder is an assistant professor of English at Kingsborough Community College at the City University of New York in Brooklyn. She recently received her PhD in English from Stony Brook University. Her research interests focus on both comparative modern drama and using digital technologies to improve students' writing skills. She is currently working on a project regarding Rachel Crothers's promotional techniques and impact on Broadway theater in the first half of the twentieth century.

Benjamin D. Carson is an associate professor and chair of the Department of English at Bridgewater State University, Bridgewater, Massachusetts. He earned a PhD in American literature from the University of Nebraska, Lincoln, in 2005, and has published essays on Edith Wharton, Gerald Vizenor, Ana Castillo, and Clarence Major. His edited collection, *Sovereignty, Separatism, and Survivance: Ideological Encounters in the Literature of Native North America*, was published by Cambridge Scholars Press in 2008.

Robert Combs teaches American drama and short fiction at George Washington University in Washington, DC. Author of *Vision of the Voyage: Hart Crane and the Psychology of Romanticism*, he has also published articles on Eugene O'Neill, Arthur Miller, William Inge, David Mamet, Israel Horovitz, Oscar Wilde, and Harold Pinter.

Thomas F. Connolly is a professor of English at Suffolk University and visiting professor at the University of Ostrava. His most recent book is *Genus Envy: Nationalities, Identities, and the Performing Body of Work.* He contributed to the *Oxford Encyclopedia of Theatre and Performance*, *The Cambridge Guide to American Theatre*, *The Encyclopedia of New England Culture*, and many other reference works. Connolly is a former Fulbright Senior Scholar and has been a consultant for the *New Yorker*, CBS, NPR, and the BBC. Connolly has served on the board of the Eugene O'Neill Society, was managing editor of *The Eugene O'Neill Review*, and review editor of *Theatre Research International*. He is the recipient of the Parliamentary Medal of the Czech Republic.

Thierry Dubost is a professor at the University of Caen Basse-Normandie, France. He is the author of *Struggle, Defeat or Rebirth: Eugene O'Neill's Vision of Humanity* (McFarland, 1997 [2005]) and *The Plays of Thomas Kilroy* (McFarland, 2007). He has coedited four books, *La Femme Noire américaine, aspects d'une crise d'identité; George Bernard Shaw, un dramaturge engagé; Du Dire à l'Etre. Tensions identitaires dans la littérature nord-américaine; Regards sur l'intime en Irlande*, and has edited *L'Adaptation théâtrale en Irlande de 1970 à 2007*, all published by Caen University Press. His translation of Wole Soyinka's *Death and the King's Horseman* was published in 1986.

Kurt Eisen is professor of English and associate dean of Arts and Sciences at Tennessee Technological University, where he teaches courses in American literature and modern drama. He holds a PhD from Boston University with a dissertation on Eugene O'Neill, published in 1994 as *The Inner Strength of Opposites: O'Neill's Novelistic Drama and the Melodramatic Imagination*. His articles and reviews have appeared in *The Cambridge Companion to Eugene O'Neill*, *Modern Drama*, *Comparative Drama*, *American Literature*, *Studies in the American Renaissance*, *South Central Review*, among others, and in *The Eugene O'Neill Review*, of which he has been book review editor since 2004. He is currently president of the Eugene O'Neill Society.

Jeff Kennedy is an associate clinical professor of interdisciplinary arts and performance at Arizona State University, where he has been teaching since 2000. As a PhD student at New York University, he was part of the renovation team in 1997 and 1998 for the Provincetown Playhouse, designing its historical gallery and authoring a monograph on its history. With Lowell Swortzell, he created and produced the award-winning *New Plays for Young Audiences* series at the Playhouse. He also created and maintains http://www.provincetownplayhouse .com, a research website on the history of the Provincetown Players. He is currently rewriting his two-volume dissertation, "The Artistic Life of the Provincetown Playhouse, 1918–1922," for book publication and serves as the vice president of the Eugene O'Neill Society.

Paul D. Streufert holds the George F. Hamm Endowed Chair in Arts and Humanities at the University of Texas at Tyler, where he directs the Honors Program and serves as associate professor of literature and languages. His research focuses primarily on drama, particularly of ancient Athens, early modern England, and twentieth-century America. He has published on a variety of playwrights, including Aeschylus, Shakespeare, and Sam Shepard. He is currently at work on a book-length study of the staging of the supernatural.

J. Chris Westgate is an assistant professor in the Department of English and Comparative Literature at CSU Fullerton, where he teaches courses in contemporary and modern drama. His book *Urban Drama: The Metropolis in Contemporary North American Plays* was published by Palgrave Macmillan in June 2011. He has published articles in *The Eugene O'Neill Review*, *Modern Drama*, *American Drama*, *Theatre Journal*, *Comparative Drama*, and *Contemporary Theatre Review*. He is currently working on a book-length project titled *Staging the Slum, Slumming the Stage* that examines the intersections of slumming and theatrical realism in Progressive Era New York City.

INDEX

CPSIA information can be obtained at www.ICGtesting.com
Printed in the USA
LVOW01s2103030815

448667LV00015B/152/P